WHAT THE HEAVENS DECLARE

What the Heavens Declare

Science in the Light of Creation

Lydia Jaeger

Translated by Jonathan Vaughan
Foreword by Cyrille Michon

 CASCADE *Books* · Eugene, Oregon

WHAT THE HEAVENS DECLARE
Science in the Light of Creation

Copyright © 2012 Lydia Jaeger. All rights reserved. Except for brief quotations in critical publications or reviews, no part of this book may be reproduced in any manner without prior written permission from the publisher. Write: Permissions, Wipf and Stock Publishers, 199 W. 8th Ave., Suite 3, Eugene, OR 97401.

Cascade Books
An Imprint of Wipf and Stock Publishers
199 W. 8th Ave., Suite 3
Eugene, OR 97401

www.wipfandstock.com

ISBN 13: 978-1-61097-034-1

Cataloging-in-Publication data:

Jaeger, Lydia.

    What the heavens declare : science in the light of creation / Lydia Jaeger, with a foreword by Cyrille Michon.

    xxiv + 202 p. ; 23 cm. Includes bibliographical references and index(es).

    ISBN 13: 978-1-61097-034-1

    1. Religion and science. 2. Creation—Biblical teaching. 3. Law—philosophical concept. 4. Philosophical theology. I. Michon, Cyrille. II. Title.

BL240.3 J3313 2012

Manufactured in the U.S.A.

To Henri Blocher,

my teacher, colleague, and friend,

on his seventieth birthday

Contents

Foreword by Cyrille Michon ix
Preface xiii
Introduction xvii

one The Idea of Creation 1
Creation as a Primary Concept in the Christian Worldview
The Freedom of Creation
The Possible and the Real
Leibniz: Rationalistic Creationism

two From Substantial Forms to Laws of Nature 25
Creation *Ex Nihilo* and the Analogy of Being
Creation as a Trinitarian Act
Critiques of the Analogy of Being in the Late Middle Ages
The Analogy of Being in Calvin's *Institutes*
The Triumph of Laws of Nature
Laws Are Not Enough

three The Order of the Created World 58
The Natural Order as a Corollary of Creation
The Creation of Matter and Mathematical Order in Nature
The Contingency of the Created Order
Covenant Causality

The Necessity of Laws of Nature
The Rejection of Reductionism
Unified Plurality
Creation and Chance
Quantum Indeterminism

four   The Relational Nature of Knowledge   94
The World as Text
The Incomprehensibility of God as the Context for Knowledge
The Noetic Effects of Sin
The Personal Nature of Knowledge
Situated Knowledge
The Relational Dimension of Creation
The Freedom of Knowledge

five   Explaining the Natural Order   123
The Physico-Theological Proof
A Probabilistic Natural Theology: Richard Swinburne
An Analytical Natural Theology: John Foster
The Pantheistic Declaration of Mystery
Scientism's Claim to Explain Everything
Intelligent Design and the "Multiverse"
Empiricism's Refusal of Explanation
The Permission to Ask Certain Questions
The Explanation of Order, *à la* Kant
The Privilege of Being Secondary

Conclusion   169
Bibliography   173
Author Index   189
Scripture Index   193
Subject Index   197

Foreword

"In the beginning God created the heavens and the earth." The first words of Genesis, intended to describe the origin of the world, are themselves the origin of a central belief shared by the monotheistic religions. Over and above the matter of a temporal origin for the universe, its beginning in time, it is the radical dependence of all that exists with respect to God that forms the basis of this belief. Christianity has placed at the heart of the faith it proclaims the doctrine of creation: "I believe in one God, the Father Almighty, maker of heaven and earth." Theological reflection over the last century has sometimes relegated this affirmation to a position of secondary importance, because it is not fundamentally Christian, because it apparently does not have crucial implications that are as obvious as the teachings found in the Gospels, or even because it could be more than just a matter of faith—since as concerns the universe, it could be a proposition open to philosophical, or even scientific, argument. Although the founders of modern science (Galileo, Descartes, Newton) adhered wholeheartedly to the biblical doctrine of creation, the theories that they developed say nothing about the universe's beginnings. Ironically, the more recent conception of a universe that is expanding after an initial explosion brings the idea of creation to mind, even if the scientific community is largely indifferent, if not hostile, to the latter. Modern atheism, even if only taken as a methodological principle, is the attitude adopted by the majority of academics today. And even if physicists seem more inclined to a form of mysticism when faced with the order of the universe, the approach that inspired Darwin—explaining the apparent purpose of living organisms through a purely mechanical process of natural selection of the fittest from among random variation of species—is the principle of another creed.

With this book, Lydia Jaeger completes a series of reflections on creation, faith, and science. After her meditation on the believer's existence (*Vivre dans un monde créé*, Farel, 2007) and her excellent treatment of religious beliefs in contemporary epistemological discussion (the subtitle of her *Lois de la nature et raisons du cœur*, Peter Lang, 2007), where she studied in detail various conceptions of the laws of nature and the relationship between these conceptions and the religious (or atheistic) beliefs of those who advocate them, the following pages aim to defend and illustrate a view of creation informed by her research on science and laws of nature. In addressing creationism in this context, Lydia Jaeger does not intend to align herself with the movement that is often described by this label to indicate a literal interpretation of the Bible's creation narrative. Rather she wishes to prevent the vital concept of creation from disappearing from view, and to present a conception of nature and its laws that is informed by the belief that all that exists is radically dependent on God.

Such a conception of creation is, in Lydia Jaeger's opinion, compatible with the discoveries of contemporary science, and can even cast light on them, without being constructed from them. Instead, the idea of creation is accepted as a *gift*: God himself reveals himself as the wise and loving creator, as the Father of all things, whose character is described by the Bible rather than by philosophers. This defense is therefore also an attack on two fronts. Jaeger leads an assault on the philosophical conceptions at the root of natural theology in its dual endeavor to provide arguments for the existence of God, and to determine an idea of God's nature. This kind of natural theology no longer possesses the aura that for centuries had surrounded it, but has nevertheless been taken up by some contemporary philosophers of religion, whose undertakings are challenged here. The other front is that of contemporary philosophy of science, whose atheistic presupposition Lydia Jaeger rightly points out. Although she refuses a concordism that leads to a God of the gaps, whose existence and nature are established on the basis of what science cannot explain, she also refuses a conception of science that from the very outset leaves no room for a creator, not just in the equations and the theory, but in the absolute.

Armed with a well-articulated theology and a clear grasp of contemporary philosophy of science, Jaeger is able to defend a paradoxical position: while rejecting the philosophical conception of theism as a natural knowledge of God, and even more so the defense of creationism based on our knowledge of nature, she upholds the intelligibility of creation, and in addition, the fecundity for science of recognizing the creation as such (an idea that we owe to the seventeenth-century founders of modern science, who never tired of quoting "God made everything with number, weight, and measure" from the book of *Wisdom*). However, faithful to Christian doctrine, reason wounded by sin cannot by itself overcome the mystery and incomprehensibility of God, except by becoming personal, situated knowledge, called forth by a revelation. A conception that remains agnostic on the (autonomous) philosophical level, therefore, seems more favorable to the affirmation of creation. Although Lydia Jaeger appeals to Kant, I would have no problem calling such a position "Pascalian," that of creation by the God of Abraham, Isaac, and Jacob, and not by the philosophers' God (a "Thomistic," or rather "Leibnizian" conception, which separates the realms of science and metaphysics). But one may prefer to associate it with the tradition that links Calvin to Kierkegaard and Karl Barth.

In any case, we should praise this initiative, of which there are very few examples, especially in France. Such issues are rarely tackled head-on, and when they are, it is not with the approach taken in this book. What is more, the concern for careful argumentation is often lacking in treatments of religion and theology. Here, in contrast, one will find a rigorously argumentative approach, even if it precisely claims to expose the limits of argumentation. "We must know where to feel certain, where to doubt, where to submit," as Pascal said. The idea of creation is both a source of intelligibility and a limit imposed on empirical knowledge, and doubtlessly on philosophy as well, when the latter wishes to become natural theology or natural atheology. This book is ambitious. Its dimensions preclude it from justifying everything. But from now on, one cannot think reasonably about creation without carefully considering the analyses and the positions that this book defends.

CYRILLE MICHON
Professor of Philosophy and Director of the "Philosophy of Experience"
Research Group at the University of Nantes

Preface

Every research project is part of a personal trajectory. For this book, it was the meeting of three disciplines that, each in its own way, seek to answer the fundamental questions of human existence: physics, theology, and philosophy. The laws of nature are, in a sense, the focal point where the three approaches converge: a fascination with the natural order has marked my intellectual journey for the past two decades; several times, it has altered its course.

This fascination took shape during my last years of high school. When choosing from the science subjects on offer, I gave priority to chemistry. In addition (and only just), I took an introductory physics course, mainly because it dealt primarily with astronomy and had less on general physics, and because my elder brother insisted that I keep doing physics. A year and a half later, I was seriously thinking about studying physics at university. Why the change? I had discovered the mystery of the cosmic order.

This fascination for physics has never wavered. Why does the pen in my hand, if I drop it, fall to the ground according to a precise mathematical formula? And we are so convinced of the orderly behavior of nature that we don't even feel the need to repeat the experiment to see if nature will obey the same rule next time? Any exploration of nature that relies on physics starts from the belief that natural phenomena are regular and can be described in mathematical language; outside of this assumption, one is outside the scope of scientific research. The revolutions that left their mark on physics in the early twentieth century have, it is true, changed our understanding of the cosmic order. Quantum mechanics introduced the idea of chance at the most fundamental level of our best scientific theories. Nevertheless, mathematical formulas are still used to describe quantum probabilities, and quantum theories do not whisk us away to a world of fairy tales where everything and anything can happen.

Having already directed me towards physics, the concept of the natural order came back again at the end of my studies in theology. With its obvious theological connotations, the metaphor of law of nature was perfect as the subject for an interdisciplinary study. The latter dealt primarily with the historical origins of the concept and the exegesis of Old Testament passages where legal terms are used in connection with natural phenomena.[1]

To go farther in the dialogue between theology and science, it quickly became imperative to bring in a third partner: philosophy, and in particular the philosophy of science. The present work is the result of considering the subject of laws of nature by taking advantage of the methods specific to each of the three disciplines. It clearly bears the marks of the two philosophical worlds in which it came about: Paris and Cambridge. If one wanted to use labels, one could say: continental philosophy, more specifically neo-Kantian, on the French side of the Channel, analytic philosophy on the other. But such categorizations do not do justice to the wealth of these traditions and the complexity of their (sometimes unexpected) interactions. Cambridge's influences doubtlessly played their part in my inability to overcome my recalcitrant (some would say naïve) realistic intuitions—both in science and in philosophy. For I cannot bring myself to believe that the great controversies that permeate the history of philosophy are meaningless. They will surface at different times during this study, for example in the discussion of competing explanations of the natural order. At the same time, the immersion in two utterly different ways of doing philosophy has increased my sensitivity to the importance of their underlying assumptions, especially when they remain unspoken, or even unconscious. This aspect clearly marks the present work as being "continental"-style philosophy.

In connection with my own scientific background, this study focuses on the notion of *law* in physics. My biologist friends assure me that the natural order receives a very different treatment in their discipline—a difference that raises fascinating questions. As it is difficult (impossible, even) to understand the specificity of a scientific domain without first

---

1. The result of this research has been published in Jaeger, *Laws of Nature*, 133–214.

knowing it from the inside, I must leave the exploration of biological order to others. Of course, the exclusion of life sciences does not imply in any way that one aims to reduce them ultimately to physics. Neither is the latter treated as a model science; it is simply a scientific discipline that is accessible by personal experience. Its pretension to be *the* fundamental science certainly provides this study with a distinctive flavor, but one should not use it as an excuse to do down other scientific disciplines.

A few comments on vocabulary: analytic philosophy of religion routinely uses the word *theism* to designate the conception of a personal and unique God, who created the world. I have followed this usage, rather than its other historical meaning, which differentiates it from the revealed monotheistic religions. The adjective *creationist* designates the worldview based on the belief that the world is created without specifying the manner of creation. This should not be interpreted in the narrower sense that the term has acquired in the United States, which ties it to a literal understanding of the six days of creation. When the text speaks of *science* without any other qualification, it is always referring to the natural sciences in their current form. "*Modern*" science designates science as it has been practiced following the upheavals of the seventeenth century that have come to be known as the "scientific revolution." For physics that postdates the formulation of the theory of relativity and quantum mechanics, the adjective "contemporary" will be used.

Works written in foreign languages are always (except in the case of accidental oversight) quoted in their English translation if this has been published. Texts that are not available in English have been translated by Jonathan Vaughan, to whom I owe deep gratitude for providing an excellent translation of this book, originally published in French. To avoid burdening the notes, the original language, which can be guessed from the title, is not indicated. To avoid unnecessary duplication of footnotes, Bible references are given in parentheses in the text. Hebrew and Greek words are transcribed into Roman characters according to the *SBL Handbook of Style*. The biblical passages are provided in an original translation.

No interdisciplinary work can do without regular contact with specialists in different domains who are in addition aware of inter-subject issues. The present volume is a *de facto* expression of the *res publica litterarum*. It has a truly "ecumenical" dimension in at least three ways: in addition to the interdisciplinary nature of the contacts, the research has benefited from the contribution of academics from all around the world, and from a wide range of religious approaches (from Judaism and different Christian denominations to Buddhism and atheism). This work constitutes my attempt at a personal response to these different influences, without trying to implement a strategy of compromise (would the latter even be feasible?). This study is therefore one of a philosophy of personal involvement. This personally-involved aspect is not in contradiction with the rigor of the study: the reader will decide if this work succeeds or not in combining overt convictions with the traditional academic ideals of listening attentively to one's sources and maintaining tightly-reasoned argumentation.

Since it is impossible to name all those who have contributed to this project, I will limit myself to those whose participation has been decisive: Michel Bitbol supervised my PhD in philosophy (Paris-Sorbonne); part of the thesis served as the basis for this book. He encouraged me throughout the process; equally, his work provided me with an example of fruitful interdisciplinary research. Under the leadership of the late Peter Lipton, mourned by friends and colleagues alike following his premature death, the Department of History and Philosophy of Science at Cambridge University has been an outstanding place for study and research, which I was able to benefit from on several visits. The warm welcome that I received on these occasions from the theological community at Tyndale House has profoundly influenced my research. Regular discussions with two of my former professors have especially contributed to the continuing interdisciplinary nature of my research: Peter Mittelstaedt, at the Institute for Theoretical Physics, Cologne University, and Henri Blocher, at the *Faculté Libre de Théologie Evangélique* (Vaux-sur-Seine, France). Intensive email discussions with the director of the Pascal Centre for Advanced Studies in Faith and Science (Ontario), Jitse van der Meer, were particularly rewarding in terms of suggestions and references. Lengthy discussions with Daniel Hillion, as well as detailed comments from John Brooke and Cyrille Michon, helped me, on more than one occasion, to better understand the key issues of concern to me. Marie-Odile Capdeville read and reread the manuscript for the original French edition of the book. My deepest appreciation goes to all these people without whom this work would never have seen the light of day. Jacques Blocher oversaw corrections to the manuscript with his valuable editorial advice. I am also grateful to the John Templeton Foundation, who helped finance its original publication in French and its translation into English.

Introduction

Science is, without a doubt, one of the dominant structural elements of modern Western society. Not only do its technical achievements affect our daily lives, it also has a profound influence on the way that we understand the world and humanity's place in it. With science so omnipresent today, we can easily forget that it is a relatively recent cultural phenomenon: despite some continuity with Greek and medieval natural philosophy, modern science as such has only been with us since the seventeenth century. Realizing this historical fact naturally makes us question the interaction between modern science and other human activities. For science is not self-evident; it is not an unconditional "given" that is independent of any external factors.

Over the last few decades, the field of philosophy of science has become more and more aware of science's sociocultural foundations. Thomas Kuhn's bestselling book, *The Structure of Scientific Revolutions*, published for the first time in 1962, has become symbolic of a holistic understanding of science, which sees not just the simple accumulation of increasingly sophisticated experimental results, but acknowledges the role of more contextual factors. This new awareness is also sustained by interpretative problems raised by contemporary physics. It is very difficult to talk about relativity, and harder still, quantum mechanics, without meeting questions of a meta-theoretical, or even metaphysical nature. The continuing disagreement over the famous measurement problem in quantum mechanics is just one sign that the relevance of distinctly philosophical questions covers the whole of scientific endeavor, extending even into the realm of the "hard" sciences.

Becoming aware of the sociocultural context in which science is done opens up several areas for study, religion being one of them. While the last forty years have seen a marked increase in studies of science and religion in English-speaking countries, francophone philosophers of science have stayed somewhat on the sidelines on this issue. The French concept of *laïcité*, which tends to relegate faith to the private sphere, is undoubtedly one cause of their reluctance to explore the role of religion. Nonetheless, one's beliefs clearly exert a strong influence on the way one thinks and acts, and this holds as much for the individual as for the community; we cannot therefore exclude *a priori* the possibility of religious influences on science.

In Western culture—where modern science emerged—religion as a cultural phenomenon is first found in its Christian form. Despite the presence of other religious traditions in the West—from the Greco-Roman cults to the modern-day attraction of eastern spirituality, without forgetting the various influences of Islamic civilization—one cannot deny that the Christian worldview, with its roots in biblical revelation, has been the strongest individual religious factor in the construction of Western identity. The churches in our cities, towns, and villages, be they stone or concrete, bear witness to Christianity's influence on the entire European landscape.

Once we realize just how strong the respective influences of Christianity and science have been, it is understandably difficult to imagine that they might have co-existed without ever having come into contact. The case of Galileo is surely the most famous (or infamous) example of the interaction between the two, which, though highly regrettable in this instance, is undeniably real. Some have inferred from this that science and Christianity are locked in a never-ending "war,"[2] but historical truth is, of course, more complicated than such clichés. Historical studies have aimed to clarify the impact of Christianity on modern science, and although the debate about the precise limits of this influence is far from over,[3] there is a consensus that Christianity is a cultural factor that

2. For example White, *Warfare*.

3. Cf. the discussions provoked by two older summaries: Merton, "Puritanism, Pietism and Science," (reprinted in Russell, *Science and Religious Belief*, 20–54) had established a link between puritanism and modern science. Russell's work also contains critical responses to his theory; see also Morgan, "Puritan Thesis Revisited," 43–74. In a series of articles, published in *Mind*, Michael Foster had emphasized the link between several themes of Christian theology and presuppositions of modern science

positively contributed to the birth of modern science. The present work, on the basis of this observation, will aim to go further than a simple historical study. Our attention will be on the debate of ideas, which is the focal point of all specifically philosophical writing. Without neglecting historical considerations, which often usefully shed light on the study of the concepts themselves, the *de facto* question of how Christianity and science have interacted will not be our first concern. Our time will primarily be spent exploring the *de jure* relationships between these two approaches to reality. Thus, the study will not simply be content to identify (or question) any contribution Christianity may have made in the past; it will seek to ask what relevance the Christian worldview has for the practice of science today.

A specific angle of attack is necessary to guide our investigation, since a study of the relationship between science as a whole and Christianity as a whole would not only be far too ambitious a project; the enterprise itself would be jeopardized if the two domains under consideration were treated as monolithic entities that could be compared as such. It is therefore preferable, in order to avoid this danger, to focus our attention on one particularly fruitful aspect of the possible relations between faith and science. The present study will choose, as its area of investigation, the natural order as observed (or brought to light?) by the sciences. For, although we are used to thinking of science as *discovering* and *describing* the "laws of nature," the very idea of a *given* order in nature is still a subject of debate. Already with Kant we find the idea that the order we find in "nature" reflects the structures of the human mind; and up to the present day, philosophers of science debate whether, and in what form, we can speak of laws of nature.[4] This very lack of agreement gives us grounds to choose laws of nature as a topic of investigation, since it shows that this central concept of scientific methodology continues to pose *problems*. We can thus hope that a study carried out from an interdisciplinary perspective—combining philosophy of science, philosophy, and theology—will help us to see the issue in a new light and therefore serve to clarify what is at stake. In return, investigating laws of nature

---

("Christian Doctrine of Creation," 446–68; "Theology and Modern Science [I]," 439–66; "Theology and Modern Science [II]," 1–27). Wybrow, *Philosophy of Michael Foster*, retraces the history of the debate inspired by the articles; cf. also Davis, "Christianity and Modern Science," 75–95.

4. Van Fraassen, *Laws and Symmetry*, provides a useful introduction to this debate.

from this specific point of view will constitute a case study that will allow us to better appreciate the possible points of contact between religious outlook and scientific practice.

Of course, choosing to study the relationship between the Christian worldview and the natural order described by the sciences does not in any way presuppose a single-cause explanation for the origin of modern science, as if all that distinguishes it from older paradigms could be credited to religion alone. Nor are we guilty of confusing categories, thinking that the Christian worldview gives a definitive answer to any question that we might ask in philosophy of science concerning the natural order. However, given the many and complex interactions between religion, science, and philosophy of science that historical studies have brought to light,[5] we should expect that areas of mutual influence exist, and that the Christian faith lends support to certain approaches to the idea of law while posing a threat to others. The fact that these interactions do not carry the force of logical constraints does not diminish the relevance of the Christian worldview for philosophical work.

Just as it is necessary to choose a precise topic in philosophy of science, in order to make our investigation more incisive, it is indispensable to identify where we stand in the diverse array of traditions that one finds within Christianity. Describing this complexity would require a historico-descriptive study, which the present work will not attempt. The philosophico-normative approach taken here cannot simply make do with either the sum total, or the lowest common denominator, of the many worldviews that bear the Christian label. Granted, there are some constants that unite the various forms of Christianity: the idea of creation in particular will play a pivotal role in our deliberation; it has structured Christian thinking about the world from the beginning, and is part of the inheritance shared by all of Christendom. Irenaeus of Lyons, already in the second century, made creation the first article of the Christian faith: "And this is the order of our faith, the foundation of [the] edifice and the support of [our] conduct: God, the Father, uncreated, uncontainable, invisible, one God, the Creator of all: this is the first article of our faith."[6] All Christendom's great confessions of faith confirm the centrality of the doctrine of creation, starting with the so-called

---

5. The historiographical works of John Brooke provide a meticulous examination; e.g. *Science and Religion*, passim, and "Religious Belief," 1–26.

6. Irenaeus, *On the Apostolic Preaching*, 43

Apostles' Creed, which opens with the famous declaration, "I believe in God the Father Almighty, Maker of heaven and earth."

Nonetheless, a certain diversity exists within Christianity concerning the exact understanding of creation.[7] Philosophical rigor demands that before going any farther we choose a sufficiently precise version of this doctrine, which will serve as a necessary backdrop for the discussion of natural order. The treatment of creation offered here chooses to follow the Augustinian tradition, on which Calvinism builds. Divine sovereignty, one of Calvin's fundamental intuitions, implies a specific treatment of the relationship between the Creator and the creature, which corresponds to a particularly radical understanding of the difference between them—the presentation that follows will clarify the meaning of this somewhat concise statement.[8] Within Calvinism, the neo-Calvinist movement, emerging in the Netherlands at the end of the nineteenth century, offers a particularly acute understanding of creation and the knowledge that humanity can have of it. Because of this, the neo-Calvinists were among the first to turn "the investigation of religion as a force which shapes knowledge" into an influential research program,[9] in line with their conviction that faith plays a distinctively foundational role in any cognitive undertaking. Starting from the Calvinist intuition of the radical difference between the Creator and the creation, these writers sought to develop a Christian worldview that encompassed all of human experience, including science, and therefore no serious consideration of the concept of laws of nature can afford to ignore their conclusions. This movement's key figures will be brought in at various strategic points of this study: the theologian and statesman Abraham Kuyper (1837–1920), the theologian Herman Bavinck (1854–1921), the lawyer and philosopher Herman Dooyeweerd (1894–1977), and the apologist Cornelius Van Til (1895–1987), to name but four. Their works, however, remain sources of inspiration only, with respect to which I do

---

7. Gay, "Medieval Views of Creation," 243–73, discusses four different understandings of creation (Augustine, Pseudo-Dionysius, Aquinas, Cusanus). Klaaren, *Religious Origins*, 46ff, 54ff, distinguishes three main kinds of understanding (voluntarist, ontological, and spiritualist) active at the time of the birth of modern science.

8. For a summary of Calvinism's particular traits, cf. Niebuhr, *Christ and Culture*, 190–96; Wolters, "Dutch Neo-Calvinism," 121f.

9. Van Der Meer, "Metaphysical and Religious Beliefs," 248. On this note, we must also point out the work of the historian of science Reijer Hooykaas (1906–94), e.g., *Natural Law*; *Religion and Modern Science*; and *Fact, Faith and Fiction*.

not consider myself bound; they do not constitute an authority for my philosophical reflections. To use their works in such a way would in fact be contrary to these authors' own intentions, since they did not aim to do anything more than distil what the Bible teaches and apply the results to life's questions.

As is fitting for the topic under consideration, the religious position is adopted as a context for thinking (and living); I shall not try to construct it, let alone defend it. The job of the systematic theologian is to studiously articulate theology's central themes (including creation) from Scripture; the apologist's task is to explain the relevance and the correctness of the Christian perspective. Neither of these efforts should take center stage in the study that follows, although one should not infer from the (relative) silence on these matters that these tasks are by any means impossible.[10] In the context of philosophy of science, it is more appropriate to "put into practice" one's chosen religious worldview, to show how the questions concerning the natural order appear against such a background. Only in retrospect will we be able to see the coherence and the fruitfulness of this approach, which is, of course, no replacement for closely-reasoned argument: it simply provides the framework that is needed to give traction to our thinking.

The style adopted from here on in is deliberately one of personal involvement. My aim will be to examine the natural order and the knowledge of it that the sciences offer, in the light of the Christian faith. In what way is the Christian worldview relevant to the concept of law? How do the arguments from different sides appear against this conceptual background? If the investigation appears biased, given the deliberate choice of religious perspective, one must remember that the requirement of neutrality is an illusion in philosophy: there is no neutral viewpoint. All rational investigation is anchored somewhere, and we must try and be as explicit as possible about the presuppositions on which our reasoning is based. Pretending that we do not have any such presuppositions only makes us more vulnerable to their unfortunate influence, inasmuch as it amounts to a choice to ignore our dependence on them. In fact, the closeness of the philosopher's convictions to the paradigm he or she is exploring—in this case, the Christian worldview—is precisely what

---

10. I have tried elsewhere to contribute to the subject: concerning the biblical evidence for the doctrine of creation, see Jaeger, *Philosophie chrétienne des sciences*, 41–50; for apologetic methodology, see Jaeger, "Apologétique de Cornelius Van Til," 27–46.

enables an in-depth and nuanced examination, on the condition that the presuppositional basis for the work be recognized as such, and that opposing points of view be sufficiently taken into account.

Let us make clear that the religious position adopted here is not confined to a particular conception of God and the relationship between him and the world, for the Christian worldview is far more than just a set of ideas: it is a way of life that requires wholehearted personal commitment. The content of our analysis will thus be different from that of some contemporary works, which follow the tradition of (analytical) philosophy of religions. It is not enough to formulate a few concepts of a religious nature, and from them to develop a line of rational argument that is supposedly neutral. This approach too often results in something resembling "materialism-plus-minds-plus-God,"[11] which does not sufficiently appreciate the distance between trinitarian theism and other conceptions.

It follows that the Bible, read in the light of the contributions made by various theological traditions, is the narrative universe inside which the understanding of the natural order will be developed. While most interdisciplinary studies encompassing science, philosophy of science, and theology limit themselves to the interplay of the finished products of these disciplines (in the form of scientific theories, philosophical analyses, and theological systems),[12] we must dare to go beneath the surface and exploit the full wealth of biblical teaching, so as to think Christianly about philosophy of science concepts. Of course, this is not to imagine that the Bible teaches a particular philosophical theory. One must be especially careful not to make the mistake of trying to deduce a worldview solely from the *words* used in the biblical text.[13] But the main themes of the Bible cannot help but resonate when brought into contact with philosophical issues. As Étienne Gilson points out, "the Bible is full of ideas about God and His divine government which, although not properly philosophical in character, only needed to fall into the right soil to become fruitful of philosophic consequences."[14] It logically followed that thinking about the structure of creation was not only for intellec-

---

11. Settle, "Stones," 331, n. 17.
12. Collins, *God of Miracles,* is one of the rare exceptions, looking at the interaction between biblical exegesis, systematic theology, and philosophy, on the subject of causality; see especially 51–53, on the issue of the relevance of the Bible for philosophy.
13. Barr, *Biblical Words for Time,* 138–41.
14. Gilson, *Mediaeval Philosophy,* 11.

tuals; the faith of every believer implied a particular worldview. The evidence for this can be seen in the way Christians were criticized for having democratized philosophy, as early as the end of the second century: "The pretension, insupportable to the philosophers, that a humble *vetula* [i.e., old woman] knew more about the universe than Plato and Aristotle . . . is an integral part of the Christian tradition."[15] The present study therefore seeks to bring the structure of the Christian worldview to bear on the question of natural order and to construct a notion of laws of nature that fits the Christian faith's framework for thinking and living.

---

15. Ibid., 429.

one

The Idea of Creation

It is not a question between mysticism and rationality. It is a question between mysticism and madness. For mysticism, and mysticism alone, has kept men sane from the beginning of the world. All the straight roads of logic lead to some Bedlam, to Anarchism or to passive obedience, to treating the universe as a clockwork of matter or else as a delusion of mind. It is only the Mystic, the man who accepts the contradictions, who can laugh and walk easily through the world.

Are you surprised that the same civilisation which believed in the Trinity discovered steam?

—G. K. Chesterton, "Why I believe in Christianity"

CREATION AS A PRIMARY CONCEPT IN THE CHRISTIAN WORLDVIEW

The biblical canon opens with the majestic declaration of creation: "In the beginning God created the heavens and the earth" (Gen 1:1).[1] Rather

---

1. I follow the traditional understanding of the text, which sees in it the absolute beginning—over against the interpretation of some modern authors, who take the verse's syntactic construction as indicating either a relative beginning ("in a beginning") or a temporal clause subordinate to the verses that follow ("When God began to create heaven and earth," NJPS). The second proposal is invalidated by the fact that nowhere

than speculating about the existence of God or offering an abstract meditation on the nature of the world, right from the outset, Scripture lays down creation as the framework within which everything that follows takes place. The creative act is therefore primary and comes before anything that biblical faith can say about the world.

Understanding the world as God's creation requires the coexistence of two truths. Firstly, everything that exists has received its being from God and remains, even after the creative act has been performed, totally dependent on him. Biblical monotheism does not allow for any compromise: apart from God himself, everything is created. Nothing and nobody can claim independence from the Creator; no being ends up halfway, partly divine, partly dependent on the Creator. Secondly, creatures have real existence, and one that is distinct from that of the Creator: "By conferring on the work of his hands a life of its own the Creator stamps it, as it were, with the seal of his own approval, and raises it above the level of a worthless and ephemeral formation to that of a permanent existence. The creation is not merely a game of caprice, something which might equally well disappear again without a trace, a divine fantasy, as in the Indian conception, but possesses a God-given right to existence in itself."[2]

The beginning of Genesis forcefully teaches these two truths—radical dependence and distinct existence. The creature's dependence follows from the text's strict monotheism. Nothing exists independently of God's creative act; nothing and nobody stands in the way of his plan. Creation happens by the divine word, which is not met with any resistance: "the text contains not the slightest hint of any battle whatsoever."[3] At the same time, God's evaluation of the creation (Gen 1:31) presupposes its real existence. The picture that is painted allows for a degree of internal autonomy in the creation: God's word confers on the earth the possibility to produce plants (Gen 1:11–12); the plants and animals are created with the ability to reproduce (Gen 1:12, 22, 28). But it is the seventh-day rest that especially underlines creation's distinct existence

---

in the Hebrew Bible do we find the initial word of Genesis' first verse with the meaning "to begin to" followed by a verb. A synonym is sometimes employed with this meaning, but in this case the verb is an infinitive construct (2 Kgs 17:25; Hos 1:2 [?]). As for the first proposal, whilst it is true that there is no definite article (at least according to the Masoretic vocalization), temporal expressions regularly omit this (cf. Isa 46:10).

2. Eichrodt, *Old Testament*, 158.

3. Blocher, *In the Beginning*, 64. Cf. Pannenberg, *Systematic Theology*, 12–14.

(Gen 2:1–3; Exod 20:11; 31:17). It expresses the "*constancy of the divine creative will.*"[4]

In this way creationism[5] introduces a radical asymmetry in its conception of reality: the creation, possessing its own solidity, is juxtaposed with its Creator, on whom everything depends, and who does not depend on anything. Thus are ruled out, right from the start, other views that do not allow for this discontinuity. The world is not an illusion; neither is it an emanation of God's nature, an extension of his being.[6] Equally, nothing exists prior to the work of creation that could limit its scope. Thus, the world is assigned its own category of being: the created order refers to God as its Creator, but is not to be confused with him: "Christian ontology requires radical separation between the Creator and the creature. God is not merely the highest or most perfect part of the world, as in all the philosophical systems of antiquity. The Christian God's being is incommensurate with that of the created world."[7]

Traditionally, Christian theology has expressed the discontinuity between the Creator and the creation by the affirmation that creation is *ex nihilo*: the creation comes from "nothing," in the strict sense of the word. God's sovereign freedom implies that he depends on nothing and nobody in order to create; at the same time, he is not obliged to create; the creation is not an extension of his essence. As pseudo-Justin remarked, "The creator . . . has no need of anything, and it is of his own power and will that he creates what is created; the demiurge gets from matter the power to carry out his work, and thus he governs what comes into being."[8] Creation *ex nihilo* therefore expresses a double denial: the

---

4. Eichrodt, *Old Testament*, 158.

5. The term "creationism" (and the adjective "creationist") refers to the belief that the world is created, without further specifying the details of how creation took place. It does not therefore imply a literal six-day interpretation, unlike the narrower use of the term common in the US.

6. There is only one biblical text that could suggest continuity between the creature and the Creator: believers are called to become "participants in the divine nature" (2 Pet 1:4). Not only is this expression unique in the biblical corpus, but the end of the verse shows that this participation must be understood in *ethical* rather than *ontological* terms: it means escaping "the corruption of sinful desire."

7. Sherringham, *Philosophie esthétique*, 105. Clouser, *Knowing with the Heart*, 197, n. 3, emphasizes that the Bible does not speak of the divine perfection in the Greek sense of the highest degree of an attribute.

8. Pseudo-Justin, *Cohortatio ad graecos*, 22, quoted by Tresmontant, *Origins of Christian Philosophy*, 48f.

creation does not rely on preexistent matter, nor is it a divine emanation. As Saint Augustine wrote, "Thou *createdst heaven and earth;* not out of Thyself; for so should they have been equal to Thine Only Begotten Son . . . And aught else besides Thee was there not, whereof Thou mightest create them, O God, One Trinity, and Trine Unity; and therefore out of nothing didst Thou *create heaven and earth*."[9] Acknowledging these twin aspects of creation *ex nihilo* is the only way to bring together the perfect sovereignty of the Creator and the total dependence of the creation, in its *real* existence.

It would be wrong to conclude that the discontinuity in the concept of being only implies divine transcendence; the idea of creation also encompasses and points to the *immanence* of God. To be sure, creation upholds the radical separation between God and all created things. Monotheism itself is at stake: an idol is none other than a creature that claims divine status. The biblical God is a "jealous" God: "I—the LORD is my name—, I will not give my glory to another, nor my praise to idols" (Isa 42:8). But the Creator God is not a distant God; he is intimately present with all of his creation, and this as transcendent Creator, to whom everything owes its existence. In fact, the two aspects of God's relationship with the world refer to one another and are incomprehensible if taken separately. As the Creator is not on the same level as his creation, his presence and action are not in competition with the creature: "God is so powerful that the more really he acts, the more reality the creature possesses in its being, in its action and in its freedom: '*Dei Providentia causas secunda non tollis sed ponit*.'"[10] Indeed, the ontological dependence of creation cannot be conceived in all its radicality without God's intimate closeness to what he has made. It is as Creator, radically distinct from his creature, that God is more present than any creature could be to itself. As Saint Augustine said, "But Thou wert more inward to me, than my most inward part; and higher than my highest."[11]

Creationism implies holding together truths that other belief systems consider antithetical: divine immanence and transcendence, absolute

---

9. Augustine, *Confessions*, XII, 7, 180.

10. Lecerf, *Dogmatique réformée*, vol. 1, 167. The Latin quote is from Johannes Wolleb, quoted by Bavinck, *Gereformeerde Dogmatiek*, vol. 2, 663 ("God's providence does not destroy secondary causes but upholds them.")

11. "*Tu autem eras interior intimo meo et superior summo meo*" (Augustine, *Confessions*, III, 6, 34).

sovereignty of the Creator and the real existence of the creature, divine aseity and divine involvement in this earthly world of change and imperfection. Should we therefore believe that this vision of reality tries to reconcile the irreconcilable?[12] It is true that creationism takes the idea of creation as its starting point; the latter does not emerge at the end of a supposedly neutral rational deduction, based on what we observe in the world. In this way, this worldview explicitly places a mystery at the heart of its interpretation of reality. However, acknowledging the mystery of existence does not mean that we abandon all responsible thinking. Is it not rather the necessary point of leverage, without which all thinking, left to itself, would fail to gain any traction? It comes down to the type of mystery that one is willing to admit. Creationism starts from the constitutive relationship between Creator and creature, instead of invoking an abstract notion of being. But "the acceptance of the ultimacy of being is a *petitio principii*; it mistakes a problem for a solution. The supreme and ultimate issue is not *being* but the *mystery* of being."[13]

The relevance of the chosen starting point cannot be demonstrated in an argument that would be independent of it. Its value is seen rather in the fruitfulness of its perspective, in how it enlightens us and directs our approach to reality. Besides, how can we expect to grasp, in an exhaustive way, the relationship between God and the world, given that this link is, from a creationist perspective, *constitutive* of who we are, right up to our ability to reason? Thus, it is only "logical" (seen from our human perspective) to accept the fact that "*the starting-point, taught by Scripture, is the Creator-creature pattern*. We cannot raise ourselves higher and dominate the constitutive structure, we cannot subsume it under an all-embracing notion of being . . . The obedience of faith, in receiving this orientation as the principle of sound thinking, does not boast that it has solved the monistic-dualistic antinomy, but humbly *refuses* it."[14]

---

12. The trinitarian perspective reconciles immanence and transcendence: although transcendence is primarily associated with the Father, and immanence to the Spirit, "the Son . . . prevents us from understanding transcendence and immanence in a dialectical fashion" (Blocher, "Immanence and Transcendence," 121–23). Gunton, *Triune Creator*, 103 (citing Cochrane, *Christianity and Classical Culture*, 367f), sees a similar idea in the writings of Athanasius (328–73). Cf. pp. 31–38 below.

13. Heschel, *Prophets II*, 43, quoted by Blocher, "Divine Immutability," 15.

14. Blocher, "Divine Immutability," 16.

Making creation the first principle of the biblical worldview does not, however, imply that we should try to deduce all of Christian doctrine from it. Indeed, such an effort would confuse immersion in a religious lifestyle with metaphysical speculation. We cannot do without revelation if we want to learn the whole structure of the Christian worldview.[15] Although the idea of creation is central to all thinking about the world, it must bring in other essential elements of the Christian worldview, like the Trinity and redemption. But such is the harmony between these various doctrines that each, to be fully understood, refers to the others. To cite just one example: the incarnation, linchpin of the Creed, "would remain strictly unthinkable and completely nonsensical," in an ontology that conceived of the deity as belonging to the impersonal category of pure being, perfectly motionless and closed on itself, with no way of relating to the world. For, in this case, how could one imagine that the deity could take the form of "a historic human individual"?[16] The doctrine of the two natures of Christ presupposes creationism as the only context in which it makes any sense.

The discussion of the natural order undertaken here will be based primarily on the idea of creation and will not involve redemption as a separate dimension—unlike the Barthian perspective—for the simple reason that redemption is seen primarily as the restoration of creation.[17] The biblical worldview resists Manichean dualism: evil is not an independent force, which stands in opposition to God's good creation. It is rather the corruption of the created order, and is therefore always parasitic. Redemption's aim is to restore the creational order, which has been disrupted, rather than replace it. This does not prevent the eschatological hope from exceeding, in its glory, the initial state; the biblical worldview rejects the pagan idea of eternal recurrence, so as to uphold a real historical perspective on the divine action of salvation. It is nevertheless possible to consider the world's created nature without broadening the perspective to explicitly include redemption, insofar as evil and God's answer in salvation are not part of the created order.

---

15. Van Til, *Survey of Christian Epistemology*, 20, notes that God is not a "master concept" from which everything else in a Christian's worldview can be deduced.

16. Sherringham, *Philosophie esthétique*, 90f.

17. Wolters, *Creation Regained*, 10, following Bavinck.

THE FREEDOM OF CREATION[18]

The face-to-face juxtaposition of God and the world, which is fundamental to creationism, is only conceivable if creation is a free and sovereign act. The New Testament emphasizes that God created everything "by the decision of his will" (Eph 1:11; 1 Cor 15:38; Rev 4:11). The freedom of creation distinguishes it from any theory that sees the world as a divine emanation; that considers the universe (or any of its parts) as an extension of the divine nature. It is important to distinguish between divine nature and divine will, unlike the necessitarian worldview, which affirms that "God . . . acts by the sole necessity of his own nature."[19] The majestic "In the beginning God created" thus stands over against any perspectives marked by pantheism; it goes against all philosophies that see the world as a result of an evolution of the divine being.

The Christian tradition has always been careful to distinguish creation from emanation: the creative act stems from the divine will, not the divine nature. Basil of Caesarea, in his fourth-century commentary on the beginning of Genesis, writes the following:

> Inasmuch as many of those who have imagined that the world from eternity co-existed with God did not concede that it was made by Him, but that, being, as it were, a shadow of His power, it existed of itself coordinately with Him, and inasmuch as they admit that God is the cause of it, but involuntarily a cause, as the body is the cause of the shadow and the flashing light the cause of the brilliance, therefore, the prophet in correcting such an error used exactness in his words, saying: "In the beginning God created." The thing itself did not provide the cause of its existence, but He created, as One good, something useful; as One wise, something beautiful; as One powerful, something mighty.[20]

It was the conception of the Trinity in particular that forced Christian theology to clarify the idea of the freedom of creation. For one must explain what distinguishes God's relationship with the world from intra-trinitarian relations. Evidently, the relationships between the Father, the Son, and the Spirit are eternal, while the relationship with the world is not. But temporal differentiation is hardly sufficient to describe what is specific to creation. For being omniscient, God knew from all

---

18. This section incorporates certain parts of Jaeger, "Nature et volonté," 109–18.
19. Spinoza, *Ethics*, first part, corollary II of proposition XVII, 11
20. Basil, *On the Hexameron* (I), 12

eternity that he would create. One must therefore make use of the stronger distinction between nature and will, between relationships that flow from God's essence and decrees stemming from his choice, in order to differentiate the creation from intra-trinitarian relations.[21]

Although the distinction between divine nature and divine will is central to the idea of creation, it is not easy to imagine how God might *freely* desire the existence of a world that is separate from him. For how is it that the necessary Being called into existence that which is contingent, that the will of the Lord "in whom there is neither change nor shadow due to change" (Jas 1:17), concerns that which is temporal and subject to change? Descartes realized this acute difficulty and his answer was to absolutize contingency. He not only affirmed the creation of "eternal truths" (i.e., mathematics)[22] but made God's nature itself dependent on his will. In so doing, he went against Augustinian tradition, which includes Platonic ideals in the deity; "the whole Cartesian system is based on the idea of an omnipotent God who, in a way, creates himself."[23] Divine freedom means indifference in the face of choices; Descartes thus abolishes any determination by categories of goodness or truth (even if they are understood as deriving from the divine nature):

> It is self-contradictory to suppose that the will of God was not indifferent from eternity with respect to everything which has happened or will ever happen; for it is impossible to imagine that anything is thought of in the divine intellect as good or true, or worthy of belief or action or omission, prior to the decision of the divine will to make it so. I am not speaking here of temporal priority: I mean that there is not even any priority of order, or nature, or of "rationally determined reason" as they call it, such that God's idea of the good impelled him to choose one thing rather than another.[24]

By absolutizing contingency, it is true that Descartes manages to exalt (a certain understanding of) freedom in the work of creation. But it resolves the difficulty by absorbing one aspect into the other; that is,

---

21. Foster, "Theology and Modern Science (I)," 444f.; Gisel, *Création*, 125.

22. Descartes, *Meditations on First Philosophy*, Fifth replies, in *Philosophical Writings*, 261; Descartes, *Letter to Mersenne*, 15 April 1630, ibid., 20s; Descartes, *Letter* (to Mersenne?), 27 May 1630, ibid., 25s.

23. Gilson, *Spirit of Mediaeval Philosophy*, 14.

24. Descartes, *Meditations on First Philosophy*, Sixth replies, section 6, 92.

by making the divine nature dependent on the divine will. As a result, creation appears to be an arbitrary act. Creationism, however, upholds two truths: God creates both *freely* and *wisely*. Even if the Cartesian solution has the advantage of being radical, it cannot, in its unilateralism, do justice to the balance of the Bible's teaching. For the Apostle Paul, God's power is shown in the works of creation (Rom 1:20). Similarly, the creation is a work of divine wisdom: personified Wisdom in the book of Proverbs calls herself "architect," "master builder" of the divine creation (Prov 8:30).[25] Of course, it is not easy to imagine that God creates both freely and in a non-arbitrary way. But we will not grasp the particularity of the concept of creation until we understand that it is a matter of divine freedom *and* divine wisdom.

It is instructive to compare Descartes' solution to Calvin's understanding of this issue. The reformer rejected the link between freedom and indifferent choice. If the ability to will presupposes the possibility of choosing between two alternatives, we cannot accept that God *wishes* something when his nature forbids him to choose the other option (owing to his goodness or his wisdom, for example). However, the idea of creation leads Calvin (and Augustine before him) to break with such a libertarian conception of freedom, when it comes to mankind. As the creature depends, even in his free acts, on the Creator, we should not oppose divine sovereignty and human freedom; predestination does not negate moral responsibility, but rather upholds it.[26] It is therefore consistent that Calvin also refuses to link *divine* freedom and the possibility of choice: "The free will of God in doing good is not impeded, because he necessarily must do good," since one must "distinguish between *necessity* and *compulsion*." Insofar as it "is owing not to violent impulse, but to his boundless goodness, that he cannot do evil,"[27] God is free when doing

---

25. Without changing the consonants of the Hebrew text, it is possible to read 'ĕmûn, "darling child" (von Rad, *Wisdom in Israel*, 152). Despite this ambiguity, the passage clearly teaches the idea of wisdom's participation in creation (v. 27).

26. Descartes embraces the same Augustinian conception of human freedom, when he writes, "For in order that I should be free it is not necessary that I should be indifferent as to the choice of one or the other of two contraries; but contrariwise the more I lean to the one whether I recognise clearly that the reasons of the good and true are to be found in it, or whether God so disposes my inward thought the more freely do I choose and embrace it." (Descartes, *Method and Meditations*, 97).

27. Calvin, *Institutes* II, III, 5, 253f.

good. Far from calling his freedom into question, the impossibility of doing evil is an expression of God's perfection.

Although this rival conception of freedom removes any contradiction between free action and creative work directed by the divine nature (God's wisdom and goodness), it does not appear sufficient to allow us to affirm the contingency of the created order as strongly as we would like. Almost without exception, throughout the various eras of church history, it was believed that the created nature of the world implies that it might not have been, or could be different. To affirm the opposite would be ceding to pantheism.[28] Are we therefore forced back to the Cartesian understanding, which makes the contingency of the world dependent on an arbitrary choice between neutral options?

When Calvin treats the question of why God did not create earlier that he did, he seems to fall back on this kind of viewpoint. He establishes a parallel with the finitude of the cosmos, since this idea seemed to him to be universally accepted. Whatever the exact size of a finite universe, "vacant space remains exceeding creation by a hundred-fold"; in the same way, "countless ages" preceded the creation of the world. The positioning of the world in time and space is thus a matter of arbitrary choice, and it should be enough for us to know that God willed it thus: "Justly does Augustine complain that God is insulted whenever any higher reason than his will is demanded."[29] This indifference does not signify a capricious will, since the rival options are equivalent to each other.

But can we extend this kind of indifference to the whole of divine action in creation, providence, and salvation? Calvin didn't seem to think so, for he maintained that God's wisdom and righteousness guide all his

---

28. There is debate about whether Aquinas does enough justice to the contingency of creation, cf. the introduction by Cyrille Michon who disagrees with Norman Kretzmann, in Aquinas, *Somme contre les Gentils*, 22, n. 22. Kretzmann believes that for Aquinas, divine freedom is limited to the form that creation takes; the fact that creation happens is a necessity. Michon considers, on the contrary, that for Aquinas creation is apposite rather than necessary: "It was proper for God, in his goodness, to create, without its introducing any necessity whatsoever" (ibid., 21). Cf. Kretzmann, *Metaphysics of Creation*, 137ff.

29. Calvin, *Institutes* I, XIV, 1, 142, quoting Augustine, *De Genesi contra Manichaeos* 2, 29 (43). This passage is perhaps indirect evidence of the consequences of the Bishop of Paris' condemnation of the Aristotelian system in 1277. Over against Aristotle, article 34 of the declaration asserted that God could create multiple worlds. This proposal led most intellectuals to postulate an empty space beyond our world, capable of hosting other worlds, if God decided to create them (Grant, "Condemnation of 1277," 243f).

actions, even if our current infirmity prevents us from seeing this. Thus he believed that God, in his providence, conducts "all things in perfect accordance with reason";[30] "the issue [will] at length make it manifest, that the counsel of God was in accordance with the highest reason."[31] This is true even for the problem of evil; "it shall be given to us to know how he mysteriously wills what now seems to be adverse to his will."[32] So the question remains as to how to reconcile God's freedom and his wisdom, in his works *ad extra*.

A reasonably speculative proposal (which does not come from Calvin) would be to seek the answer by understanding monotheism in a particularly exact way: it is God himself who determines the possible options, the choice itself owing its existence to him, since aseity belongs to God alone. In this way God freely creates the choice in response to which his will is exercised. Even if God's nature leads him to choose one option rather than the other, the contingency of this choice is maintained insofar as the existence of a choice is dependent on God's will. Compared to Descartes, this proposal pushes divine indifference back a step. Instead of postulating that God could have chosen the other option, it maintains that God could have decided not to create the choice. This proposal, which may at first glance seem extravagant, assumes that modality depends on actuality: what is possible depends on the ontological basis by which we understand reality. It thus becomes possible to postulate that creation does not happen in the context of a pre-existent range of possibilities, but that creation itself brings about the network of choices to which it belongs.

Understanding the *freedom* of creation as an expression of the divine nature points us to the personal character of God. Only in the case where ultimate reality is a *person*, can we understand how creation can be both free and a matter of divine wisdom. Compared to the Cartesian idea, it is less a matter of *abolishing* the dichotomy, and more a case of *refusing* it. The divine nature is not absorbed by the divine will; rather, God's nature and will find themselves in perfect harmony. God is what he wants and wants what he is: "for Calvin, God's will is never arbitrary since it is expressive of God's nature, while God's nature is never to be identified with impersonal law because God's nature is never taken in

---

30. Calvin, *Institutes* I, V, 8, 57.
31. Ibid., I, XVII, 1, 183.
32. Ibid., III, XXIV, 17, 257.

separation from God's will. It is thus that *complete personalism and therefore complete stability are combined.*"[33]

Thus creation leads us to think of the divine as a Person; only a free and voluntary choice can maintain the necessary distinction between creation and begetting, between the relationship with the world and intra-trinitarian relations. Creationism implies an understanding of God diametrically opposed to that of Greek philosophy, which identifies the deity as "pure being, the self-sufficient and closed-on-itself fullness of absolutely stable and immobile being."[34] A personalistic understanding of God is the only one that leaves room for a contingent world.

THE POSSIBLE AND THE REAL

By refusing any blurring of boundaries between God and the world, creationism emphasizes the contingency of the natural order. It therefore becomes possible to distinguish between logical (or metaphysical) necessity and physical necessity—a distinction unknown to the ancient world.[35] The argument used by Spinoza against miracles is representative of the difficulty that all pantheistic conceptions have in making room for such a distinction. As Spinoza does not maintain sufficient distance between nature and the Necessary Being, for him the laws of nature stem directly from the divine nature: "All things which come to pass, come to pass solely through the laws of the infinite nature of God, and follow . . . from the necessity of his essence."[36] Thus the world is governed by the strictest metaphysical determinism: "Things could not have been brought into being by God in any manner or in any order different from that which has in fact obtained."[37] In such a perspective, it is as nonsensical to postulate events contrary to nature's laws, as it is to imagine that the Necessary Being might change: "if anyone were to assert that God does anything contrary to the laws of nature, he would at the same time be compelled to assert that God acts contrary to his own nature, than

---

33. Van Til, *Survey of Christian Epistemology*, 100.

34. Sherringham, *Philosophie esthétique*, 91.

35. Funkenstein, *Theology and Scientific Imagination*, 119. The contingency of the created order is a key concept in Pannenberg's theology of nature (e.g., Pannenberg, "Contingency and Natural Law," 72–122, and Pannenberg, "Kontingenz der geschöpflichen Wirklichkeit," 1049–58). See Russell, "Contingency in Physics," 23–43.

36. Spinoza, *Ethics*, first part, scholium to proposition XV, 10.

37. Ibid., prop. XXXIII, 18, cf. prop. XXIX, 16.

which nothing is more absurd."[38] If creationism, on the contrary, holds to the possibility of miracles, it is because they manifest the freedom of the Creator, something fundamental to this worldview.[39]

The contingency of the created world can be related to the experimental approach, the latter being characteristic of modern science when compared to its Greek and medieval predecessors. For the contingency of the natural order implies that we cannot know it by pure speculation; the difference between logical and natural necessity makes experimentation absolutely vital.[40] Thus it is almost certain that the condemnation issued in 1277 by the Bishop of Paris, Étienne Tempier, contributed to the rise of the experimental method. Against an Aristotelian worldview, marked by determinism and rationalism, the condemnation exalted the freedom of the Creator. The rejection of the argument that God cannot act against the natural order figured prominently.[41]

The conviction that the natural order is contingent is the foundation of Newton's empiricism. In one of his unpublished manuscripts, we read: "The world might have been otherwise then it is . . . Twas therefore noe necessary but a voluntary & free determination yt it should bee thus."[42] In doing so, he takes the opposite stance to that of his rival Leibniz, whom he considered too rationalist in his approach to nature. Roger Cotes, who oversaw the publication of the second edition of the *Principia*, championed this view by writing in the preface that we find in the laws of nature, established by the will of God, "many traces indeed of the most wise contrivance, but not the least shadow of necessity. These therefore we must not seek from uncertain conjectures, but learn them from observations and experiments."[43] One who imagines he can deduce science rationally "must either suppose that the world exists by necessity, and by the same necessity follows the laws proposed; or if the order of Nature was established by the will of God, that himself, a miserable reptile, can tell what was fittest to be done."[44]

---

38. Spinoza, *Theological-Political Treatise*, chap. 6, 83.

39. Tresmontant, *Etudes de métaphysique biblique*, 225. The fact that miracles are *real*, and not just possible, is not a question of creation, but rather of salvation history.

40. Torrance, "Beliefs in Science," 163.

41. This is found in proposition 17 (Hyman et al., *Philosophy*, 542).

42. Quoted by Davis, "Newton's Rejection," 117.

43. Cotes, 1713, in Newton, *Principia mathematica*, xxxii.

44. Ibid.

The distinction between logical and natural necessity, which creationism requires, implies that the possible goes beyond the real. Thus, the Bible repeatedly suggests that history does not exhaust the possibilities open to an almighty God (Matt 3:9; 19:26; 26:53; Luke 1:37). Whereas "Aristotle identifies... *being* with the *real*, and correspondingly makes the *possible* a *not-yet-real*,"[45] the contingency of the created world forces us to imagine possibilities that are never realized—creationism does not sit comfortably with the plenitude principle, according to which everything which is possible happens in reality. While this principle (with variations) provided a influential philosophical framework, since at least Aristotle, via Plotinus, through to Spinoza,[46] such an approach to potentiality appears reductionistic when compared to seeing the world as creation. It is thus important to seek the conceptual tools that allow us to express this "thickness" of potentiality that surrounds the created world, without equating the former with the latter.

The work of Simo Knuuttila has highlighted the unique contribution that the idea of creation has made in the development of modal theories. With Saint Augustine we see the beginnings of a new understanding of modality, which seeks to do justice to the contingency of the created order. To uphold God's omnipotence, whose scope is not limited to what actually happens, one must be able to affirm that something is possible that in fact never occurs. With the old understanding of modality, which identifies the possible with what exists at a given moment, such a thing is unthinkable. To this objection to Christian doctrine, Augustine replied that something that does not happen is still possible, if God can do it.[47]

---

45. Gisel, *Création*, 247. Simo Knuuttila sees three modal models in Aristotle's writings: the statistical interpretation of possibility, the understanding of possibility as potentiality and (perhaps) the idea of "diachronic modalities." In none of the three conceptions are there synchronic possibilities, i.e., mutually exclusive rival options that cannot simultaneously occur but that coexist as possibilities (Knuuttila, *Modalities in Medieval Philosophy*, vii, 1ff, 19ff, 31ff).

46. Lovejoy, *Great Chain of Being*. With Spinoza, this principle is a direct consequence of his metaphysical determinism. As he denies the Creator's freedom, "from God's supreme power, or infinite nature, an infinite number of things—that is, all things have necessarily flowed forth in an infinite number of ways, or always flow from the same necessity" (Spinoza, *Ethics*, first part, scholium to prop. XVII, 11).

47. Knuuttila, *Modalities in Medieval Philosophy*, 67–69, and Knuuttila, "Time and Creation," 107, which cites Augustine, *De spiritu et littera*, 1–2, and Augustine, *De civitate Dei*, XXI, 5–8, and XXII, 4 and 11.

Duns Scotus (c. 1268–1308) subsequently developed this idea, in order to exalt as far as possible God's omnipotence, which we should not limit to what we see happen in our world. Negating the plenitude principle had become commonplace in medieval theology, but Duns Scotus seems to have been the first to use this negation as a basis on which to develop a new modal theory. In order to have at his disposal a language in which to describe the conviction that the possible goes beyond the real, he developed a semantic system that shows striking similarity to the modern formalism of possible worlds. In particular, he arrived at the concept, new in Western thought, of *synchronic* possibilities: mutually exclusive rival options that coexist as referents of the divine mind.[48] For Duns Scotus, the possibilities are not dependent on God's choice: "the absolute totality of intelligiblity" would be "similarly actualized by any omniscient intellect."[49]

So we see that creationism required a broadening of the notion of what is possible. However, one must wonder whether representing creation as a choice among several possibilities in existence before the divine decree is sufficient to fully account for the contingency of the created order. To express the contingency of the created order, the Bible never uses, to my knowledge, the language of unrealized potential; it does not say that our world could have been different. Rather, it emphasizes the sovereign power of the Creator: nothing and no one can thwart his plans (Isa 14:27; 43:13; Eccl 7:13); he accomplishes all he wishes, according to his good pleasure (Isa 46:10; Ps 115:3; 135:6); he has never needed any help to achieve his work (Isa 40:13f; 44:24; Jer 10:12; 27:5; 32:17). Scripture repeatedly emphasizes that God can overturn the natural order, for he maintains perfect control of it, being its Creator (Joel 3:3–4; Amos 8:9; Ps 97:5; Job 26:11; 2 Pet 3:10–13). But even if events contrary to the natural order are possible, the biblical texts do not explicitly state that nature's ordinary state could have been different. God's omnipotence may go beyond the course of history, but our world is still the framework within which these unrealized possibilities are described.

---

48. Knuuttila, *Modalities in Medieval Philosophy*, 138ff, and Knuuttila, "Time and Modality," 236; Langton, "Scotus and Possible Worlds," 241.

49. Knuuttila, "Duns Scotus," 137. Not everyone follows Knuuttila on this point. William of Ockham thought Duns Scotus defended the creation of possibilities by God, and criticized him for this idea (ibid., 142, 145). See Adams, *William Ockham*, 1075–78, which discusses the intricacies of Duns Scotus' position and Ockham's response.

It is not impossible that the Bible's restraint in this matter is linked to monotheism: when one imagines the contingency of creation in terms of choice between various possibilities, some of which are not realized, polytheism is perhaps not far away. Even if the worlds, among which God made a choice when creating, are merely possible and not real, they conjure up the specter of realities that are independent of God and co-eternal with him.[50] But as an opponent of Christianity succinctly put it (finding here an argument against such a conception of God): "If we ask what exists outside of an omnipotent God, independently of his will, the answer must be: Nothing whatever. There are not even possibilities. There is nothing at all."[51]

To fully honor the idea of creation *ex nihilo*, however, it is not enough to situate the possible worlds within God. Admittedly, in so doing we avoid postulating the existence of eternal entities outside of God—but we run the risk of necessitarianism. For if we include all possibilities inside the divine nature, we find ourselves back at a version of the plenitude principle: this time, it is not the created world that realizes all possibilities, but the divine nature. Neither understanding accounts for the contingency of creation with sufficient rigor. According to Etienne Gilson, the condemnation of 1277 is lucid on this point when it identifies the source of the errors as "the Aristotelian identification of reality, intelligibility and necessity, not only in things, but first and above all in God."[52]

Creationism requires us to maintain a distinction between the divine nature and the free creative decree, to make room for contingency. Including the created order in God—even as a thought or possibility—does little to clarify this distinction. Ultimately, we find ourselves up against the mystery of creation: how can the self-sufficient and unchangeable[53] God call into (real, not illusory!) existence something that

---

50. Henri Blocher, private discussion, which here continues Cornelius Van Til's thinking on God's self-sufficiency. Cf. the medieval debates about whether something is (im)possible because God can(not) do it, or whether God can(not) do something because it is (im)possible: Adams, *William Ockham*, chap. 25.

51. McTaggart, *Some Dogmas of Religion*, sec. 169, 207; cf. sec. 170, 208, for the argument against the existence of such a God.

52. Gilson, *History of Christian Philosophy*, 407.

53. The fact that divine immutability is not an idea that is foreign to biblical thought, which Christian theology would have imported from Greek philosophy, can be seen in texts like 1 Tim 6:15–16; Heb 1:11f; Jas 1:17. However, there is debate about how the

does not participate in his eternity? Situating potentiality in the divine nature does not get us any nearer to the solution. It is more satisfactory (even if, of course, it does not make the mystery disappear) to imagine that the creative act gives rise to the modal "thickness" that accompanies reality. Rather than thinking of creation as a choice among existing options, creation establishes the network of possibilities in relation to which it can be understood.[54]

This proposal may seem paradoxical at first sight, and yet it becomes intelligible if we accept that the possible is affected by the ontology that we choose. Not only do we often learn what is possible by contemplating reality, but also, potentialities depend crucially on the ontological basis that one adopts. Quine's inclusion of the principle of contradiction itself in the network of truths established *a posteriori*[55] can be interpreted as a belated victory for Descartes' position, which included even mathematical truths in God's free act of creation.[56] Such an understanding can easily accept that the possible is a matter of divine decision, and thus escape the rampant necessitarianism of a worldview that places modality in God himself.

One noteworthy consequence of such an approach to modal ideas is that it allows us to attribute necessity to God, in a very specific sense. God is necessary inasmuch as no attribution of modality has any meaning independently of him. The standard proofs of God's existence are therefore radically transformed: since the notion of possibility is based on God himself, it makes no sense to ask whether it is possible, necessary, or probable that God exists, given a particular fact. No probability calculation can be placed "above" God, the source of all modality. As Cornelius Van Til stressed: "When one opens his mouth about possibility he also

---

biblical understanding of divine immutability differs from the Greek idea of the perfect Being: Blocher, "Divine Immutability," 1–22, and Helm, "Impossibility of Divine Passibility," 119–40.

54. See Clouser, "Religion, Metaphysics and Science," 67, and Clouser, *Myth of Religious Neutrality*, chap. 10 (with biblical arguments); Ross, "Crash of Modal Metaphysics," 251–79.

55. Quine, "Two Dogmas of Empiricism," 196–213. Hilary Putnam's critical response, "There is At Least One *A Priori* Truth," 153–70, does not, in the end, come down one way or the other, despite what the title says.

56. See p. 8 above. The possible contingency of the laws of logic is a complicated subject; for a comparison of Descartes' position with that of Calvin (who maintains, it seems, a certain link between the principle of contradiction and the divine nature) see Jaeger, "Nature et volonté," 111f.

opens his mouth about God. God is either the source of possibility or he comes out of bare possibility."[57] But this latter understanding amounts to granting modal considerations a value that is independent of, or even superior to, God himself, thereby giving modality quasi-divine status.[58]

LEIBNIZ: RATIONALISTIC CREATIONISM

One can hardly discuss the understanding of modality, from a Christian perspective, without mentioning Leibniz's name. As is evidenced by the famous phrase: "Everything is for the best in the best of all possible worlds,"[59] the idea of unrealized possibility played an important role in the German philosopher's work. It is this notion that, as Leibniz himself says, pulled him out of Spinoza's "abyss," in which everything happens by necessity; it is what enabled him to distinguish "between the infallible, or what is known with certainty to be true, and the necessary," even though his worldview showed such a strong fascination with the ordering force of reason.[60]

Leibniz shows himself to be a rationalistic philosopher (or rather, theologian), in the way he closely links God and the rules of logic (in particular, the principle of contradiction): these laws are included in the divine essence. He explicitly rejects the Cartesian conception of the creation of the necessary truths of logic and geometry. The latter are not "the effects of the will of God," but rather (and exclusively) "the consequences of his understanding, which certainly does not depend upon his will any more than does his essence."[61] To say that the divine mind depends on his will means "that he is deprived of his wisdom and justice" and leaves only "a certain unmeasured power from which all emanates, which deserves

---

57. Van Til, *Survey of Christian Epistemology*, 107. See Van Til, *Christian Theory of Knowledge*, 251. A rational apologetics remains possible in a Van Til-style view, see Jaeger, "L'apologétique de Van Til."

58. Chap. 5 will investigate in more detail the meaning of proofs of God's existences from a creationist perspective.

59. The slogan is a combination of two expressions frequently used in the philosophical tale *Candide*, in which Voltaire ridicules (a caricature of) Leibniz's optimism: "the best of possible worlds" and "everything is for the best in this world."

60. Leibniz, "On Freedom," 263.

61. Leibniz, "Discourse on Metaphysics," § II, 304. See § XIII, 311: "Necessary truths, by contrast, are based on the principle of contradiction and on the possibility or impossibility of essences themselves, without considering in this relation the free will of God or of the creatures."

rather the name of nature than that of God."[62] It follows that the sum of all possible things does not in any way depend on God's choice.

So as not to abandon his attempt at a theistic approach to this question, Leibniz places the principles of logic, and with them all possible things, within the divine mind. He thus avoids (at least formally) making them into a principle that would be a rival to God. In his "Conversation with Steno on Freedom," he speaks of "the constitution of ideas established in the divine mind, which express the nature of possible things."[63] This conception is faithful to Augustine's incorporation of Platonism; Leibniz thus asserts plainly that "the Holy Scriptures and the Fathers ... were always more Platonists than Aristotelians."[64] In fact, he goes as far as identifying the *possibilia* with God himself when he writes to Wedderkopf in May 1671: "the Essences of things are like numbers and contain the very possibility of Beings, which [possibility] God does not make, but he makes existence: since rather these possibilities themselves or the Ideas of things coincide with God himself."[65]

For Leibniz, the essence of an object not only contains its immutable characteristics, but also encompasses its entire history: "For in the perfect notion of an individual substance, considered in a pure state of possibility by God before every actual decree of existence, there is already whatever will happen to it if it exists, and indeed the whole series of things of which it forms a part."[66] This understanding is ideally suited to the doctrine of monads: because of the divine creative act which is extended in time, all each substance does is to deploy, in its historical development, what it already carries within it; there is no interaction (in a literal sense) between two creatures: "Each substance is as a world apart, independent of everything outside of itself except God."[67]

Therefore, for a human being, every act is already written into his or her essence. One should not ask how a certain individual can do this

---

62. Russell, *Philosophy of Leibniz*, 250.

63. Leibniz, "Conversation avec Sténon," 123. Cf. Russell, *Philosophy of Leibniz*, 250: "The truths of the ideas contained in his essence" are the object of God's understanding.

64. Leibniz, "Discourse on Metaphysics," § XXVIII, 321.

65. Leibniz, "Letter to Magnus Wedderkopf," quoted in Mercer, *Leibniz's Metaphysics*, 241.

66. Leibniz, "Specimen of Discoveries," 78.

67. Leibniz, "Discourse on Metaphysics," § XIV, 312. To employ an image that Leibniz himself uses: a monad has neither doors nor windows (ibid., § XXVI 319–20, for the human soul).

or that, but rather why a certain essence, existing only as a possibility in the divine mind, is actualized. Leibniz applies this kind of reasoning to the theological problem of sin, exemplified by Judas, the paradigmatic sinner: "How does it come that this man will certainly commit this sin? The reply is easy; it is that otherwise he would not be this man. For God foresees from all time that there will be a certain Judas, whose idea or concept which God has contains this future free act. There remains then only this question: Why does such a Judas, a traitor, who is merely possible in the idea of God, actually exist?"[68]

Therefore, in Leibniz's system, creating a certain person means: "it has pleased God to choose this one person for actual existence among an infinity of other equally possible persons."[69] Leibniz only keeps hold of one of the two aspects of creation *ex nihilo*: nothing external to God provides material for the creative act. Since he places the potentialities in God, he comes close to the idea of emanation, which links the world to the divine essence. The reason he does not stray into pantheism is that, for him, God confers existence on the essence that was only in his mind, and therefore did not exist *stricto sensu* (it only existed as an unrealized possibility). Nevertheless, the creative act happens against the backdrop of all possible things. Creation is a matter of voluntary decree, which avoids Spinoza's "abyss," the all-encompassing necessity of pantheism. But this backdrop, which serves as the context for creation, depends only on God's *essence*, not his *will*.

Identifying the *possibilia* with the deity is not the only thing that threatens the contingency of creation in Leibniz's system. Another difficulty comes from the predominant place that the principle of reason holds in his philosophy. How can the philosopher for whom "the first principle of all reasoning" is the assertion that "one can find a reason for everything,"[70] or again that "nothing is without reason,"[71] make room for the freedom of the creative act's decree? Does he not assert that "it is . . . a mistake to imagine absolute decrees without any reasonable

---

68. Ibid., § XXX, 322. According to Leibniz, "no answer can be expected here on earth" to this question. Nevertheless, he remains convinced of the "general" explanation that God permits sin because he "will draw a greater good from it" (ibid., 322). See ibid., § XXXI, 323, for similar expression of a limit to what the human mind can understand of God's detailed reasons.

69. Ibid., § XXXI, 323, cf. Leibniz, "Specimen of Discoveries," 78.

70. Leibniz, "Conversation avec Sténon," 125.

71. Ibid., 119.

motive"⁷² —and this even in relation to the election of some to salvation, even though this decree is often seen as the paradigm of a divine decision that eludes rational determination?

The idea of possible worlds helps Leibniz to make the distinction between the necessary and the contingent: God, of course, always chooses the best, and so the domain of historical contingency also has its "principle of truth" and should not be confused with a totally arbitrary or random series of events.⁷³ But this principle of truth is not the principle of contradiction: the unfolding of history is not determined by pure logic. Our world is but one of the possible worlds. Even if the other possible worlds are not actualized, they remain *possible* nonetheless. Recall that, for Leibniz, God's "decrees do not change the possibility of things." What prevents the realizing of all possible worlds, rival to ours, is not their impossibility, but their *imperfection*.⁷⁴

Placing our world in amongst the vast set of possible worlds allows us to have a creation decree that is not logically determined. But is it enough to make it a *free* decision, given that the reason for it is to seek what is best? The question arises, and is of crucial importance, since for Leibniz, what is best does not depend on God's will. For he not only subtracts "the eternal truths of geometry" from the "free ... choice of the will of God," but also "the eternal truths of ... morals, and consequently also the rules of justice, goodness and beauty."⁷⁵

In order to maintain the freedom of the creative act, Leibniz must refuse to think of freedom as indifference when faced with a choice. For him, it makes no sense (even for God) to talk of "acting out of pure pleasure," that is, an exercise of the will that does not in some way seek what is intrinsically good.⁷⁶ For "the will never acts except towards an end. But an end is an apparent good."⁷⁷ Seen this way, an act need not be undetermined for it to be free. On the contrary, it is determined by its

---

72. Leibniz, "Discourse on Metaphysics," § XXXI, 323.

73. See Leibniz, "On Contingency," 112.

74. Leibniz, "Metaphysics," § XIII, 311.

75. Leibniz, "[On Cartesian Philosophy]," in Russell, *Philosophy of Leibniz*, 211. cf. Leibniz, "Discourse on Metaphysics," § II, 304.

76. Leibniz, "On Contingency," 112. See Leibniz, "[On Cartesian Philosophy]," in Russell, *Philosophy of Leibniz*, 212: "How can [God] have a will which has the idea of the good, not for its object, but for its effect?"

77. Leibniz, "Conversation avec Sténon," 120.

aim—that which is truly good in God's case, that which appears to be good in the case of a human agent, inasmuch as human judgment is fallible.[78] Whereas other understandings of freedom opt for the principle of indifference faced with a choice, Leibniz believes that no exercise of will is possible when the two alternatives are perceived as being equally good: "We want more what seems best, so the greater the equality, the less we want this instead of that, and when [the equality] is total, we want nothing."[79]

Leibniz's understanding of freedom allows him to admit that there can be a reason behind contingent things, without their ceasing to be contingent. In fact, such things find their determination (without logical necessity) in the good sought by the free agent. Thus reason holds sway even over what is contingent, without its being bound by necessity: it is not the principle of contradiction that prevails (the alternative choice would not be logically contradictory), but rather the pursuit of what is best. As Leibniz refuses to make chance an additional source of causality, alongside free acts (by God and rational creatures), his analysis of freedom enables him to affirm the distinction between contingent and necessary, without having to give up the rationality of the whole of reality. However, Leibniz pays a high price for making reality subordinate to reason. In doing so, he separates the pursuit of good, which governs contingent events, from the divine will, since God no longer determines what is good. Granted, he asserts that the choice "always to do what is most perfect" is "the first free decree of God"; it constitutes the foundation of all God's other free decrees.[80] But is reason therefore absent from this first decree? The principle of reason, so dominant in Leibniz's system, will hardly allow such an answer. Is the decree motivated, then, by the desire for what is best? If this were true, it would be its own foundation. It is difficult to see any other alternatives open to Leibniz on this point. As such, the decree depends on nothing but itself; it possesses aseity, and thus has divine status. Logically, Leibniz should include it in the divine essence—but that would amount to equating God's nature with his *ad extra* works, and we are back to Spinoza's abyss.

78. By this statement, Leibniz plays down the effects of sin on the human will. He does not seem to imagine the possibility of a corrupted will, i.e., a will that consciously chooses what it believes to be bad.

79. Leibniz, "Conversation avec Sténon," 120.

80. Leibniz, "Discourse on Metaphysics," § XIII, 311, cf. Leibniz, "On Contingency," 111–13.

Creationism, on the other hand, must refuse to drive a wedge between the divine will and moral principles. The divine nature is, of course, not amoral: goodness is one of the obvious attributes of God. But this does not imply that the divine will is exercised in relation to moral distinctions that precede it; on the contrary, "God . . . is a law to himself."[81] God's free decrees (in creation, redemption, etc.) certainly express his character, but it would be wrong to imagine his will's being subject to a moral law outside his control—even if it were internal to the divine essence. We thus arrive at a radically personalist conception of God; the only one that enables us to fend off necessitarianism. God is what he wants, and he wants what he is; how he can, by his free decrees, will a creature *distinct* from him, is the mystery of creation, which cannot be resolved by subjecting the divine will to the principle of reason.

We see just how far Leibniz goes in his subordination of reality to reason when he says that all true propositions are true *a priori*. This assertion, which is relatively trivial in the field of mathematics, is surprising when applied to contingent propositions, those with which natural science and history are concerned. In fact, his enlargement of the domain of *a priori* truth is a direct result of his doctrine of monads: everything that happens to a creature and all that it does is contained in its essence. Essence therefore dictates a being's entire history. Once again, one might be inclined to think that Leibniz falls prey to Spinozism, which subjects reality to mathematical necessity. He only avoids it (or hopes to do so) by an ingenious use of mathematics and its methods of proof. For Leibniz, events appear contingent to us when we, finite beings, cannot deduce them from the essence of things, because the number of intermediate steps in the deduction is infinite. However, everything is necessary from God's point of view, since he is able to traverse "an infinite series in one stroke of the mind."[82]

Does this ingenious idea make it possible to affirm the contingency of creation, with as much force as we would like? Admittedly, the distinction that Leibniz sets up is not merely epistemic: that one can prove a proposition in a finite number of steps is a *logical* truth; it depends

---

81. Calvin, *Institutes* III, XXIII, 2, 227.

82. Leibniz, "On Contingency," 111; Leibniz, "Specimen of Discoveries." Adams, *Leibniz*, 23–42, recounts the meanderings that finally led Leibniz to prefer this approach for explaining contingency; he also discusses the difficulties that remain in the philosopher's reasoning, with respect to the accommodation of contingency.

only on the proposition and not our intellectual abilities.[83] Nevertheless, this is at best a softer version of contingency, which only explains the *appearance* of contingency. For the distinction he makes seems to be of no importance for an infinite mind. And yet it is God who sees things as they really are. If for him everything is necessary, then everything *is* necessary. Unless human reason usurps the place of the Creator, the finite nature of our understanding cannot legislate over reality.

When one seeks to identify the key ideas of Leibniz's philosophy, which combine to deny the full contingency of the created order, one first recalls the way he absolutizes what is possible by including the possible worlds in the divine essence. Also of note is the unwavering rule of the principle of reason, and in correlation, the independence of the idea of good, with respect to the divine will. A third aspect stems from the handling of the difference between necessary and contingent propositions, both of which are true *a priori*: Leibniz essentially understands contingency as a lesser degree of necessity. Since contingent propositions only differ from necessary ones by the (infinite) number of steps needed to prove them, they are essentially of the same kind. Such an understanding of contingency, which is quantitative rather than qualitative, overlooks the radical discontinuity between the created and the uncreated, insofar as Leibniz has identified what is divine with what is necessary. Thus Leibniz's worldview, which is impressive in terms of the scope of its attempted systematization, is not able to do justice to the contingency of the creationist worldview. Even if Leibniz the Christian wants to maintain the distinction between God's understanding and his sovereign decrees,[84] Leibniz the philosopher's attempts to rationalize the world cannot help but swallow up divine freedom.

---

83. Adams, *Leibniz*, 28.
84. Leibniz, "Discourse on Metaphysics," § XIII, 310.

two

From Substantial Forms to Laws of Nature

But to speak strictly, . . . to say that the nature of this or that body is but the law of God prescribed to it, is but an improper and figurative expression . . . Nothing but an intellectual being can be properly capable of receiving and acting by a law . . . It is intelligible to me that God should at the beginning impress determinate motions upon the parts of matter, and guide them as he thought requisite for the primordial constitution of things; and that ever since, he should by his ordinary and general concourse maintain those powers which he gave the parts of matter to transmit their motion thus and thus to one another. But I cannot conceive how a body devoid of understanding and sense, truly so called, can moderate and determine its own motions, especially so as to make them comfortable to laws that it has no knowledge or apprehension of.

—Robert Boyle, *A Free Enquiry into the Vulgarly Received Concept of Nature*

CREATION *EX NIHILO* AND THE ANALOGY OF BEING

Placing the mystery of creation at the center of one's worldview means accepting, as a first principle, the distinction between Creator and creature —a radical distinction, in the literal sense of the word, since it provides the basis for creation's being. The difference between God and the world is not quantitative but qualitative: "The world is more God's other than it is his opposite. It is not *less*, with God being *more*. It *is*, but differently."[1] Thus the idea of creation stands over against any worldview that sees the world as an extension of the divine being: the doctrine of creation *ex nihilo* rules out the notion that the created order came out of the divine essence. It follows that the doctrine of creation rejects a graduated view of being: it sees reality as a (necessarily asymmetric) juxtaposition of the divine and the profane, rather than a hierarchy of beings who fill the spectrum from non-being and potentiality at one end to the perfect Being at the other. Of course, different modalities of existence within the created order are not excluded,[2] but these do not correspond to varying degrees of divinity. Creatures are not more or less divine: they are not divine *at all*. Far from diminishing the world's importance, rejecting the confusion of pantheism restores "the created order to profanity,"[3] and means it can be assigned its own category of existence. At the same time, scientific study is not hindered by the reverent submission that we would owe to nature were it to participate in the divine nature.

Creationism therefore comes into conflict with a rival approach to reality, which has been, over the centuries and in its many forms, an influential perceptual framework: the so-called *analogia entis*. Arthur Lovejoy's study of this concept has been of significant influence.[4] He believes that the analogy of being has its origins in the *Timaeus*, which sees the "Self-Sufficing Perfection" of the supreme Idea of Good in terms of "Self-Transcending Fecundity." Not being jealous of anything, the divine being cannot deny existence to anything that is possible and, as a result, the demiurge shapes a world in which *all* potentialities are realized.[5] Aristotle adds to this the concept of a hierarchy of all beings, which are placed on a graduated scale according to their degree of perfection. By the principle of plenitude (already implicit in Plato's work), all degrees of

---

1. Gisel, *Création*, 118.

2. We shall see that creationism encourages a plural approach to the world, see pp. 77–82 below.

3. Gisel, *Création*, 119f.; the author underlines that historically, the demythologization of the world involved the secularization of the heavenly bodies.

4. Lovejoy, *Great Chain of Being*. Cf. however, on the origin of this idea in Greek antiquity, the nuances introduced by Maula, "On Plato and Plenitude," 12–50, and Hintikka, "Lovejoy on Plenitude," 5–11.

5. Lovejoy, *Great Chain of Being*, 49. For the *Timaeus* see especially section 41c.

potentiality are realized, all the way up to the *ens perfectissimum*. From that time on, the analogy of being has influenced a wide range of philosophers, such as Plotinus, Spinoza, Leibniz, and Schelling.[6]

The biblical worldview, however, cannot accommodate this kind of graduated approach to reality. Not only is it at odds with the asymmetric distinction between God and the created order, granting a measure of divinity to entities in the world; the analogy of being amounts to admitting, alongside God, the existence of a second underived principle. In order to discern the dualist nature of this scheme, which might at first glance go unnoticed, one must realize that a being can only be *more or less* divine if it possesses a second (non-divine) component in addition to its divine part. When one imagines the idea of being on a scale that runs from the deity to nothingness, from pure reality to pure potentiality, one has in effect established God's opposite as an independent reality. By giving nothingness its own existence, this kind of worldview is—despite the similarity of language—diametrically opposed to creation *ex nihilo*. Someone who believes that everything that exists owes its entire being to God cannot accept the idea of a gradation, from the potentiality of the *materia prima* to the full actuality of God. The fundamental distinction is that between creature and Creator. Inside creation, everything receives its (exhaustive) definition from the creative act.[7]

To study the comparison between a graduated metaphysics of being and creationism in more detail, it is instructive to consider the writings of Thomas Aquinas, who attempted a synthesis of Aristotelian and Christian worldviews. From its contact with the Arab world, the West had rediscovered the works of Aristotle, and the early thirteenth century saw young intellectuals, on the basis of their interpretation of these texts, critique traditional Christian thinking, which had up to that point been overwhelmingly dominated by Platonism. Aquinas thus worked hard to present Christian doctrine in a rational way, drawing on the conceptual tools that Aristotelian philosophy made available to him. His *Summa contra Gentiles* specifically targets Muslim commentators of Aristotle, and the critique of Christian theology that their texts might inspire.

In keeping with church tradition, Aquinas asserts that the world as a whole owes its being to God, that "everything besides God derives

---

6. Lovejoy, quoted by Oakley, *Omnipotence, Covenant, and Order*, 37f.
7. Dooyeweerd, "Philosophie scolastique," 41f.

its being from Him."⁸ Thus he is obliged to part ways with Aristotle, in order to deny the eternity of matter and affirm creation *ex nihilo*: "God brought things into being from no pre-existing subject, as from a matter."⁹ At the same time, he accepts the dualism between form and matter, which underlies Aristotelian philosophy. But wanting to remain faithful to the received doctrine, he must not identify God with either of these two structuring principles. On the one hand, he asserts that "God is not matter," which follows from creation *ex nihilo*, because "God has created all things, not out of His own substance, but out of nothing."¹⁰ Thus there cannot be any continuity between the matter of the created world and the divine essence. On the other hand, he rejects "the error of certain persons who said that God is nothing other than the formal being of each thing."¹¹

However, a shift occurs when Aquinas follows Aristotle's definition of God as that which "is only in act and in no wise in potency"¹² and identifies matter with passive potency: "Whatever matter is, it is in potency."¹³ Thus matter threatens to become a principle that is foreign to God. Their mutual relationship is that of "opposite differences . . . : one is pure act, the other is pure potency, and they agree in nothing."¹⁴ The creation of matter then becomes problematic, for how could God create something that stands in opposition to him? Aquinas is obviously aware of the difficulty, when in the *Summa theologiae* he deals with the resulting objection: "Further, action and passion are opposite members of a division. But as the first active principle is God, so the first passive principle is matter. Therefore, God and primary matter are two principles divided against each other, neither of which is from the other."¹⁵

Greek philosophy had solved the problem by positing the eternity of matter, a route that Aquinas cannot take without breaking from received doctrine. He has to affirm the creation of matter, even if this fact makes little sense in the conceptual framework he has inherited from

---

8. Aquinas, *Summa contra gentiles*, II, XV, 1.
9. Ibid., II, XVI, 1; cf. II, XIX, 5.
10. Ibid., I, XVII, 1 and 6.
11. Ibid., I, XXVI, 1.
12. Ibid., I, XVI, 7.
13. "Quia materia id quod est, in potentia est." (ibid., I, XVII, 2).
14. Ibid., I, XVII, 7.
15. Aquinas, *Summa theologiae* Ia, q. 44, art. 2, obj. 2.

Aristotle.[16] He then tries to evade the objection raised: "Passion is an effect of action. Hence it is reasonable that the first passive principle should be the effect of the first active principle, since every imperfect thing is caused by one perfect."[17] But does it make sense to postulate that a cause has an effect that is fundamentally dissimilar to it? It seems difficult to accept that a pure act gives rise to something that is passive, the perfect to the imperfect: the relationship between God and matter remains enigmatic, as long as one adopts this kind of antithesis to describe the difference between the Creator and the creature. Aquinas' answer is little more than begging the question; it simply repeats the conviction that matter finds its cause in God, without really clarifying the relationship that holds between them. Aquinas no doubt moves towards a solution when he says that matter is not created on its own, but is always attached to a form.[18] But even this statement fails to give a satisfactory answer to the question of principles: if "what is potential in it [i.e., in every creature] should be created"[19] how is it that a pure act confers existence on something that stands in opposition to it, in its very essence?

Identifying God with pure action doesn't just cause problems with respect to the creation of matter. For the opposition between action and passion is not limited, in Aquinas' mind, to material beings, as is clear from his doctrine of angels: these are distinguished from God not by their participation in matter, but by the fact that they receive their being from God. As a result, essence and being do not coincide in their case; they are composite beings, tainted with potency. God alone is pure action, since being and essence are identical in him.[20] Aquinas places created beings on a scale that runs from pure passion at one end, to pure action at the other: "the more distant a thing is from that which is a being by virtue of itself, namely, God, the nearer it is to non-being."[21] Thus immaterial beings are closer to the first principle than material beings. For "when we find a form that cannot exist except in matter, this happens because such forms are distant from the first principle, which is primary

---

16. Dooyeweerd, *Critique of Theoretical Thought*, vol. I, 180, 182.
17. Aquinas, *Summa theologiae* Ia, q. 44, art. 2, rep. 2.
18. Ibid., rep. 3.
19. Ibid.
20. Aquinas, *On Being and Essence*, IV, 7; cf. Renault, *Dieu et les créatures*, 44f.
21. Aquinas, *Summa contra gentiles*, II, XXX, 6.

and pure act."²² However, immaterial things exist necessarily (once the creative act has happened); they are "totally devoid of potentiality to non-being." Being "the most remote from non-being," they are "nearest to God."²³ Yet, "they differ one from another with respect to their grade of perfection according to how far each recedes from potentiality and approaches pure act."²⁴ Human beings are located between immaterial and material substances. Since "among intellectual substances, the [human] soul has the most potency, it is so close to material things that a material thing is brought to participate in its existence: that is, from the soul and the body there results one existence."²⁵

By affirming that God alone is pure act, Aquinas seeks to respond to a fundamental belief of creationism: that it is impossible to include the Creator and the creature in the same category of being. In this regard, it is significant that the term *analogia entis* is not found in his writings: divine transcendence rules out a general concept of being, under which God and the world can be subsumed.²⁶ Nevertheless, Aquinas's graduated understanding of reality leads him to adopt an antithetical formulation of the relationship between creation and Creator. Understanding this relationship in terms of participation, to a greater or lesser extent, in pure action runs the risk of conceiving this relationship as a mixture of two heterogeneous principles: passion can become a principle that is independent of God, and which stands in opposition to him. To assimilate it with non-being does not avoid giving this principle its own metaphysical status, thereby threatening the monotheistic nature of Aquinas' proposal.

As a result of the dichotomous relationship between God and the world, the creature both resembles his Creator and is distinct from him: "God gave things all their perfections and thereby is both like and unlike all of them."²⁷ It follows that Aquinas' scheme is not without a certain ambiguity: by focusing on the aspect of resemblance, one may try to subject God to human reason, while affirming the dissimilarity leads us

---

22. Aquinas, *On Being and Essence*, IV, 3.
23. Aquinas, *Summa contra gentiles*, II, XXX, 6.
24. Aquinas, *On Being and Essence*, V, 7; cf. ibid., IV, 8.
25. Ibid., IV, 9.
26. Cf. Aquinas, *Summa contra gentiles*, I, XXXIV, 4.
27. Ibid., XXIX, 2.

towards negative theology, making it problematic to speak meaningfully about God.

In the end, one might ask whether Aquinas' project is attempting to do the impossible: to rationally explain the relationship between God and the world, starting from our experience of the world. By making the mystery of creation the starting point for philosophical reflection, creationism dissolves, rather than solves, the issue that Aquinas seeks to address. The divine and the created are both categories without which our human experience remains incomprehensible. It is not possible to construct an understanding of God on the sole basis of concepts resulting from one's encounter with the world. The experience of the created order's dependency on its Creator is one of the primordial elements from which our worldview must be constructed. Not only is the Divine primary on an ontological level; the relationship with the Uncreated constitutes a basic, underived, component of knowledge. Thus the mystery of creation is not so much a problem to be solved, but rather a constitutive relationship; one that grounds our existence.

CREATION AS A TRINITARIAN ACT

As someone who was particularly virulent in his critique of the analogy of being, Karl Barth (1886–1968) had no trouble writing, in the preface to his monumental *Church Dogmatics*: "I regard the *analogia entis* as the invention of Antichrist."[28] This accusation, although shocking at first sight, highlights the fact that in the understanding of creation, the analogy of being plays the role that many New Testament texts assign to the Son. It is in this sense that Barth links it to the Antichrist, the one who takes the place of Christ. The prologue of John's Gospel assigns creation to the Word, which is distinct from the Father *and* intimately connected with him (John 1:3). Similarly, the Epistle to the Colossians speaks of creation and providence "in the Son" (Col 1:16); the author of the Epistle to the Hebrews discerns his work in providence, which extends the work of creation (Heb 1:3). Other biblical texts broaden the trinitarian perspective and link the creation to the Spirit. At the very beginning, the first creation narrative mentions the Spirit hovering over the waters (Gen 1:2). The psalmist says that beings are created when God sends his Spirit (Ps 104:30), and the believer understands that he is

---

28. Barth, *Church Dogmatics*, I.1, xiii.

formed by the Spirit (Job 33:4). Thus the Scriptures present creation as the work of the triune God.

Aquinas' metaphysics of participation stands out against this biblical background. Admittedly, the notion of similarity is not absent from the creation accounts. If we start with the notoriously mysterious account of the Fall, God says: "The man has become like one of us" (Gen 3:22). The point of comparison between God and man (in his fallen state!) concerns the knowledge of good and evil. The most probable meaning is that of the ability (real or imagined) to decide what is good or evil, rather than receiving the definition from someone else. This meaning fits the five other passages that use a similar expression (Deut 1:39; 2 Sam 14:17; 19:36; 1 Kgs 3:9; Isa 7:15f). Ontological resemblance is therefore not in view.

More relevant to our study are the narratives that underline humanity's privilege of being created "as the image and likeness of God." Although ancient and medieval theologians tended to make a distinction between these two words (giving them various meanings),[29] the two terms seem largely interchangeable in Scripture: the first creation narrative uses both words in God's declaration of intent; in what follows, only the first term is used to describe the fulfillment (Gen 1:26ff). When the theme returns, in the fifth chapter of Genesis, only "likeness" appears (Gen 5:1), whereas the birth of Adam's son, two verses later, is described using both. The ninth chapter upholds the sanctity of human life by referring only to image (Gen 9:6). In the New Testament, both terms are used in the various allusions to the texts of Genesis (1 Cor 11:7 uses "image" and "glory," Col 3:10 "image," Jas 3:9 "likeness").

As to the meaning of "image," there are two options open to us: does it refer to God's "shape" which was the prototype according to which man was formed, or is it actually the effigy that is made, i.e., human beings? The term used (*ṣélém*) generally denotes a concrete image, a statue, or an idol (Num 33:52; Ezek 16:17); on two occasions, it means shadow, a dreamed image (Ps 39:6; 73:20). It is therefore hard to see how it could refer to the model according to which something is formed; the usage suggests rather an image made in accordance with the original. The preposition is thus the *beth* "of essence" (as in Exod 6:3: "I appeared . . . *as* God Almighty"). Paul seems to understand it in this way when he says "man . . . is the image and glory of God" (1 Cor 11:7). The second term (*demût*, "likeness") specifies what kind of image it is: there

---

29. See Berkhof, *Systematic Theology*, 202f.

are similarities between the original and the image (without their being identical).

Several different understandings of the nature of this similarity have been favored at different times in the history of theology: reason, original righteousness, dominion over the earth, sexual differentiation (which constitutes a "being-in-relation"). Today, most theologians understand the *imago Dei* relationally: a human being is the image of God, since he or she is called to live in communion with God and to represent him in the visible sphere of creation. It follows that human beings can only find total fulfillment by living in relationship with their Creator, with other human beings, and with the rest of the creation.[30]

Without explicitly using the same terms as the creation narratives, other biblical texts confirm a certain likeness between humanity and God. Paul's speech at the Areopagus quotes a verse from Aratos' *Phenomena* (third century BC): "We are his offspring" (Acts 17:28). Certain categories of people (and celestial beings) are given the title "sons of God" (Ps 2:7; Job 1:6; cf. Ps 82:6 quoted in John 10:34). The genealogy of Jesus found in Luke's Gospel suggests a parallel between begetting and creation, using the same formula: "... of Enosh, of Seth, of Adam, *of God*" (Luke 3:38). Peter's Second Epistle goes as far as saying that the Christian participates in the divine nature, even if, in context, the scope is clearly moral rather than ontological (2 Pet 1:4).

The vocabulary of likeness, used for humans, underlines the fact that we can legitimately speak of a certain kind of comparison between God and creation, and more specifically, between God and humans. But the metaphysics of participation finds little real support, since in the Bible the notion of likeness does not refer to the overall comparison of creature to Creator. In particular, nothing suggests that this likeness might vary in its degree and thus explain the diversity of creatures. Since many of the major New Testament texts concerning creation relate it to the Son of God, it is more worthwhile considering creation and the Trinity together and looking at how the two mysteries shed light on each other: God can call into existence a creature that is genuinely distinct from him—without alienating himself, without changing his character—since he is not a monolithic unity, but is constituted by multiple internal relationships. Hence the possibility of creating something that is separate from him and that appears in many forms:

---

30. Burkhardt, *Einführung in die Ethik*, vol. I, 67–70, 96–99.

> If God's being is to be conceived as *pros ti* [in relation to something] and yet to remain protected from being dependent on the *heteron* [other] without the relation becoming the accidental property of a substance existing in and for itself, then God's being will have to be understood essentially as *doubly* relational being. This means that God can enter into relationship (*ad extra*) with another being (and in this very relationship his being can exist ontically, *without* thereby being ontologically dependent on this other being), because God's being (*ad intra*) is a being related to itself.[31]

Even the Jewish theologian Abraham Heschel was led to conclude: "*God's being One means more than just being one.*"[32]

One finds in Aquinas' writings an analogy between trinitarian relations and the Creator's relation to the world. Of particularly interest, on this theme, is his early work, the commentary on Peter Lombard's *Sentences*.[33] One reads, for example: "The procession of the [divine] persons is the reason for the production of creatures by their principle, and is also the reason for their return at the end,"[34] and again: "The procession of creatures has as its exemplar the procession of the divine persons."[35] In this way, "as streams are derived from a river, so the temporal procession of creatures is derived from the eternal procession of persons."[36] The trinitarian perspective not only sheds light on the fact that creation occurs, but also on the structure of the created order. Using the idea of vestiges of the Trinity, Aquinas draws a comparison between order in the world and order in the Trinity.[37] In the *Summa theologiae*, this same theme is related to the persons: "But in all creatures there is found the trace of the Trinity . . . As it is a created substance, it represents the cause

---

31. Jüngel, *God's Being*, 114 (I have transliterated the Greek terms).

32. Heschel, *Prophets II*, 47, quoted by Blocher, "Divine Immutability," 17.

33. All the quotes that follow are taken from the classic study by Emery, *Trinité créatrice*. He translates from *Scriptum super libros Sententiarum* (Emery, *Trinité créatrice*, 36, n. 4). Aquinas taught the *Sentences* from 1252 to 1254, in Paris; the writing of his commentary no doubt extended beyond this time (to 1256?; ibid., 35).

34. Aquinas, I *Sent.* dist. 14, qu. 2, art. 2, cited by Emery, *Trinité créatrice*, 25.

35. Aquinas, I *Sent.* dist. 29, qu. 1, art. 2, qla 2, trad. Emery, *Trinité créatrice*, 552. Cf. Aquinas, *Summa theologiae* Ia, q. 45, art. 6, 59–62.

36. Aquinas, I *Sent.*, *Prologue* (commenting Sir 24:30), trad. Emery, *Trinité créatrice*, 532f.

37. Aquinas, I *Sent.* dist. 3, commented by Emery, *Trinité créatrice*, 352–59; and ibid., 353, for the development of Aquinas' thinking on this subject.

and principle; and so in that manner it shows the Person of the Father, Who is the 'principle from no principle.' According as it has a form and species, it represents the Word . . . As it has relation of order, it represents the Holy Ghost, inasmuch as He is love."[38] For creatures endowed with reason there is an additional image of the Trinity, "as there is found in them the word conceived, and the love proceeding."[39]

However, trinitarian theology is not the only source of Aquinas' thinking on the subject of creation. The act of creating (and of revealing oneself) can be conceived of in a framework of unitary monotheism: "Even if one ignores the distinction between persons, the divine intellect can still manifest itself to itself and to others. To others, as for example by creating the creature or by inspiring knowledge into his creature; to itself, according to the way by which one reflects on what one knows."[40] The multiplicity of the created order is thus related to the imperfection of the creature. In a perspective that takes simplicity as being fundamental to God, multiplicity distances creation from the divinity: "God . . . brought things into being in order that His goodness might be communicated to creatures, and be represented by them; and because His goodness could not be adequately represented by one creature alone, He produced many and diverse creatures, that what was wanting to one in the representation of the divine goodness might be supplied by another. For goodness, which in God is simple and uniform, in creatures is manifold and divided."[41]

For Aquinas, creatures are multiple, since they can only express the divine nature imperfectly, and so they must complement each other to compensate, in some way, for this lack. But from a radically trinitarian perspective, one no longer needs to oppose divine simplicity and the multiplicity of creation. Cornelius Van Til formulated the conviction that in God, the One and the Many are equally ultimate, in his expression: "God is our concrete universal," that is: "In the ontological trinity there is complete harmony between an equally ultimate one and many.

---

38. Aquinas, *Summa theologiae* Ia, q. 45, art. 7, 65f. This theme does not contradict Aquinas' belief that the Trinity is not accessible to natural knowledge, since the trace is only recognized by faith (ibid., 63, 67).

39. Ibid., 65.

40. Aquinas, I *Sent.* dist. 27, qu. 2, art. 2, qla 1, ad 2. The Latin text is given in Emery, *Trinité créatrice*, 311, n. 5, the translation is my own.

41. Aquinas, *Summa theologiae* Ia, q. 47, art. 1, xxxf. On divine simplicity, see Renault, Dieu et les créatures selon Thomas d'Aquin, 38f.

The persons of the Trinity are mutually exhaustive of one another and of God's nature. It is the absolute equality in the point of ultimacy that requires all the emphasis we can give it."[42]

As a result, it becomes possible to think of God as the sole basis of reality, while granting a real existence to what is not divine: "The doctrine of the Trinity is fully monotheistic insofar as it does not merely think of God, in the Platonic way, as the One opposed to the Many and thus only as the world's opposite, which would amount to attributing to the world or at least to matter, as God's vis-à-vis, the equivalent of a divine dignity and a divine primitiveness."[43] The trinitarian perspective makes it possible both to eliminate from one's understanding of reality every principle that is independent of God, and avoid a pantheistic fusion whereby God encompasses the world. Trinitarian creationism avoids both dualism and monism.

It is important to distinguish the trinitarian understanding of creation from one that dominated the patristic and medieval eras to a large extent: many theologians tried to explain creation by means of Platonic ideas. Philo of Alexandria (c. 25 BC–AD 50) prepared the way with his understanding of the *logos*. Seeking to reconcile Greek philosophy with Jewish faith, Philo saw in the *logos* the source of the intelligible world, composed of ideas.[44] The synthesis became particularly clear with Augustine, for whom the Platonic doctrine of ideas followed logically from Christianity's faith in the *Logos*: "Plato, indeed, did not err in saying that there is an intelligible world ... He called the intelligible world that eternal and unchangeable plan according to which God made the world. It follows, therefore, that anyone who denies this says that God has made what He made without plan, or that when He made it or before He made it, He did not know what He made if He did not have a plan for making it."[45]

Without recourse to the ideas that preexist the world of the senses, the doctrine of creation is unintelligible for Augustine. Contained in the mind of God, these ideas share his attributes: they are "fixed and unchangeable, which are not themselves formed and, being thus eter-

---

42. Van Til, *Common Grace and Gospel*, 8.

43. Pannenberg, "Die Subjektivität Gottes," 101, n. 34.

44. Wolfson, *Faith, Trinity, Incarnation*, 257. Ibid., 257–86, for a detailed treatment of the different conceptions of Platonic ideas in the writings of the church fathers.

45. Augustine, *The Retractations*, book I, chap. III, 2, 14f.

nal and existing always in the same state, are contained in the Divine Intelligence."[46] However, such an understanding threatens the freedom of the creative act. At the same time, it endangers the strictly monotheistic nature of creationism: if the divine mind already contains the world—even if only in the form of ideas—, the world thereby becomes (quasi-)eternal and ends up on a par with God. When we try to identify why Augustine would adopt a scheme whose consequences go against his fundamental intentions, we find the reason in the false dichotomy in which he traps himself. On the basis of creation *ex nihilo*, he rules out the possibility that the creative act depends on something external to God; from this he concludes that creation depends on what is in God: "Individual things are created in accord with reasons unique to them. As for these reasons, they must be thought to exist nowhere but in the very mind of the Creator. For it would be sacrilegious to suppose that he was looking at something placed outside himself when he created in accord with it what he did create."[47] However, the idea of creation *ex nihilo* goes against the two alternatives that Augustine imagines: the world has its unique origin in God, *without* extending the divine essence in any way. Admittedly, the difficulty that Augustine wrestles with is real: how can the necessary Being possibly imagine that which is contingent? But this is but a variation on the mystery of creation: how can God confer existence on, and maintain a meaningful relationship with, a world that is distinct from him? We get no further in our understanding of the mystery by making a shadowy duplicate of the contingent world by means of Platonic ideas. The dichotomy between Creator and creature must be kept intact if one wishes to remain faithful to biblical monotheism and its vision of a freely-performed creation.

The inadequacy of Augustine's proposal becomes obvious in the difficulty it has differentiating between creation and the incarnation: such an understanding "must define the Creation as the material embodiment of the Word, and it can define the Incarnation in no other way."[48] Of course, being a Christian theologian, Augustine maintains the link between creation and God's will; thus, he says: "[the Creator's] will is what imposes necessity on things." But the dependence on ideas in the divine mind makes it difficult to distinguish properly between intra-

---

46. Augustine, *Eighty-Three Different Questions*, q. 46, 80.
47. Ibid., 81.
48. Foster, "Theology and Modern Science (II)," 9.

trinitarian relations and God's *ad extra* works, which leads John Milton to conclude that "this tension between a theology which emphasized the free-creative will of God and a philosophy in which explanations were ultimately grounded on the intrinsic necessity of the Ideas was never adequately resolved by Augustine."[49] Since the Johannine writings speak of the *Logos*, in whom the world was created, referring to the second person of the Trinity (John 1:1, 14; 1 John 1:1; Rev 19:13), Augustine's proposal has the effect of attributing the Son of God's role to ideas. One runs the risk "that the coeternal and personal mediator of God's creating work is effectively replaced by the *almost* eternal Platonic forms. The Logos is crowded out by the logoi."[50]

CRITIQUES OF THE ANALOGY OF BEING IN THE LATE MIDDLE AGES

Although it is possible to cite the sixth-century Christian philosopher and physicist John Philoponus as an early critic of the hierarchy of beings (and with it the metaphysical framework of Aristotelian science),[51] it is not until the last centuries of the Middle Ages that we see a substantial critique appear. The leading scholars belong to the nominalist movement.[52] Duns Scotus attacks the idea of analogy: rather than understanding the world in terms of a metaphysics of participation, one must take as one's starting point the category of being, which can be applied to God and the world. The difference between the Lord and his creation becomes a quantitative difference, of infinite degree. The univocal nature of being seems at first glance to be a narrowing of the distance between the Creator and his creature: both "are," in the same sense. But ultimately, this idea prevents any actual resemblance between God and the world: an immeasurable gulf separates the world from God; there is no common measure that allows for any comparison. It follows that nothing in creation can serve as a symbol of divine reality and procure

---

49. Milton, "Laws of Nature," 188.

50. Gunton, "Trinity," 93.

51. Gunton, *Triune Creator*, 72f.; Gunton also emphasizes the questioning, from the perspective of creation, of a graduated metaphysics of being, in the writings of Basil of Caesarea and Gregory of Nyssa.

52. On the difficulty of defining this movement and the diverse perceptions of what is called nominalism in the Middle Ages, see Putallaz, "Historiographie du nominalisme médiéval," 233–46.

us any knowledge of his true character (even by analogy). "The 'same' becomes the radically disparate and unknowable."[53] Hence the inadequacy of all human language to describe God.

One can therefore no longer derive the natural order from the fact that all creatures participate in the rational divine essence. The identification of (neo-)Platonic ideas with the Son-*Logos* disappears at the same time; the refusal to situate ideas in the divine essence is particularly clear in the writings of William of Ockham (1285?–1349?), who identifies them directly with creatures.[54] Admittedly, not all regularity is eliminated. Nature is not the domain of chaos; it remains subject to God's will. The inscrutable will of God becomes the only ordering source, as much in the moral realm as in nature: "If the natural world that such men studied was no longer conceived as a luminous world fraught with purpose by virtue of its own indwelling rationality, they did see it, nonetheless, as possessing an order that God, by virtue of his ordained power, had freely imposed upon it. And to *that* contingent order, as Buridan insisted against Autrecourt, the empirical investigations of the scientists . . . could be taken to be a safe guide."[55]

Thus the very foundations of Aristotelian science are shaken: "The unmoved Mover . . . cedes his place to the inscrutable Lawgiver."[56] Rather than imagining a specific nature for each class of entities (as determined by the unique place they occupy in the hierarchy of beings), all natural things are subject to the same divine law. For the nominalists, "the order of creation was conceived in terms of law . . . rather than in terms of symbols with varying degrees of mind and soul which participated in the divine Logos."[57] In this way, they anticipate the universal laws that modern science would formulate to describe the natural order. Natural entities no longer have an intrinsic meaning, which refers to the supernatural Beyond, but are linked together by imposed laws: "In this new

---

53. Pickstock, *Liturgical Consummation of Philosophy*, 123. It was Catherine Pickstock who first aroused my interest in the relationship between the *analogia entis* and the doctrine of creation (discussion on 17 July 2000, Cambridge).

54. Adams, *William Ockham*, 1050–56.

55. Oakley, *Omnipotence, Covenant, and Order*, 83f, referring to Buridan, *In metaphysicen* [sic] *Aristotelis Quaestiones*, II, q. I, fol. 9r.

56. Oberman, "Reformation and Revolution," 409.

57. Klaaren, *Religious Origins of Science*, 36.

language of nature [of Newton and Descartes], syntax has triumphed over semantics."[58]

The nominalist approach to science was part of a more general atmosphere that followed the condemnations of 1277: the Bishop of Paris, Étienne Tempier, had at that time rejected several Aristotelian positions, including some affirmed by Thomas Aquinas. Although the condemnation's legal validity was limited to the jurisdiction of the Bishop of Paris, the declaration contributed to a growing suspicion of reason's powers of speculation, well beyond its official zone of influence. It encouraged skepticism about humankind's ability to know the essence of things, which made the deductive method more precarious and gave a greater place to experimentation in the sciences. But insofar as people continued to believe that the sovereignty of the Creator imposed its law on nature, the effort to describe the empirical facts in an orderly manner was not abandoned.[59]

It is therefore not surprising to find the idea of laws imposed by God on nature in the writings of many late Middle Age authors. William of Ockham frequently uses legal metaphors when talking about natural phenomena. Pierre d'Ailly (1350–1420) often uses expressions like "by the common laws and naturally," and "naturally, or by the ordained law."[60] It remains to be seen to what extent such phrases really indicate the emergence of the new concept of natural law, which only fully emerges with Descartes.[61] For most medieval authors, the idea of law with respect to nature is very general, without any particular connection to scientific practice. One must not forget that the use of legal expressions for natural phenomena was well established, as a result of well-known examples in the text of holy Scripture and Roman sources inspired by the Stoics.[62] It

---

58. Harrison, *Bible, Protestantism and Science*, 264. He believes that the rejection of allegorical interpretation and sacramental theology in the Protestant Reformation favored the new attitude (ibid., 4, 161f).

59. Duhem, *Reflux de l'aristotélisme, passim*; Grant, "Condemnation, Power, and Thought," 211–44.

60. Oakley, *Omnipotence, Covenant, and Order*, 83 (referring to D'Ailly, *De libertate creaturae rationalis, De Trinitate*, and *Sent*. I, qu. 1, art. 2, JJ, fol. 96r). One even finds the clock metaphor, so familiar to eighteenth-century deism, in the writings of several nominalist authors (for Nicole Oresme and Jean Buridan, see Oberman, "Reformation and Revolution," 410, and 427, n. 53; for Pierre d'Ailly, see Oakley, *Omnipotence, Covenant, and Order*, 83, which refers to *Sent*. IV, qu. 1, art. 1, N, fol. 188r, and *Tractatus de legibus*).

61. See Jaeger, *Laws of Nature*, 181.

62. Ibid., 176f.

is possible nevertheless that some late medieval authors sowed the seeds of the modern concept. Having examined a vast corpus of original texts, Anneliese Maier concludes that Jean Buridan had eliminated the ancient concept of final causes, inherent in things, so as to explain the course of natural events by means of efficient causes alone, thereby anticipating the modern idea of causal law.[63]

THE ANALOGY OF BEING IN CALVIN'S *INSTITUTES*

Although the Protestant Reformation, in the sixteenth century, contributed primarily to renewal in terms of theology and ecclesiastical practice, it is interesting to position it in relation to the movement that went from the medieval nominalists to the "philosophers of nature" who participated in the scientific revolution in the seventeenth century. As a whole, the Reformation was characterized by its efforts to purify the church's teaching of the weight of tradition, in order to refocus on the Bible's message. It is therefore not surprising that it reacted against the importing of metaphysical categories, when these distorted the biblical message.[64] Regarding the analogy of being, the reformers criticized the complex hierarchy of intermediaries that medieval theology had introduced between God and the world. Their handling of the movement of heavenly bodies is particularly significant in this regard: whereas Thomas Aquinas still tended towards attributing souls to the stars, the reformers agreed with the critique of astrology, which emerged in the early church, denying that stars were living beings.[65] Rather than making the stars' movement dependent on a hierarchy of intermediate causes, they believed that God's Word undergirds the whole of reality. As Luther wrote, in conscious opposition to earlier writers: "Although Aristotle makes the Prime Mover the cause of all these, while Averroes declares that forms which assist from without are the causes of the motions, we follow Moses and declare that all these phenomena occur and are governed simply by

---

63. Maier, *Metaphysische Hintergründe*, 334f.

64. For the (complex) relationships between the reformers and scholastic theology, see Trueman and Clark, *Protestant Scholasticism* (in particular the articles on Luther, Melanchthon, and Calvin).

65. Klaaren, *Religious Origins of Science*, 40. Although Philo of Alexandria had already discussed the question of whether the stars were living, Christian thinkers are the first in antiquity to explicitly deny it, according to the texts we have in our possession (Dales, "De-animation of the Heavens," 532). For Aquinas' position, see ibid., 543f.

the Word of God."⁶⁶ His close collaborator Melanchthon (1497–1560) speaks of "perpetual laws" that govern celestial motion. God maintains complete freedom of action with respect to "physical necessity [which] is the ordinary mode of action in natural causes," because God is "a most free agent, not, as the Stoics used to teach, bound by secondary causes."⁶⁷

It is not inconceivable that the growing predominance of legal categories to describe nature received support from Protestant soteriology, for as regards the doctrine of salvation, the Reformation placed renewed emphasis on legal concepts. Following, in particular, Paul's Epistle to the Romans, salvation was understood as the justification of the sinner, which in no way implied deification. The change is therefore legal and moral, and not a matter of the human essence. Without confusing the order of creation and the order of salvation, it is not unlikely that the emphasis placed on the legal aspect of salvation indirectly encouraged the use of legal metaphors when considering natural phenomena.

Calvin, the second-generation reformer, builds on Luther's discoveries to develop a genuine system of thought that seeks to reflect the structure of biblical revelation as closely as possible. It is therefore instructive to see how Calvin treats the metaphysics of participation, with respect to the doctrine of creation. When we turn to the *Institutes*, we find no in-depth discussion of the analogy of being. This silence (which is not absolute, as we shall see) can be interpreted as a significant indication of the paradigm shift that occurred at the Reformation, not only in the understanding of salvation, but also in the way of looking at the world.

Calvin takes as his starting point the fundamental distinction between Creator and creature, which allows for no confusion whatsoever between the two. His work is shot through with holy fear of the Creator God: he sings his praises, defends his justice, and worships his grace manifested in the salvation of humanity. He opposes pantheism, which talks of "a secret inspiration quickening the whole world," and he does not hesitate to call "diabolical" the idea that "the world, which was made to display the glory of God, is its own creator."⁶⁸ He concedes

---

66. Luther, "Lectures on Genesis," 29f.

67. Melanchthon, *Initia doctrinae physicae*, 206f. Oakley, "Theology and Newtonian Science," 445, points out similar affirmations in the writings of the Zurich reformer, Ulrich Zwingli.

68. Calvin, *Institutes* I, V, 5, 54. The term "diabolical" is found in the French version

the expression that "'Nature is God,' may be piously used, if dictated by a pious mind." Nonetheless, it is an "inaccurate and harsh" expression, and so it is preferable to say that nature is "the order which has been established by God" since "it does harm to confound the Deity with the inferior operations of his hands."[69]

His rejection of any idea of emanation becomes particularly clear in a passage where he attacks the Manichean idea (which Michel Servet revived in Calvin's day) whereby the human soul is part of God's essence, "a secret influx of divinity." No participation in the divine nature should be envisaged, even for the noblest of creatures: "Souls, notwithstanding of their having the divine image engraven on them, are created just as angels are. Creation, however, is not a transfusion of essence, [as if one were to draw wine out of a cask into a bottle;] but a commencement of it out of nothing."[70]

Calvin understands that creation *ex nihilo* not only rules out the use of pre-existing material, but also excludes any idea of the creation as divine emanation. The created world is not an extension of God, by which he pours out his glory and love; the creative act gives existence to something "out of nothing."

Calvin sometimes describes the distance that separates the creature from his Creator in terms of imperfection. Without giving up his fundamental conviction that the world is good, because it is created,[71] Calvin uses the idea of a double righteousness: the requirement of the Law is what God demands of the creature, but the latter's righteousness cannot be compared to God's righteousness: "God . . . has . . . two kinds of righteousness. One is that which he has declared to us by his Law: I say righteousness to deal with men, and to judge them . . . But there is another kind of righteousness which is stranger to us: when God wishes to deal with us not according to his Law, but according to what he can righteously do . . . The Law is not something as perfect or exquisite, as this infinite righteousness of God."[72]

---

of the *Institutes* but is absent from the Latin version (on which nearly all English translations are based).

69. Ibid., 55.
70. Ibid., I, XV, 5, 166. The text in brackets is found in the French version only.
71. Cf. the passages quoted in Stauffer, *Dieu, création et Providence*, 183, 218f.
72. Calvin, 88th sermon on Job, quoted in ibid., 118f.

The first righteousness is what is required of us "according to our human reach"[73] when "our life is brought to the standard of the written law."[74] But "there is a higher righteousness in God that surpasses all creatures . . . For what comparison can there be between an infinite thing and one which is finite?"[75] This righteousness is "incomprehensible" and "transcends all our thoughts."[76] It is in this respect that every creature, even those that are not fallen, can be declared imperfect: "When one wishes to compare what creatures have with what is in God, one finds that one is nothing, and the other is everything. Just as the heavens will never be clear, creatures will always have imperfection, there will be no reason they can stand before God, or before this infinite glory that is in him."[77]

In Calvin's writings, the concept of dual righteousness comes in the commentary of a group of passages from the book of Job. In response to the complaints of Job, who pleads his innocence in the face of the adversity he suffers, Job's friends assert the imperfection of all that is created: neither the heavens nor the stars are pure in God's sight (Job 15:15; 25:5), even the angels are tainted with folly (Job 4:18). However, such statements are difficult to reconcile with the goodness of every creature, one of the leitmotifs of the biblical worldview (Gen 1:31; 1 Tim 4:4). Moreover, they presuppose that the righteousness of the Creator can be placed on the same scale as the righteousness of the creature, albeit at infinity. Not only is the antithetical pair finite-infinite that Calvin uses absent from the Bible's vocabulary, it is also rather too reminiscent of the univocal nature of Scotus' category of being, for us to hope to use it in understanding the relationship between God and the world. Let us note that the epilogue of Job does not give its approval to all that Job's friends have said—they have not spoken about God "what is right" (Job 42:7)—and it is wiser not to accept the idea of the imperfection of the creature, compared to the justice of the Creator.

---

73. Calvin, 69th sermon on Job, quoted in ibid., 118.

74. Calvin, *Institutes* III, XII, 1, 62. I am grateful to Henri Blocher for having pointed out the reference, contra Stauffer, *Dieu, création et Providence*, 118, who asserts that the distinction between the two kinds of righteousness is absent from the *Institutes*.

75. Calvin, 58th sermon on Job, quoted by Stauffer, *Dieu, création et Providence*, 192.

76. Calvin, *Institutes* III, XII, 1, 61.

77. Calvin, 58th sermon on Job, in *Sermons sur Iob*, 726f. Calvin even speaks of guilt, with respect to angels, in the 16th sermon on Job (Stauffer, *Dieu, création et Providence*, 191).

With Calvin, one finds the traditional view—which can be traced back to the Apostle Paul (Rom 1:19f), or even the psalmist (Ps 19:1ff)—that creatures express something of God's character. For the world, and all that is in it, owes its being to the creative act; we can therefore expect that the Artisan left his mark on it. "The worlds are images of invisible things, . . . [and] the invisible Godhead is indeed represented by such displays."[78] Thus we can "contemplate [God] in his works, by which he draw near, becomes familiar, and in a manner communicates himself to us."[79] Calvin exhorts us not to "decline to take a pious delight in the clear and manifest works of God. For . . . it is, in point of order, the first evidence of faith, to remember to which side soever we turn, that all which meets the eye is the work of God."[80]

The teaching received from "such holy meditation" is not limited to the recognition of the created nature of the world; no, we must also "contemplate the immense treasures of wisdom and goodness exhibited in the creatures as in so many mirrors," for the "wisdom, power, justice, and goodness of God, in the formation of the world" are "inestimable"![81] All are called to seek God "by tracing the lineaments of his countenance as shadowed forth in the firmament and on the earth."[82] Nevertheless, Calvin makes no concession to the idea of participation. The Lord's character is expressed by his action; beings, which originate from it, bear its mark. But this does not imply participation in the divine being; the distinction between the Creator and the creature will not allow any mixing. The image of the mirror, which Calvin employs frequently, helps to express the distance: the creature *reflects* the glory of God, precisely by means of its difference, because it stands facing the Creator. Moreover, Calvin applies the same image to the linguistic representation of creation, that is, the creation narrative of Genesis: "That invisible God, whose wisdom, power, and justice, are incomprehensible, is set before us in the history of Moses as in a mirror, in which his living image is reflected."[83] The mirror metaphor does not indicate a sharing of nature,

---

78. Calvin, *Institutes* I, V, 13, 62, commenting Heb 11:3.
79. Ibid., I, V, 9, 57.
80. Ibid., I, XIV, 20, 156.
81. Ibid., I, XIV, 21, 156.
82. Ibid., I, V, 6, 56.
83. Ibid., I, XIV, 1, 141.

but rather the message transmitted: the creation is God's mirror because it declares the glory of the Lord.[84]

If there is one place where one might be tempted to accept (some kind of) continuity between the Creator and the creature, it is in humanity, which from the very start of the Bible is called the "image" and "likeness" of God.[85] But here again, Calvin resists the temptation. Granted, he says that God "has adorned us with divine endowments."[86] Memory, imagination, and inventiveness are "sure indications of the agency of God in man."[87] Nevertheless, such expressions must be understood as speaking "not [of] substance, however, but [of] quality."[88] Arguing against Andreas Osiander (1498–1552), Calvin clarifies that Adam's privilege of being created in the image of God did not lie in the fact that "God dwelt in him essentially." Instead, he adopts a relational interpretation—Adam "bore the image of God, inasmuch as he was united to God"—adding the reference to the "marks of superiority with which God has distinguished Adam above the other animals."[89] He even deviates from Saint Augustine on this point (whom he normally holds in high esteem), rejecting the latter's "speculation, that the soul is a mirror of the Trinity, inasmuch as it comprehends within itself, intellect, will, and memory."[90]

To give a complete "definition of this image," Calvin considers humanity's original state: "At the beginning the image of God was manifested by light of intellect, rectitude of heart, and the soundness of every part." The goal of redemption is the restoration of this image, severely damaged by the fall, so "as to bear the image of God in knowledge, purity, righteousness, and true holiness."[91] Calvin therefore understands this expression firstly in a moral sense—the perfection of humanity in relation to God and to his law—and then in the sense of a harmonious

84. Ibid., I, V, 1, 51, commenting Ps 19:2–5.

85. For Calvin, the privilege of being created in God's image extends to angels (ibid., II, XII, 6, 406; cf. ibid., I, XIV, 5, 144–5). But as he is wary of vain speculations which lack any scriptural basis, he only treats the expression with respect to humankind (ibid., I, XV, 3–4, 162–65).

86. Ibid., I, XV, 5, 166.

87. Ibid., I, V, 5, 54.

88. Ibid., I, XV, 5, 166.

89. Ibid., II, XII, 6, 405.

90. Ibid., I, XV, 4, 165.

91. Ibid.

and full-bloomed functioning of all facets of human nature, especially (but not exclusively) of human reason. It amounts to the perfection of humankind as humankind, that is, of what human beings are by virtue of their creation, radically distinct from the Creator. Humans, while being the image of God, are not and should not seek to be God, even in a very weakened sense.

In harmony with this understanding of humanity, the multiplicity of created beings is not according to a linear order, based on the criterion of proximity to, or distance from, God. For Calvin, no creature is closer to the first principle than any other. Each creature, without exception, receives its being in its entirety from the creative act. As such, there is no room for mixture, of differing degrees, between actuality and potentiality, where actuality alone would come from God, the latter being pure act. Instead of a linear order, Calvin sees plurality in the created sphere; each being has a specific role to play in the orchestra of the universe: "God, by the power of his Word and his Spirit, created the heavens and the earth out of nothing; that thereafter he produced things inanimate and animate of every kind, arranging an innumerable variety of objects in admirable order, giving each kind its proper nature, office, place, and station."[92]

There is one way in which the hierarchy of beings receives some attention in the *Institutes*, although Calvin touches on the issue only in passing. The subject that concerns him is the knowledge that we can have of angels. Rejecting the speculation of the scholastics, he refers to Scripture as the sole source of reliable information: "Since the Lord has been pleased to instruct us, not in frivolous questions, but in solid piety, . . . let us rest satisfied with such knowledge" and "not indulge in curiosity, . . . studying things of no use."[93] Some books, however influential they may have been during the Middle Ages, should not be allowed to lead us in perilous directions: "None can deny that Dionysus (whoever he may have been) has many shrewd and subtle disquisitions in his *Celestial Hierarchy*, but on looking at them more closely, every one must see that they are merely idle talk. The duty of a Theologian, however, is not to

---

92. Ibid., I, XIV, 20, 156. In the 153rd sermon on Job, quoted by Stauffer, *Dieu, création et Providence*, 178f, Calvin uses the diversity of creatures to affirm, against pantheism, that the world's origin has a personal cause.

93. Calvin, *Institutes* I, XIV, 4, 144. The same warning is found in Calvin's preaching (Stauffer, *Dieu, création et Providence*, 192f).

tickle the ear, but confirm the conscience, by teaching what is true, certain, and useful. When you read the work of Dionysus, you would think that the man had come down from heaven, and was relating, not what he had learned, but what he had actually seen."[94]

Calvin is convinced that with respect "both to the ranks and numbers of angels, . . . the full revelation . . . is deferred to the last day." Since Scripture says nothing about these questions, "how is it possible . . . to ascertain the gradations of honour among the angels to determine the insignia, and assign the place and station of each?"[95] Similarly, the reformer warns against the worship of angels: "Away, then, with that Platonic philosophy of seeking access to God by means of angels, and courting them";[96] there can be no place, in Reformed theology, for a ministry of mediation other than that provided by the God-Man, Jesus Christ. Angels are not beings situated on a spectrum of creatures between humans and God. Despite all the glory and splendor they display, they can never serve as intermediaries;[97] man, created in the image of God, is assured of *direct* access to his heavenly Father.

Even in these few passages where Calvin considers the hierarchy of beings, he does not directly attack the conceptual framework underlying it: the contrast between actuality and potentiality, and the ranking of creatures with respect to their greater or lesser proximity to the Creator. On one hand, this is doubtlessly owing to the pastoral concerns of the *Institutes*: the work does not aim to discuss philosophical questions in themselves, but wants to help the reader in his or her understanding of biblical faith. On the other hand, such restraint stems from the formal principle of Calvinist theology, that of *sola Scriptura*. Given that the conceptual framework of the *analogia entis* is absent from biblical revelation, but is part of the heritage that the Middle Ages took from Greek philosophy, Calvin does not feel the need to discuss it. More fundamentally, we can link this silence to his major presupposition: the radical distinction between Creator and creature. His starting point determines the topics of importance that must be considered. As a result,

---

94. Calvin, *Institutes* I, XIV, 4, 144.
95. Ibid., XIV, 8, 147.
96. Ibid., XIV, 12, 150.
97. Ibid., XIV, 10, 148f.

the hierarchy of beings remains foreign to him; for Calvin, "all creation was egalitarian because of its ultimate dependence upon God's power."[98]

THE TRIUMPH OF LAWS OF NATURE

It is not difficult to understand how the nominalistic emphasis on God's will, in the work of creation and the governing of the world, might have helped the transition from substantial forms to laws of nature, which was so characteristic of the beginnings of modern science in the seventeenth century. The writings of Robert Boyle are a prime example. They clearly reflect the influence of medieval discussions about the *potentia absoluta*. For him, "the ordinary course of things mainly depends" on mechanical laws;[99] they refer to "that order of things that, at the beginning, [God] most wisely instituted." However, God can invalidate them "for weighty ends and purposes" (which in actual fact has rarely happened).[100] For his omnipotence is equivalent to his ability to do "all that is not truly contradictory."[101] Boyle thus aligns himself with the more recent understanding of absolute power, which sees in it the miraculous action of God. In the old sense of the term (common from the mid-thirteenth century onwards), the expression designated divine omnipotence, when it went beyond the divine decree. Although there was no doubt that God can do what he *wants*, this name was used for God's power beyond and independent of his will.[102] In the medieval debates about the pope's power to suspend ecclesiastical law—a power that evoked parallels with God's absolute power—we see the beginnings of a shift towards the second understanding, where the *potentia absoluta* no longer refers to what God *could*, but does not, do, but to his miraculous action, as distinct from general providence. The *potentia ordinata*, the counterpart to absolute power, now designates not ordained power, but the ordinary power of God.[103]

---

98. Klaaren, *Religious Origins of Science*, 40. Ibid., for the modesty of Calvin's doctrine of angels, who are instruments of the divine will, but do not constitute intermediaries.
99. Boyle, *Enquiry into Nature*, sec. VI, 216.
100. Ibid., sec. VII, 223; Boyle, *Reason and Religion*, part I, sec. III, 161.
101. Boyle, *Reason and Religion*, part I, sec. II, 159.
102. Courtenay, "Dialectic of Divine Omnipotence," 4–6.
103. Ibid., 10–12.

In his essay *Origin of Forms and Qualities according to the Corpuscular Philosophy*, published for the first time in Oxford in 1666, Boyle incorporates some of his articles written during the 1650s, which develop the theoretical and experimental foundations of the new corpuscular philosophy. In it we see the replacement of substantial forms by laws of nature, as the explanatory principle. In particular, Boyle refuses the need to explain the persistence of an object's properties; only *change* requires the action of an agent: "These accidents being once . . . introduced in the matter, we need not seek for a new substantial principle to preserve them there, since, by the general law or common course of nature, the matter qualified by them must continue in the state such accidents have put it into, till by some agent or other it be forcibly put out of it."[104]

The law imposed by the sovereign action of God, rather than the intrinsic nature of things, is used to explain natural phenomena. This shift in emphasis is accompanied by the rejection of necessitarianism, when Boyle writes that "the laws of motion, without which the present state, and course of the world, could never be maintain'd, did not necessarily spring from the nature of matter, but depended upon the will of the divine author of things."[105]

In the same vein, Descartes replaces scholastic concepts with laws of nature, to explain order in the world. The transition is particularly clear in his book *The World*, written in the early 1630s, but only published posthumously. Descartes invites the reader, in chapter VI of this treatise, to imagine a world whose matter can be described geometrically, but which is devoid of any forms in the scholastic sense of the word. The purpose of the exercise is, of course, to convince the reader that this world is not an imaginary one, but our own. And yet, as Andreas Hüttemann notes, "the abolition of the ontological inventory traditionally used to explain natural phenomena, such as real qualities and substantial forms, and the introduction of the geometric concept of matter,

---

104. Boyle, *Origin of Forms*, 62.

105. 105 Boyle, *Christian Virtuoso*, in Boyle, *Works*, vol. 5, 521. This doesn't prevent Boyle from saying that the creation stems from the divine wisdom, and making reference to divine ideas, in this context: God's "almighty power, still accompanied with his infinite wisdom, did at first frame the corporeal world according to the divine *ideas*, which he had, as well *most freely* as *most wisely*, determined to conform them [the different parts of the universe] to." (Boyle, *Enquiry into Nature*, sec. IV, in Boyle, *Works*, vol. 5, 190).

create the problem of explaining order and regularity in nature. The geometric objects of the Cartesian world move, but they move arbitrarily."[106]

The introduction of laws of nature addresses this very problem; they ensure the transition from "the most confused and muddled chaos that any of the poets could describe" to the harmonious world we know:

> For God has established these laws in such a marvellous way that even if we suppose that He creates nothing more than what I have said, and even if He does not impose any order or proportion on it but makes it of the most confused and muddled chaos that any of the poets could describe, the laws of nature are sufficient to cause the parts of this chaos to disentangle themselves and arrange themselves in such a good order that they will have the form of a most perfect world, a world in which one will be able to see not only light, but all the other things as well, both general and particular, that appear in the actual world.[107]

Other scholars of the time make the same transition from substantial forms to laws of nature. Of course, Descartes' conviction that even mathematical laws depend on God's will[108] remained in the minority, but others affirm, as clearly as he does, that the laws of nature express the exercise of divine omnipotence. Besides, for example, John Locke,[109] we must especially mention Isaac Newton, insofar as his adoption of this way of describing the natural order marks its decisive victory over other, older understandings. Rejecting an exclusively immanent explanation of movement, Newton stresses that "ye motions wch ye Planets now have could not spring from any naturall cause alone but were imprest by an intelligent Agent."[110]

Admittedly, the use of legal metaphors with respect to nature is not restricted to those of a creationist worldview. The Stoics (especially the

---

106. Hüttemann, "Chaos und Naturgesetz," 522.
107. Descartes, "Treatise on Light," 23.
108. Cf. p. 8 n. 22 above.
109. Locke, *Law of Nature*, 108f.
110. Newton, First letter to Bentley, 16 Dec., 1692, 431. Cf. Jaeger, *Laws of Nature*, 182, and Jaeger, *Philosophie chrétienne des sciences*. Whilst it is difficult to deny the influence that voluntaristic theology had on Newton's thinking, specialists do not agree about the possible persistence of the neoplatonist hierarchy of beings: whereas J. E. McGuire discerns it in his writing, Richard S. Westfall finds no trace in his later works (Westfall, "World of Newtonian Industry," 179; cf. Guerlac, "Voluntarism and Biological Analogies," 219–29).

Romans) had already spoken of *laws* in this context. But a similarity of vocabulary does not necessarily indicate that their thinking was the same. Not only does the expression become, in the seventeenth century, the *standard* way to describe nature's ordinary course (previously it had remained in the minority), but, above all, its meaning undergoes major changes: it no longer designates the intrinsic orientation of each kind, but refers to a universal order, imposed from outside.[111] Thus what characterizes the transition from substantial forms to laws of nature is the abandoning of a hierarchical vision of the world, in favor of the universal reign of the law imposed from outside. Rather than explaining the behavior of things by principles that are inherent and specific to each kind, the new natural philosophers adopt a worldview characterized by the fundamental asymmetry of Creator and creation. As a result, the same law can govern all natural phenomena, all being subject to divine providence.[112]

The historian of science Alexandre Koyré (1882–1964) summed up these two concepts in an incisive way with the terms "Cosmos—a closed whole with a hierarchical order" and "Universe—an open ensemble interconnected by the unity of its laws."[113] In a similar way, Bas Van Fraassen describes the new understanding of laws using the metaphor of the "choreographed universe."[114] Others have used the contrast of biology versus craftsmanship to express the difference between the two views: nature is not an animal that generates its motion by an inherent vital principle, but an artifact made by the Lord who imposes the form he chooses.[115] Closely related to this is the belief that everything is created, and in this sense, an artifact. Thus one should not exclude artifacts from the operation of ordinary laws, as Aristotle imagined.[116]

Equally, we must abandon the Aristotelian distinction between natural motion and violent motion. Aristotle believed that all bod-

---

111. Beuttler, "Neuzeitliches Naturverständnis," 13f.

112. Osler, "Immanent Natures," 403, and Hampe, "Gesetz, Natur, Geltung," 243f. Joseph Needham discerns, in the lack of notions of Creator-Legislator and imposed laws, a principal reason for the different direction in which science developed in China compared to the West (Needham, "Human Law," 299–331).

113. Koyré, *Galileo Studies*, 131.

114. Van Fraassen, "Tragedy and Science," 31.

115. Collingwood, *Idea of Nature*, 5; Foster, "Theology and Modern Science (I)," 446, 450f.

116. Milton, "Laws of Nature," 193f.

ies of the universe have a defined place, which corresponds to their nature. Should they find themselves out of their "natural" place, they naturally try to come back to it. For example, heavy objects naturally try to approach the earth; once they arrive, they remain at rest. Other phenomena are at odds with this natural order; they are thus driven by a "violent" movement. It is only this second type of movement, against nature, which requires a causal explanation involving an outside agent, the "motor"; natural movement arises from an object's nature. Modern physics has abandoned the Aristotelian distinction between natural and violent motion; it sees all kinematic phenomena as being governed by the same universal laws of mechanics. Such a perspective resonates with the concept of a created world, subject in its entirety to God's providential action. When the Bible distinguishes orders of events, it emphasizes the difference between orders of creation and redemption. It follows that the ordinary course of things includes what Aristotle calls natural and violent movements; only miracles are considered separately, since they do not come under general providence but play a pivotal role in salvation history, which seeks to restore everything in creation that has been corrupted by evil.

In a worldview of laws imposed on nature, it also becomes possible to imagine phenomena that resist local explanation,[117] as well as forces of interaction that depend on the relative distance of two objects. Such notions were unthinkable for Aristotle, for whom any change had to be explained in terms of the properties of entities considered individually. For substantial forms rely on the particular place and the inherent properties of things; external circumstances can play no part in this context.[118] Needless to say, all these different facets of the new perspective were essential for the development of the modern method of physics in the seventeenth century.

LAWS ARE NOT ENOUGH

Although the replacement of substantial forms by laws was an important step in the development of modern science's interpretive framework, it must be acknowledged that the concept of law is not without its difficulties. The problem of the so-called *ceteris paribus* laws is particularly

---

117. For example, forces of inertia in classical physics.
118. Cassirer, *Individual and Cosmos*, 176.

significant in this domain. Most laws (perhaps even all) that we know of today are idealizations. They do not describe situations that occur in real life, but apply to very specific "ideal" experimental conditions, and typically include, even in this context, approximations. They are only true *ceteris paribus*, all other things being equal. To give just one example: Coulomb's law states that two electrified spheres will move towards each other, with an acceleration inversely proportional to the square of their relative distance—provided that nothing stands in their way, that we ignore the resistance of the atmosphere in which they are placed, that they are not magnetized, that they are not too close to each other, that we can ignore any atomic forces, and so on. Given the variety of interfering factors that are ignored, it is impossible to list them all. This raises the question of knowing how "All Fs are G *ceteris paribus*" differs from "All Fs are G, except in cases where F is not G"—the latter not exactly being an earth-shattering statement! If, however, we imagine that laws only concern idealized objects and situations, the reasons why scientific laws are able to guide us in real life become mysterious, since practical applications always imply non-ideal conditions. Given the difficulty of finding a satisfactory formulation of such laws, several authors recommend introducing the notion of disposition, which describes a tendency to do something or act in a certain way. The disposition is therefore present even in situations where other factors interfere.[119] Other philosophers of science are skeptical of the idea of dispositions, seeing in them little more than the analogy of the true, but trivial, explanation of opium's soporific effects by invoking its sleep-inducing powers.

To decide whether it is worthwhile introducing the idea of dispositions, it is not enough to question their explanatory power; we must make sure that they can be adapted to fit the interpretive framework of modern science. Alan Chalmers considers that dispositions do no more than express the belief, implicit in any practice of science, that natural objects can act. He tries to show that the followers of the new science had, in fact, made use of the same idea: while Robert Boyle ardently defended the idea of laws imposed from outside, he did not stick to this belief in the actual development of his science. Thus, he had no trouble using dispositional properties such as acidity or the elasticity of the air,

---

119. For example, Cartwright, *Nature's Capacities, passim*; Chalmers, "Laws Needn't Lie," 196–205; Hüttemann, "Laws and Dispositions," 121–35; Lipton, "All Else Being Equal," 155–68; Woodward, "Realism About Laws," 181–218.

when describing his experiments.[120] In fact, he admitted explicitly that a description in terms of laws of motion is incomplete: it "gives us but a very defective *idea* of *nature*, since it omits the general fabric of the world and the contrivances of particular bodies, which yet are as well necessary as local motion itself to the production of particular *effects* and *phenomena*."[121]

When we consider this issue with respect to different theological systems of thought, it is of vital importance to understand the difference between a perspective that absolutizes the divine will and creationism. In the Bible, divine sovereignty is never in conflict with the creature's power to act; for the latter is radically dependent on the Creator and yet is endowed with a full and complete existence of its own. Quite the contrary: the creative act is constitutive for the creature; the fact that it receives everything from God *upholds* its very capacity to act.[122] As a result, there is no need to limit ourselves to the false dichotomy whereby either the creature acts in accordance with its nature, or it obeys a law imposed by an external authority. The law given by the Lord is precisely what gives it its nature; divine action is not external to the creature but constitutes its being, as Calvin puts it: "Each species of created objects is moved by a secret instinct of nature, as if they obeyed the eternal command of God, and spontaneously followed the course which God at first appointed."[123]

It is worrying that on this point, some nominalists did not do justice to the finely-balanced nature of the biblical worldview. One must completely escape from the antitheses inherited from the Greeks—matter and form, potency and act—in order to articulate the relationships between freedom and wisdom, and the divine will and divine essence, without confusing or opposing these concepts. Hence the resurgence of the "scholastic dilemma: if the sovereign will of God is not linked to his metaphysical essence and the divine mind, it must be entirely contingent and capricious . . . The conception of God as pure form is replaced by its polar opposite: the incalculable *anangkè* [sic] of an orderless will."[124]

We should not, therefore, be surprised to see some give priority to God's unlimited power, to the point of reaching a "vision of a

120. Chalmers, *This Thing Called Science*, 220.
121. Boyle, *Enquiry into Nature*, sec. II, 181.
122. Cf. p. 4 above.
123. Calvin, *Institutes* I, XVI, 4, 176.
124. Dooyeweerd, "Philosophie scolastique," 45f.

world so thoroughly impregnated by the divine will that the very idea of a natural order becomes a quasi-blasphemous intrusion." In Islamic scholarship, we can cite the example of Al-Ash'ari in the tenth century; on the Christian side, during the same period, Peter Damian, and in the fourteenth century, Nicolas of Autrecourt.[125] The occasionalists of modern times, Malebranche (1638–1715) and Berkeley (1685–1753), continued the medieval legacy of skepticism in this direction.[126]

The opposition between law imposed by sovereign decision and natural order is, however, totally foreign to biblical thought. The two concepts—divine action and established order—refer to each other and cannot be understood separately, so that biblical authors often speak of them in the same breath, without the slightest problem (Jer 5:22–24; Ps 119:89–91; Job 26:5–14; 38:4—39:30). It is, therefore, perhaps no coincidence that this finely-balanced position of creationism seems to have played a decisive role at a strategic time in the emergence of the modern concept of natural law: in this regard, Descartes' writings show the influence of the Augustinianism of the Oratory,[127] which underlines precisely this harmony between the two key concepts of the creationist view. On April 15th, 1630, he writes to Mersenne that mathematical truths are created: "It is God who has laid down these laws in nature just as a king lays down laws in his kingdom." What is more, he has placed them in our soul, "just as a king would imprint his laws on the hearts of all his subjects if he had enough power to do so."[128] In a letter to Newcastle in April 1648, Descartes compares these innate ideas to "graces"; they are given to us freely.[129] In the Augustinian worldview, grace does not constrain a human person; it permeates the will, so that he or she comes to accept salvation. In the same way, providence is by no means a capricious and unpredictable reign and shows itself in the stability of the natural order.

That said, Aristotelian natures are not welcomed back into the framework of a created world. It is true that divine action is constitutive for the creature, so that the laws instituted by God are, so to speak, part of his "nature." But they do not arise from this nature, as was the case

---

125. Oakley, *Omnipotence, Covenant, and Order*, 78.

126. Collins, *God of Miracles*, 29ff, 107ff.

127. A French secular order founded in 1611 by the cardinal Pierre de Bérulle, and devoted to the application of Augustinian theology.

128. Letter quoted in Moyal, *René Descartes*, 37.

129. Letter quoted by Lecourt, "Loi (Epistémologie)," 204.

for the substantial forms of Aristotelian science. It follows that humans cannot go by their reason alone in their quest to discern order in nature. He must instead, "go and see" what God freely decided to create, and this corresponds to the empirical approach favored by the new science. It is nevertheless true that the Lord "is the author of the essence of created things no less than of their existence."[130] To see in the laws of nature an external constraint, which is arbitrary and unrelated to the nature of things, would be to maintain an antinomy that has no place in creationism.

The idea of the world as creation thus makes it possible to re-evaluate the understanding of the concept of laws of nature and constitutes a promising starting point from which one can tackle the problems arising from the notion of law, despite all its advantages. As regards the laws' only being valid *ceteris paribus* (that is, in the absence of interfering factors), this theological framework provides grounds for acknowledging the dispositions of natural agents, without falling back into necessitarianism, where properties are linked to a thing's essence. The relevance of theological reflection on this matter is not invalidated by the fact that creationism provides only the interpretive framework, and that the philosophical analysis of *ceteris paribus* laws remains to be done. To expect the doctrine of creation to provide *ipso facto* an epistemological explanation would be to confuse religious and philosophical domains. However, the writings of several main figures in modern science testify to the fruitfulness of this interpretive framework, which gives the scientist a broader vision of the world.

---

130. Descartes, Letter (to Mersenne?), *Philosophical Writings of Descartes*, 25.

three

The Order of the Created World

> To say that a line in nature is not quite straight means for a Platonist that it is an approximation to a straight line, the result of a praiseworthy but not altogether successful attempt on the part of some natural thing to construct a straight line or to travel in one. For a Christian it cannot mean that. The line was drawn or constructed by God; and if God had wanted it to be straight it would have been straight. To say that it is not exactly straight, therefore, means that it is exactly something else . . .
>
> Thus the possibility of an applied mathematics is an expression, in terms of natural science, of the Christian belief that nature is the creation of an omnipotent God.
>
> —Robin G. Collingwood, *An Essay on Metaphysics*

THE NATURAL ORDER AS A COROLLARY OF CREATION

Will the ball in my hand drop to the ground again, according to Galileo's law of falling bodies, the next time I let go of it? In fact, the belief that natural phenomena are consistent with exact rules is so obvious to us that we do not feel the need to repeat the experiment to check that the object's movement continues to follow the same equation. The nomological regularity of nature's behavior provides a presupposition that is not questioned by scientific research programs. The revolutions that took place in physics at the start of the twentieth century did, it is true, affect our understanding of the cosmic order in a profound way. Quantum mechanics introduced the idea of *chance* at the most basic level of our physical theories. Nonetheless, quantum probabilities can still be described by strict mathematical formulae. Quantum theory has not left us in a disturbing world of fairy tales, where anything can happen.

There exist a variety of philosophical attitudes to the regularity that the sciences perceive. Most scientists and philosophers of science clearly see it as a "given" of nature, which we can discover and describe. Others place greater emphasis on the creative activity of the human subject. For them, the natural order is not so much discovered as *constructed:* by means of the constraints imposed by our experiments and reasoning, we participate in the emergence of scientific laws, in a kind of partnership with nature. But the majority agree that something in reality outside the knower makes it possible to formulate the description of orderly behavior. If nature were a completely chaotic mixture, no kind of scientific practice would be feasible. While Kant is in some sense the founder of "emergentist" approaches, he seems to be aware of the difficulty of accounting for scientific description if *nothing* in the world outside of human beings corresponds to this description. Indeed, he imagines a chaotic world where sensations could not be organized into a coherent system; in such a world, science would not be possible.[1]

So it is significant that creation implies the existence of an objective order in the created world. This is apparent in the first creation story, at the beginning of Genesis, which shows the creative act as having a six-day structure. The plants and animals are each produced "according to their kinds." God's word is of particular importance: ten times the narrative refers to this word, which brings forth a structured creation. The creative endeavor encounters no obstacles, in contrast to other cosmogonies of the time: whereas in Babylonian cosmology the world is the byproduct of a battle between the gods, the monotheism of Genesis depicts a creative act that meets no resistance, so that "God saw everything that he had made, and behold, it was very good" (Gen 1:31).

The prologue of John's Gospel alludes to the beginning of Genesis when it gives Christ the title of *logos* and emphasizes his role in creation:

---

1. Kant, *Critique of Judgment*, First Introduction IV, 13ff; cf. Bitbol, "Lois de la Nature," 112.

"In the beginning was the Word, and the Word was with God, and the Word was God... All things came through him, and nothing that has come came without him" (John 1:1-3). By choosing this title for Christ, the evangelist assigns him a name that is laden with significance in both the Jewish and Hellenistic traditions. Against the background of the Old Testament, the term incorporates both the idea of creation by the word, and the theme of wisdom's presiding role at the beginning of the world (Prov 8:22-31), since *logos* has a rich spectrum of meaning, being used to express both word and thought, speech and reason. After the closure of the Hebrew canon, the Jews continued to ruminate on the idea of creative wisdom, as evidenced by the book of Sirach (24:1-22) and a passage in the Qumran Community Rule, which bears a strange resemblance to the opening of John's Gospel: "By his knowledge everything came into being, and everything that is, he established by his thinking, and without it nothing has been made" (I QS XI, 11). As to the significance of the expression for the Greeks, it is noteworthy that the Stoics (who, at the time, exerted considerable influence on the entire Mediterranean basin) used *logos* to designate the universal Reason that governs and confers harmony to the world. Of course, the evangelist frees the concept of the *logos* from any kind of pantheistic connotations; eternal Wisdom, in the person of the Son of God, "in-forms" the world.

The conviction that we live in an ordered world is found elsewhere in the canon. The poetic books' teaching is particularly interesting in this respect. God's first speech to Job opens by his comparing the act of creation with the construction of a building, thereby emphasizing the stability and accuracy of his work (Job 38:4-6). The firmness of the earth's foundations is a recurring theme in the Psalms (Pss 24:2; 93:1; 96:10; cf. 1 Sam 2:8; 1 Chr 16:30). In times of trial and adversity, the believer consoles himself with the immutability of the natural order, guaranteed by God (Ps 119:89-91). The laws that the Creator has given to natural phenomena are even described in quantitative terms:

> He determined the weight of the wind,
> And fixed the water's measure.
> When he determined a law for the rain
> And a path for lightning and thunder,
> He saw wisdom and made it manifest
> He established it and searched it out.
> (Job 28:25-27; cf. 38:25)

Since Israel's neighbors considered the sea to be a symbol of the forces of chaos, many texts insist on the limit imposed on the sea and the laws that its waves must obey (Jer 5:22; 31:35–36; Ps 104:9; Job 26:10; 38:8–11; Prov 8:27–29). To say that the sea is subject to the order established at creation is to affirm the universality of this order. Certain Bible passages explicitly affirm the conviction that creation's laws are universal (Jer 33:25; Ps 119:91; Ps 148, by the use of enumeration).[2]

From these biblical texts, it follows that God's active omnipotence and omnipresence do not threaten the natural order in any way. Of course, as Creator, he maintains full control, in such a way that the ordinary course of events cannot limit his action. Miracles are still possible, but they stand out from the background of an ordered creation that is maintained in existence as such. It is therefore inadequate to see laws of nature as simply God's "habits," to reduce the natural order to successions of isolated acts that God performs with a certain regularity;[3] creationism lends no support to occasionalism.[4] Once one grasps the uniqueness of creationism, one understands why one should not eliminate the creature's power to act, in an attempt to exalt God's sovereignty. For God's power does not threaten the veritable existence of his creatures, but upholds it. Opposing divine action and the natural order amounts to perpetuating an antithesis that the concept of creation gives us grounds to reject.

Thus we see that the existence of an objective natural order is linked to the very heart of creationism. In fact, nothing less than our understanding of God is at stake. On one hand, the natural order expresses God's faithfulness and wisdom. The work of creation demonstrates that the Lord "is not a God of disorder but of peace" (1 Cor 14:33). On the other hand, the universality of this order is a direct consequence of monotheism. As the Lord alone is God, nothing and no one can escape

---

2. For a more thorough treatment of the biblical arguments for an objective natural order, see Jaeger, *Philosophie chrétienne des sciences*, 59–62, and Jaeger, *Laws of Nature*, 139–69 (with a particular focus on texts which employ lawlike metaphors).

3. Bilynskyj, *God, Nature and Miracle*, 82f., shows that such a conception of laws runs into the same problem as do Humean approaches: it is unable to distinguish between a law of nature and an accidental generalization.

4. Collins, "*Miqreh* in 1 Samuel 6:9," 144–47, contributes an original exegetical argument against occasionalism: the use of the word *miqre(h)* ("coincidence," "chance") assumes that in this pericope the narrator distinguishes between the ordinary course of events and miraculous intervention—a distinction that occasionalists cannot accept.

his reign. Whereas polytheistic gods are incapable of giving structure to the world, since they are but copies of it,[5] the one and only God combines in himself attributes that are often dissociated: he is both wise *and* powerful. Thus, no obstacle can prevent his establishing the order that he has decided in his wisdom. In this way, the recognition of God's transcendence led the biblical authors to "see the universe as a unity, organized and internally related in all its parts, and permeated as well by a single will."[6]

THE CREATION OF MATTER AND MATHEMATICAL ORDER IN NATURE

The clarification that creation is *ex nihilo* rules out any trace of polytheism in one's worldview: no independent principle or being is left, since God is the Creator of every aspect of reality. He is therefore in total control of it; nothing can escape his sovereignty. In answer to the predominant conceptual framework of their time, the church fathers placed particular emphasis on the creation of matter. While the antithesis between form and matter governed, for the most part, the different Greek ontological schemas, Christian theologians had to reject the analogy of the demiurge, in order to describe creation: God did not give shape to preexistent matter. Commenting on the Bible's opening verses, Saint Augustine precisely formulates the difference that the doctrine of creation requires, compared to the Greeks' understanding. It is not enough to say that God is the origin of all forms, for formless matter precedes any determination: "Before Thou formedst and diversifiedst this formless matter, there was nothing, neither color, nor figure, nor body, nor spirit . . . Yet [it was] not altogether nothing; for there was a certain formlessness, without any beauty."[7] To uphold the belief that God is the Creator of *all* that exists, one must consider that matter itself is created. Augustine seeks biblical support for this doctrinal conviction in his particular understanding of the *tohû wābohû* (Gen 1:2): this designates "the formlessness of matter —which [God] didst create without shapely form."[8]

---

5. Gisel, *Création*, 121.

6. Eichrodt, *Old Testament*, 112.

7. Augustine, *Confessions* XII, 3, 179; cf. XI, 5, 162.

8. Ibid., book XII, 4, 229. For the controversial exegesis of this verse, see Hamilton, *Genesis*, 108–17.

The affirmation of creation *ex nihilo*—and with it the creation of matter—upset the matter-form schema of Greek science. For the Greeks, matter was only intelligible to the extent that it was given form, whereas a substance created by a God of order and wisdom cannot be an inherent obstacle to rational understanding. In fact, at the time when modern science emerged, debate arose about the status of matter.[9] Several times in his imaginary dialogues, Galileo dramatizes the disagreements about the supposed imperfection of the material world. Salviati, Galileo's spokesman, insists that mathematical description applies to material objects as they really are. If a spherical material object touches a plane more than one point, this is not because it is material, but because it is not truly a sphere.[10]

At first glance, the difference may seem trifling: one view holds that the material object is an imperfect instance of an ideal sphere, the other that is not an exact sphere. But the radical divergence of these perspectives in shown by the different ways they handle deviation from the spherical form: for Simplicio, who defends the traditional view, material imperfection is a dead end, with no possible explanation.[11] Salviati, however, has no problem seeking an exact mathematical description of how the material object deviates from the ideal form. If it is not exactly a sphere, it is exactly something else! Hence the revolutionary assertion that the book of *nature* is written in mathematical letters: "The book of philosophy is that which is perpetually open to our eyes. But being written in characters different from those of our alphabet, it cannot be read by everyone; the characters of this book are triangles, squares, circles, spheres, cones, pyramids, and other mathematical figures, the most suited for this sort of reading."[12]

---

9. The concept of matter had progressed: in the Aristotelian conception, matter is the substrate of form, which confers on it all determination (including its spatial dimensions) and makes it a body. With John Philoponus one can see the transition to the modern concept of matter, which includes its spatial attributes in the concept of matter itself; it becomes a "material body." Its extension in three-dimensional space itself becomes the substrate of other properties, classed as secondary (Bitbol, "Corps matériel," 188f., based on Sorabji, *Matter, Space and Motion*).

10. Galileo, *Two Chief World Systems*, Second Day, 204; cf. Galileo, *Two New Sciences*, First Day, 2f.

11. For the imperfect realization of mathematical forms in material objects, see also Plato, *Timaeus* 50b, 53b, 56c, 39, 43, 48.

12. Letter to Fortunio Liceti, January 1641, quoted in Palmerino, "Galileo's Book of Nature," 30.

Refusing to link material instantiation with imperfection produces a novel attitude to experimental data: the belief that nature allows a precise mathematical description means that one expects to discover an order that is more far-reaching and more universal than the "obvious" one. To use Kant's terms, confidence in the mathematical structure of the world functions like a regulating principle for Galileo: it leads him to scrupulously examine the setting up of his experiments, in his quest for a natural order that can escape the normal observer's distracted and inexperienced gaze.

It is instructive to compare such an approach with the idea of the "dappled" world, which the American philosopher of science Nancy Cartwright has contributed to the contemporary debate about laws of nature. Her most well known claim is that "the laws of physics lie."[13] Far from being a key concept in the sciences, as she sees it, laws of nature only provide an adequate description in a small number of situations. Nature as a whole resists universal description, and science should take into account the fragmentary and partial nature of the natural order. The metaphor of the dappled world thus means, in her writing, a world (ours) where universal laws are absent. Of course, Cartwright accepts the amount of order that the sciences currently bring to light; she refuses to interpret this as a sign that there is a *universal* order. Instead, the picture that the sciences are currently giving us must be taken seriously: "Science as we know it: . . . pockets of great precision; large parcels of qualitative maxims resisting precise formulation; erratic overlaps; here and there, once in a while, corners that line up, but mostly ragged edges; and always the cover of law just loosely attached to the jumbled world of material things . . . The dappled world is what, for the most part, comes naturally: regimented behaviour results from good engineering."[14]

This focus on "all things counter, original, spare, strange"[15] induces an attitude diametrically opposed to that normally taken in modern science: in Cartwright's understanding there is no (productive) tension that encourages an ongoing distillation of more and more of the natural order out of a mass of seemingly chaotic experimental data. In current scientific practice researchers are, of course, aware of the approximate

---

13. Cartwright, *Laws of Physics Lie*. Cf. Jaeger, *Lois de la nature*, chap. 4 (esp. 198–201; 240f.; 249–52).

14. Cartwright, *Dappled World*, 1.

15. Cartwright, "Reply," 271, quoting Hopkins, "Pied Beauty."

nature of any mathematical description of a given situation; the number of factors involved in each real situation is simply too great for them to describe it completely. But a mature research program always includes methods of self-correction. In cases where more precision is required, one does not have to abandon the theoretical framework; instead, a more refined model is developed to incorporate the additional complexity. In fact, the Galilean trick of using idealizations is based on the belief that mathematical description applies to the concrete material world: "The very deviation of the real from the ideal can be measured and explained with an ever more complicated model."[16] The process of idealization, in modern science, makes no concessions whatsoever to Greek science's world of ideas; it only makes sense as part of a scientific approach that is thoroughly rooted in our "mundane" material world.

While creation *ex nihilo* would eventually undermine the Greek antithesis between matter and form, one cannot deny that Christian theology was slow to make use of the incredible leverage contained in this key doctrine. The writings of Thomas Aquinas once again provide an example of a kind of creationism that has not yet managed to draw all the conclusions that one might wish. His view of order in the world shows, in many places, the influence of a latent dualism, foreign to the Bible's monotheism. Thus, he gives matter the role of resisting being formed. Movement always takes a certain time because of "a defect of the matter, which is not suitably disposed from the beginning for the reception of the form."[17] Similarly, matter explains the failures that an agent encounters in its attempts to act: "Things referred to matter as their primary cause fall outside the intention of the agent concerned—monsters, for instance, and other failures of nature. The form, however, results from the agent's intention. This is evident from the fact that the

---

16. Funkenstein, *Theology and Scientific Imagination*, 178; cf. ibid., 167f. According to an observation that Ernan McMullin shared with me, Galileo was not entirely consistent on this point. At one stage, he conceded that "these conclusions proved in the abstract will be different when applied in the concrete," but that demonstrations made in the abstract should be enough for the goals of scientific description (Galileo, *Two New Sciences*, 251).

17. Aquinas, *Summa contra gentiles*, II, XIX, 6; cf. ibid., II, XXV, 3: "Hence, there is potency with respect to being only in those things which have matter subject to contrariety."

agent produces its like according to its form, and if it sometimes fails to do so, the failure is fortuitous and is due to the matter involved."[18]

Perhaps matter's resistance can also explain Aquinas' reluctance to postulate a universal natural order: "The things produced by God have a mutual order among themselves which is not fortuitous, since this order is observed always *or for the most part*."[19] However, granting matter the power to oppose the ordering action of the Creator is foreign to biblical monotheism. Creation *ex nihilo* goes hand in hand with God's perfect control over all parts of reality. Here Thomas pays the price of his attempted synthesis with Aristotle's ideas. One cannot arrive at the universal reign of God's law over nature if one allows for an element that remains radically foreign to God: matter understood as pure potentiality.

THE CONTINGENCY OF THE CREATED ORDER

The possibility of exact science is not the only consequence of the creation of matter. The idea of creation also implies a different way of understanding the contingency of the natural order. A demiurge's work is only contingent to the extent that he doesn't manage to impose the *telos* he had decided on preexisting matter. If there is deviation as concerns the rational essence of things, this is a matter of imperfection: its cause is in the limitations of the demiurge. Working on matter that precedes his action, the demiurge is not omnipotent, but must cope with matter's resistance. In no way can the world produced by the demiurge be the object of empirical science. Inasmuch as it is "successful," his work is completely transparent to thought; the essences of things can be grasped rationally, since they are the planned result of a (finite) mind, which gave form to matter. Consequently, no experiments are necessary in order to understand nature. Inasmuch as it is imperfect, the world of the demiurge does not allow for science—neither empirical nor rational—since the divergence from the original *telos* doesn't obey any rules, but arises from an irrational principle.[20]

---

18. Ibid., II, XL, 3. Notice that Aquinas also sketches out the solution to the problem of *ceteris paribus* laws, by means of dispositions (see pp. 53f. above): he thinks of actions whose "necessity results from the form, so far as the power to act is concerned; if fire is hot, it necessarily has the power of heating, yet it need not heat, for something extrinsic may prevent it" (ibid., II, XXX, 12–14).

19. Ibid., II, XXIV, 4 (italics mine).

20. Foster, "Theology and Modern Science (II)," 4–7. Foster quotes two passages from the writings of Francis Bacon, which demonstrate how the idea of divine omnipotence

However, creation as the voluntary act of an omnipotent Intelligence *can* provide the basis for the empirical method that governed the new scientific approach from the seventeenth century onwards. The idea of creation combines rational work and free act, so that the contingency is no longer a matter of imperfection; it expresses the freedom of the Almighty Creator: "The transformation of the concept of contingency is that the contingent is now no longer based on the indeterminacy of matter, but on the freedom of God's will as the creative ground of the world and all its parts."[21]

Thus, creationism considers that what is contingent—as contingent—is intelligible, and this makes it possible to ground the empirical approach of modern science. For, on the one hand, reality can be described scientifically since it finds its origin in God, who is both omnipotent and rational. On the other hand, rational speculation is not enough to understand the natural order, since the latter is the result of a free act and is therefore not necessary: scientists must learn, through their experiments, what laws God has actually established in the creation.

Not only does the fresh perspective that creationism brings to contingency encourage the empirical approach, it also opens up a promising way to reconcile "hard" sciences with a historical view. From the nineteenth century in biology and the twentieth in cosmology, the place granted to historical evolution has become a key question in the natural sciences. It is therefore noteworthy that the idea of creation is compatible with, and indeed requires, the historicity of the natural order.[22] Up until at least the Enlightenment, the civilizations that benefited from biblical revelation understood the world as being created, with a clearly defined beginning and end. Time and space do not possess eternal existence, but flow from an act of the Creator who will also one day bring them to an end. The natural order itself is the result of a historic act, and is therefore neither eternal nor necessary. Although assertions of

---

made it possible to move from the ancient conception of imperfectly realized forms to one of forms that allow scientific description and that are effectively given in nature (ibid., 7, n. 1).

21. Pannenberg, "Kontingenz der geschöpflichen Wirklichkeit," 1052. This alternative appreciation of contingency constitutes, for Pannenberg, one of Christian theology's major contributions to philosophy of science; e.g., Pannenberg, "Creation and Modern Science," 36f., and Pannenberg, "Contingency and Natural Law," 115f. For the role that contingency plays in the created order in Newtonian empiricism, see p. 13 above.

22. Pannenberg, "Theological Questions to Scientists," 21, and Pannenberg, "Contingency and Natural Law," 78, 90; Peters, "Cosmos as Creation," 101.

uniqueness are always difficult—given how many different worldviews there are—it seems that the concept of a linear historical development of the world was indeed introduced to humanity by the Bible. Thus Pierre Duhem writes: "Whether . . . Indian or Chaldean, Greek or Latin, almost all the pagan philosophies of Antiquity seem to agree on one doctrine: The World is eternal; but since it is not immutable, it returns periodically to the same state . . . Christian philosophy alone would reject this idea that the universe is eternal and cyclical."[23]

Already with Augustine we see an insistence on the opposition between the "once and for all" of salvation history and the circular repetitions found in pagan stories.[24] It also bears mention that the founder of "Newtonian" science, saturated with Scripture as a result of his regular reading, did not agree with the worldview of an eternal physics, which certain Enlightenment scholars developed on top of his scientific foundation. Newton was convinced that the laws of nature change over time, given the biblical prophecies that foretell radical upheavals in the future. Since, as far as he was concerned, the natural order is not final, such changes remain possible because of divine omnipotence.[25]

Situating the laws of nature in a historical perspective enables one to avoid the antithesis between natural sciences and history: to the extent that the natural order itself is a matter of history, there is room in the exact sciences for a historical dimension. Even though some Christians resisted Darwin's theory of the evolution of species, one should not conclude from this that the creationist worldview implies fixity. Indeed, other Christians, among the most conservative, agreed with the new biological paradigm,[26] and more besides: it is likely that the contingent understanding of the natural order implied by creationism facilitated the acceptance

---

23. Duhem, *Système du monde*, 295f. Laubier, *L'Eschatologie*, 16, also affirms that "the linear conception of history . . . [is of] biblical origin." Many nineteenth-century philosophers advocated a cyclic eternal universe (Jaki, *Science and Creation*, 309f, 311-13, 319-22, names in particular Schelling, Engels, and Nietzsche). Jaki believes that the resistance of many scientists to the finite universe of general relativity stemmed from the attractiveness of the Greek idea of a cyclic universe (ibid., chap. 14).

24. Augustine, *City of God*, XII, 13, 354f.

25. Force, "Newton's Holy Alliance." 266-68. See Pannenberg, "God and Nature," 63, for the temporal dependence of the natural order in the works of Samuel Clarke.

26. Such as Benjamin B. Warfield (1851-1921), systematic theologian at Princeton Theological Seminary, known for his unstinting defense of biblical inerrancy (Warfield, *Evolution, Science, and Scripture*). Cf. Livingstone, *Darwin's Forgotten Defenders*, and Livingstone, "Evangelical Responses to Evolution," 193-219.

of the idea of a dynamic universe in astronomy. One should not forget that Georges Lemaître, who in 1927 introduced the idea of Big Bang for the first time, was a Catholic priest, whereas Einstein's Spinozism was undoubtedly a factor in his initial resistance to cosmological evolution. Whatever the (strongly different) attitudes adopted by Christians faced with the historicizing developments in the natural sciences in the nineteenth and twentieth centuries, there is no reason, within the creationist worldview, to see the relationship between the scientific and the historical as antithetical. On the contrary, since the web of laws of nature is itself part of history, natural sciences must allow for a historical element.

COVENANT CAUSALITY

In the Bible's presentation of history, the category of covenant plays a preponderant role. The covenants that God makes with humankind punctuate the salvation history narratives: the covenant with Noah after the flood, to ensure the stability of the creational order (Gen 6:18; 9:8–17); the covenant with Abraham, with a view to blessing all the peoples of the earth (Gen 12:3; 15:18; 17:2ff; cf. Acts 3:25); the Sinai covenant with the people of Israel (Exod 24); the covenant with David, guaranteeing his descendants a perpetual royal line (2 Sam 7:12–17; Ps 89:3, 28–37); and finally the "new" covenant, announced by the prophets and fulfilled in Jesus the Messiah (Jer 31:31–34; Ezek 37:26; Matt 26:28; Heb 8–9). It is therefore no coincidence that the Latin term *testamentum*, which translates the Greek *diathēkē* ("covenant," "testament") has come to designate the two parts of the Christian Bible.

The category of covenant is found in the realm of nature, even if it remains exceptional in this context. After the flood, the Genesis text mentions the covenant that God makes, not just with Noah's family but with all the animals. Their habitat will never again be destroyed; in particular, God promises to maintain the yearly and daily cycles: the succession between seasons and between day and night (Gen 8:21f; 9:9–13). The prophet Jeremiah undoubtedly makes allusion to this passage when he mentions the "covenant with the day and the night" that the Lord has established and which serves as a guarantee of his covenant with the Jewish people, who are suffering the Babylonian exile:

> Thus says the LORD: If you can break my covenant with the day and my covenant with the night, so that day and night will not come at their appointed time, then also my covenant with David

> my servant may be broken, so that he shall not have a son to reign on his throne, and my covenant with the Levitical priests my ministers...
>
> Thus says the LORD: If I have not established my covenant with day and night and the laws of heaven and earth, then I will reject the offspring of Jacob and David my servant and will not choose one of his offspring to rule over the offspring of Abraham, Isaac, and Jacob. For I will restore their fortunes and will have mercy on them.
>
> (Jer 33:20–21, 25–26)[27]

The way that Jeremiah applies the Noahide covenant, in order to console his contemporaries, is remarkable: this interpretation of the "laws[28] of heaven and earth" in terms of covenant, with such a high degree of precision, is unique in the biblical corpus. We can compare it with a novel understanding of causality, which some medieval authors adopted. The Dominican theologians Richard Fishacre and Robert Kilwardby defended this view at Oxford around 1240, to respect God's entire freedom in sacramental theology. While they did not deny the effective action of the sacraments (they were not occasionalists), they based it not on the nature of the sacrament, but on the promise of God, who faithfully promised to respect the pact made with the church. In this way, the sacraments do not act by an inherent virtue that they possess; it is the Lord's contractual commitment that ensures their efficacy. Fishacre uses, as an illustration, the token that the king's minister gives to a pauper in reward for some specified work, and which provides access to the banquet (cf. Matt 20:1ff; 22:1ff).[29] The image is certainly inspired by his reading of Saint Augustine: to show that God can be the (temporal) creature's Lord, without changing his essence, Augustine uses the

---

27. This passage comes from the largest section of the book of Jeremiah that the Septuagint has not conserved (Jer 33:14–26). The (complex) relationships between the Hebrew and Greek versions of Jeremiah are not our concern here, inasmuch as the passage quoted is part of the received text of Scripture, both Jewish and Christian, and has therefore contributed to its influence throughout history; the Vulgate, for example, includes it. For the exegesis of this passage, see Jaeger, *Laws of Nature*, 165–69.

28. *Ḥuqqôt*, the plural of *ḥuqqâ*, a word which is close, in terms of etymology and meaning, to *ḥōq* (cf. p. 86 below).

29. Courtenay, "King and Leaden Coin," 191–200, presents this proposition against the background of the economic mores of the time. The image that Fishacre uses is "the earliest medieval example of a distribution of tokens for any purpose whatsoever" (ibid., 199). Rosier-Catach, *Parole efficace*, 120–24, finds a similar conception of causality in William of Auvergne's work *De legibus* (1230).

example of the coin that becomes "the price of . . ." without undergoing any intrinsic change whatsoever.[30] The fact that Fishacre changes the coin, made of precious metal, into a tin token, highlights the fact that its effectiveness comes from outside, from God's promise.[31]

Franciscan theologians, especially Bonaventure (1221–74), developed this proposal in more depth. The image is now that of a token given to the poor. According to the king's command, the token may be exchanged for 100 marks anywhere in the kingdom. One can see, in this illustration, the first justification of fiduciary currency, whose value is not based on the price of the metal used, but on the promise of a superior. In contrast to certain modern monetary theories, the value of that currency is not purely contractual; it is guaranteed by the king's promise to redeem, on request, the token at the price indicated. The effective wealth of the king is therefore essential for the currency to function properly.[32] Thomas Aquinas cites, in his discussion of the sacraments, this notion of causality (called *"sine qua non"*),[33] in order to reject it. His version of it—a leaden coin—became the standard term for the idea in debates about sacramental efficacy, and has remained so to the present day.[34]

Sine qua non causality offers a promising way of understanding the stability of the natural order, in a theistic framework. The idea allows one to hold together both the stable character of the laws of nature and the full freedom that God maintains, even after the act of creation has happened. Such an understanding avoids the mistake of absolutizing the fixity of the laws; they remain dependent on God's continuing faithfulness, which honors the commitment made at creation. We therefore escape the false dichotomy of divine action and immutable order, in which modern thinking easily gets trapped. Describing the natural order in terms of covenant enables us to understand how God freely chooses to ensure the perennial character of the laws of nature. Far from imposing constraints

---

30. Augustine, *The Trinity*, book V, XVI, 201.

31. Rosier-Catach, *Parole efficace*, 108.

32. "King and Leaden Coin," 200–202, 207. A similar conception concerning the sacraments is found in the work of certain nominalists, e.g., William Ockham and Pierre d'Ailly (Courtenay, "Covenant and Causality," 99f, 116–19).

33. Rosier-Catach, *Parole efficace*, 103, also calls it "pact causality."

34. Courtenay, "King and Leaden Coin," 185f., 207–9. Courtenay believes that Aquinas did not understand how causality *sine qua non* differed from occasionalism and that he rejected it for this reason. Cf. Rosier-Catach, *Parole efficace*, 135ff.

on God's action (as deists imagine), the existence of the natural order is an expression of God's faithfulness.

At the same time, an understanding of the natural order based on covenant helps us not to confuse the divine with the created. In fact, this understanding depends, crucially, on the distinction that creationism places at the heart of its vision of reality, since a covenant involves two partners who stand face to face. By avoiding occasionalism, this approach sheds light on the scientific process; granting full existence to the creation includes the acknowledging of its causal network. It is therefore important not to oppose fiduciary and ontological understandings of causality: the covenant by which God guarantees the natural order does not eliminate or replace the creature's causal powers. Indeed, the Noahide covenant protects the rhythms in place from the beginning of creation: just as the transition between day and night structures the work of creation in the first chapter of Genesis, God promises in his covenant to maintain the daily and yearly rhythms.

It is noteworthy that with respect to nature, Scripture reserves the category of covenant for providential action, and does not use it to describe the initial act of creation. The "covenant with the day and the night" guarantees the stability of the created order. It is in no way an arbitrary legal framework, but expresses the creatures' nature. A voluntaristic interpretation, which limits the causal powers in creation to a *sine qua non* causality, is therefore simplistic. Rather, this kind of causation sheds light on an aspect of how the natural order works, and must be complemented by taking into account the causal network, which is inherent in creation. The category of covenant is, however, a reminder that "inherent" does not mean "independent" in this context: we should not imagine the validity of laws without providential action. In this way, *sine qua non* causality conceives of the natural order in the framework of a resolutely theistic understanding of reality, since it does not separate natural order from continual divine action.

THE NECESSITY OF LAWS OF NATURE

When we speak about order, or laws, we do not simply state what *is*; we are pretentious enough to formulate what *should* be. While such a distinction poses few problems when applied to the behavior of morally responsible beings, endowed with freedom, it is not at all clear what meaning it can take in a scientific context. The necessity of laws of nature is therefore a hotly debated question, and continues to interest modern-day philosophers of science.[35] Intuitively, we place the necessity of laws at an intermediate level, between the necessity of mathematical propositions and the contingency of individual events. But the centuries-old debate—which has been rolling since Hume pointed out the problem, if not before then—has still not reached a consensus about the exact formulation of nomological necessity. Whereas some try to describe the natural order in a way that avoids any kind of necessity, others consider such Humean[36] analyses inadequate. In particular, the latter prove incapable of distinguishing between natural law and accidental regularity: it so happens that all the coins in my pocket are made of copper; although this assertion is true, we would not want to call such accidental generalization a law. For a regularity to merit the honorific title "law of nature," it must include a necessity over and above the fact that no exception to the rule exists—this is, in any case, the strong conviction of all those who are not ready to abandon the idea of nomological necessity.[37]

Does placing these laws in a theological conceptual framework provide a satisfactory basis for nomological necessity? Our first instinct would be to say yes, since one can invoke God's will in order to explain nomological necessity: laws apply necessarily, since this is what God has decided. However, upon reflection, one must understand that this is merely shifting the problem: simply referring to God's will does not provide the required distinction between the necessity of a particular event and the necessity of laws, because both (if they are effective) are decreed by God. One must find a way of saying how God's will is different in these two cases, if one wants to explain why there are two distinct types of necessity at work here. Hence the difficulty that many philosophical approaches have in justifying nomological necessity is shifted, without going away, when considered in a theological framework involving God's will.

Is it an admission of weakness to acknowledge that the divine will does not *ipso facto* provide a basis for nomological necessity, in its distinction from other forms of necessity? Not really, for one must take care

---

35. See for example Van Fraassen, *Laws and Symmetry*, 28–30.

36. The term "Humean" is not employed here in a historical sense; the question of whether Hume himself ruled out all nomological necessity is not of interest here.

37. Armstrong, *Law of Nature*, 1–73, discusses in detail the principal objections that can be raised with respect to Humean analyses.

not to confuse theology and the natural sciences. Of course, both involve the same reality; to say that the world is God's creation rules out any compartmentalization of our endeavors. Theology speaks of the Creator of the world that the sciences try to describe, so it is not appropriate to consider in isolation these different modes of interaction with the real world.[38] But at the same time, the idea of creation brings out the "profane": by demythologizing the world, it reveals a sphere of reality that is not divine and is thus open to scientific investigation. The strict duality of God and the world, which creationism upholds, makes it possible to hold together God's sovereignty and the integrity of the natural order. One would, in fact, drastically underestimate the Creator's power if one imagined it to be in conflict with his creatures' ability to act. As Creator, God's intervention in the world is not like the intrusion of a foreigner; he doesn't need to impose any external constraints to force the creature to do his will. In this way, his providential action does not negate the network of secondary causes, but upholds it.

In creationism's logic, the task of describing natural phenomena using concepts specific to creatures remains undiminished.[39] It is no surprise, therefore, that the difficulty of accounting for nomological necessity also persists. Placing the question in a theological framework does not provide a shortcut in the philosophical debate. The question of the necessity of laws must find its answer by careful evaluation of the philosophical arguments advanced for and against the various descriptions of nomological modality. With this precaution in place, one can nevertheless expect that the weight one gives to various arguments will depend on their wider perspective. One particular trend among contemporary writers is of interest to us in this context: that of broadening their ontological basis in an attempt to find a strictly immanent basis for the natural order, so as to avoid the need to refer to a divine Legislator.

The Australian philosopher of science David Armstrong has developed a detailed account of the laws of nature, in the context of naturalism, that is, his belief that our spatiotemporal world is *all* that exists.[40] Naturalism leads him to postulate what he calls the "truthmaker

---

38. Pannenberg, "Theological Questions to Scientists," 16.

39. Thorson, "Naturalism in Science (part I)," 7–10; Van Till et al., *Portraits of Creation*, 261; and Jaeger, *Philosophie chrétienne des sciences*, 88–91.

40. Armstrong, *Law of Nature*, 75–191; Armstrong, *States of Affairs*, 220–62. Cf. Jaeger, *Lois de la nature*, chap. 2 (esp. 112f.).

principle"; that is, the belief that "for every true statement, or at least for every true contingent statement, there must be something *in the world* which makes the statement true."[41] Of course, naturalism does not inexorably imply the adoption of the truthmaker principle: there are some atheist philosophers who resist the generalized requirement for explanation that follows as a consequence. But for someone with strong non-Humean intuitions, who does not accept brute facts,[42] rejecting a transcendent foundation means seeking an immanent explanation for every aspect of the world. Regarding his theory of laws, the truthmaker principle provides one of the strongest motives for invoking universals: "For it to be a law that an F is a G, it must be *necessary* that an F is a G, in some sense of 'necessary'. But what is the basis in reality, the truthmaker, the ontological ground, of such necessity? I suggest that it can only be found in *what it is to be an F* and *what it is to be a G*."[43]

Armstrong is aware of the rival explanation adopted by many pioneers of modern science: nature "obeys" the laws established by the Creator.[44] But his atheism rules out a theistic explanation of the natural order, and leads him to rely on universals, in order to account for the laws of nature.

In the case of Nancy Cartwright, it is even clearer how atheism has played a part in her adoption of a broader ontological basis: she explicitly states that capacities alone (which she prefers to universals) allow one to understand the natural order, without referring to God. In a lecture that she gave in Varenna (Italy) in October 2004, she examines four approaches, which she calls "empiricism" (which includes David Lewis' theory),[45] "Platonism" (represented by Armstrong), "instrumentalism," and "Aristotelianism" (which corresponds to her own approach).[46] Of these four ways of interpreting the natural order, only Platonism claims to possess a strong concept of law, sufficient to say that such laws "govern

---

41. Armstrong, "Dispositions as Categorical States," 15 (italics mine).

42. Armstrong replies to those who see no need to explain natural regularities, "Perhaps the regularities need no explanation? If you believe that, I say, you will believe anything." (Armstrong, "Reply to Van Fraassen," 229).

43. Armstrong, *Law of Nature*, 77.

44. Armstrong, "Reply to Van Fraassen," 229.

45. Lewis, *Counterfactuals*, 73, and Lewis, "Theory of Universals," 41–43. Cf. Jaeger, *Lois de la nature*, chap. 3.

46. Cf. Jaeger, *Lois de la nature*, chap. 4 (esp. 254–56).

events in Nature."[47] However, Cartwright rejects such a claim: "Abstract relations [on which Platonism is based] are not the kinds of things that can make other things happen; they are not the kinds of things that have powers."[48] She concludes from this: "None of the four contemporary accounts . . . can make sense of laws of Nature without God. The last, Aristotelianism, can offer a stand-in for laws—natural powers—that satisfies the major requirements on the laws without the need to call on God."[49] Hence her primary motivation for understanding the natural order in terms of capacities.

Such chains of argument have little effect on believers: they have no need to reify, as universals or as capacities, the cause of the order revealed by their practice of science. They are content to attribute it to God's continuous providential action, which ensures the functioning of ordained laws. Granted, it is not impossible that Christians, by other means, come to believe that universals or capacities are good tools to describe reality. But their conviction will not stem from the diktat of having to find an immanent basis for the legal order.

Conversely, we can also assume that creationism goes against one argument in favor of the Humean worldview: the difficulty of finding an immanent basis for nomological necessity has led some to adopt a Humean conception—sometimes it is convenient to deny outright the existence of what one has trouble explaining! However, for the creationist, there is no place for such a motive. For even if the divine will does not provide a philosophical analysis of nomological necessity, it allows one to *conceive of* the difference between the necessity of law and the contingency of individual events: we can situate an intermediate level of necessity, reserved for laws, inside the divine decree itself, when God not only decides two events A and B, but also ordains a link of necessity between the two, such that B necessarily follows A.

Such an approach is similar to philosophical descriptions that lay down certain modal concepts as being primitive, alongside factual elements (such as objects or states of affairs). Instead of trying to explain, for example, the necessity of laws of nature by other types of necessity—in particular logical necessity and the "necessity" of individual events—such systems postulate nomological necessity, without seeking to define

47. Cartwright, "No God, No Laws," 4.
48. Ibid., 14.
49. Ibid., 24.

it or explain it in other terms.⁵⁰ Considering the matter from a theological perspective can remove the unease that some feel at the primitive, unexplained nature of nomological necessity in such philosophical systems.⁵¹ This advantage is not, of course, of a philosophical nature: a theological context does not move the philosophical analysis forward as such. However, we can see how it might stand up to the idea that one must find, at any cost, an immanent explanation for the necessity of laws. Admittedly, taking the broader perspective of creationism as the context for this philosophical reflection does not mean one has to treat modal notions as being unexplained. To describe them one can still invoke, for example, universals or capacities. But in that case, one must find other justifications than the mere need to explain the natural order.⁵²

THE REJECTION OF REDUCTIONISM

Let us leave, for now, the thorny problem of nomological necessity, and return to the natural order that the idea of creation leads us to expect. It is clear that the biblical view is not the only religious conception to produce such an expectation. To cite but one example: Werner Heisenberg (1901–76), one of the founders of quantum mechanics, links the Pythagorean religion to the belief—shared by many physicists—that we can understand natural phenomena in simple mathematical terms.⁵³ Given the range of religious views that encourage us to assume that nature is ordered, it makes good sense to deepen our investigation and try to discern the *particular kind* of natural order that creation leads us to expect.

In the previous chapters, we have already seen that the Bible's strict monotheism suggests the universality of the natural order. The critique of the Greek matter-form antithesis eliminates, in particular, the irrational

---

50. The approach to laws of nature that John Carroll adopts (in Carroll, *Laws of Nature*) provides an example of such a system.

51. For example, Chalmers, *This Thing Called Science*, 225, writes, after having rejected the theistic explanation of laws of nature, "What makes systems behave in accordance with the law of conservation of energy? I don't know. They just do. I am not entirely comfortable with this situation, but I don't see how it can be avoided."

52. In a Christian thought-framework close to Thomist Aristotelianism, Bilynskyj, *God, Nature and Miracle*, *passim*, advocates a conception of laws based on the dispositions of things. For the different types of necessity which Calvin distinguishes and their possible explanations, see Jaeger, "Diverses formes de nécéssité," 54–69.

53. Heisenberg, *Physics and Philosophy*, 71–73.

and chaotic aspect of formless matter, thus paving the way for a comprehensive description of the natural order in precise terms. One imagines that such a perspective may have helped the transition from substantial forms to laws of nature at the beginnings of modern science. But does the universality of the natural order imply scientific reductionism? Does creationism provide support for the hegemony that physics often aspires to? This is hardly plausible, given the combination of the universality of the natural order with other themes that are equally, if not more, characteristic of the biblical vision, and which militate against the imperialism of physics.

Of course, we must first mention the duality between God and the world, which stands at the center of the creationist worldview. This duality alone destroys any pretense that science might have of being able to understand all that exists. The traditional doctrine of divine incomprehensibility means that any description of God in purely scientific terms impinges on his transcendence. This inherent limit of science is reflected inside creation: just as some medieval artists represented themselves in their stained-glass windows or paintings, human beings, as God's image, are a reminder that the Person transcends the objectifying method of the scientific approach. The traditional doctrine of the duality of human nature[54]—body and spirit—tries to express this dual truth: humans, who are part of the visible creation, are also in special relationship with their Creator, and this implies a reaching beyond the confines of the natural order. With their bodies, human beings are immersed in the material world; with their spirit, they lift their gaze to God and rule over nature (Gen 2:7; Matt 10:28; 2 Cor 4:16; Col 2:5a; 1 Pet 3:4). Our intellectual creativity, ability to love, and moral responsibility will never find a comprehensive description in the physical or chemical categories that are the fruit of our encounter with the non-human part of creation.[55]

Once we have acknowledged this aspect of differentiation inside creation itself, it becomes likely that the human realm is not the only one to escape the imperialism of physics, but that created reality can be seen to be composed of many facets. The first creation story contains several clues that suggest a plurality of realms in the created world. The

---

54. Duality does not necessarily mean (Cartesian) dualism, cf. chap. 4, sec. 7 below.

55. For the proof of this assertion, see Jaeger, *Philosophie chrétienne des sciences*, 64–67; ibid., 74–78 develops the biblical and philosophical arguments in favor of the multifaceted nature of reality.

theme of separation is a central way of presenting creation: the separation between light and darkness (Gen 1:4, 18), between day and night (Gen 1:14), between the water above and water below the "firmament" (*rāqîaʿ*, Gen 1:6), between the sea and dry land (Gen 1:9). Moreover, plants and animals are created "according to their kinds" (Gen 1:12, 21, 24). The magisterial architecture of the whole chapter gives the work of creation a six-day structure and suggests a multifaceted reality.[56]

It follows that creationism encourages a non-reductionist view of order in creation: different aspects of reality have their own structuring principles. The (relative) independence of different regions goes together with distinct methods of investigation, so that no view of reality should claim to be superior to another. The number and delineation of these different facets of existence are not, it is true, determined solely by theological considerations; we cannot do without an empirical examination of reality. It is nevertheless true that creationism opposes any particular science's claim to hegemony; more specifically, physicalism is incompatible with a multidimensional view of reality.

Opposition to reductionism is one of neo-Calvinism's key themes. Abraham Kuyper speaks of different "spheres" of creation, among which are science, family, church, and state. Each is autonomous in the sense that the other spheres must not interfere with it nor impose laws that are alien to it. Not only does this "sphere sovereignty" forbid the natural sciences from having jurisdiction over matters of morality and religion; but also, the church is the community of believers: it must renounce all pretensions of temporal government. Kuyper was convinced that the Christian faith must cover all aspects of human life, and no less convinced that the church should not meddle with the "secular" spheres of human existence. Thus, the Free University of Amsterdam, which he founded to promote a Christian approach to academic disciplines, maintained a strict independence from the church.[57]

Herman Dooyeweerd, on the other hand, speaks of "modal aspects, [which] delimit . . . the special viewpoints under which the different branches of empirical science examine the empirical world." They are not distinctive domains of reality, but arise inside the temporal horizon of

---

56. Wolters, "Creation as Separation," 347–52, based in particular on Beauchamp, *Création et séparation*.

57. Kuyper summed up his beliefs in his inauguration speech at the Free University: Kuyper, "Sphere Sovereignty," 461–90; see Kuyper, *Stone Lectures on Calvinism*, 29.

human experience. He sees the *ego* as "a supra-temporal, central unity," but human experience "is refracted in the order of time into a rich diversity of modi, or modalities of meaning, just as sunlight is refracted by a prism in a rich diversity of colors."[58] Dooyeweerd lists fifteen modal aspects—arithmetic (number), spatial, kinematic (extensive movement), physical (energy), biotic (organic life), psychic (feeling, sensation), logical, historical (cultural, formative), lingual (symbolic), social, economic, aesthetic, jural (justice, retribution), ethical (temporal love, loyalty), and pistical (faith)—which are organized in a hierarchy of modes of experience. In a given context, one of these modal aspects will be predominant, although others will never be completely absent.[59]

Without our being obliged to accept these neo-Calvinist approaches in their entirety,[60] we can see that they are in harmony with the multidimensional approach to reality that creationism encourages: no single mode of interaction is able to exhaust the richness of creation; the multiplicity of reality must be mirrored by a plurality of practices. Does this then mean a hierarchical view of reality, analogous to that which results from the *analogia entis*? In fact, this is not the case: although the idea of creation stands in opposition to all monistic interpretations, the appreciation of multiplicity to which it gives rise is not of the same kind as the hierarchy of beings. The latter explains multiplicity by means of two heterogeneous principles: the actual and the possible, reality and nothingness. Creationism, on the other hand, affirms that everything that exists is radically dependent on God. Thus the various aspects of reality are related, in an equal way, to the creative act; no realm or being is ontologically closer to God than the others. It is the Bible's radical monotheism that allows us to conceive of the unity of creation's multiplicity: everything comes from the one God, whose differentiated activity brings a multiform creation into being.[61] The creation of multiplicity can be understood more specifically from the trinitarian nature of Scripture's monotheism: since God is three persons in one nature and

---

58. Dooyeweerd, *Twilight of Western Thought*, 7f.

59. Ibid.; cf. Clouser, "Dooyeweerd's Philosophy of Science," 83–86.

60. As concerns Dooyeweerd, I have certain reservations about the precise list of modal aspects that he proposes and the linear order he gives them, as well as, more fundamentally, the idealistic inclination of his work. For an incisive evaluation of Dooyeweerd, see Young, "Herman Dooyeweerd," 270–301.

61. Collingwood, *Essay on Metaphysics*, 213.

thus expresses within his very being the one and the many, he can call forth a world that is both unified and multifarious, without alienating himself or needing to resort to a heteronomous principle.[62]

In this way, creationism allows for a view that is simultaneously more unified and more differentiated than the analogy of being. It is more unified, since it rejects any latent dualism and bases the plurality of the real world on God's creative act. It is more differentiated, because it does not require that the different realms be arranged in a linear hierarchy, but is able to acknowledge the diverse relationships between them. An encounter with reality, rather than a preconceived idea, is what must give us the "map" of areas of knowledge.[63] Why then should we attempt to arrange the various sciences in linear order, as if some were more "scientific" and could give us privileged access to knowledge? This doesn't rule out the possibility that some modes of interaction with reality prove more fundamental than others. But none should pretend to possess unique, or even simply privileged, access to knowledge. On the contrary, a creationist worldview allows for the complimentarity of various approaches to be fully recognized, and banishes the nostalgia of reductionist programs that seek to impose one approach over the others.

It is interesting to compare this perspective with the emergentist movement (British, for the most part) in the first half of the twentieth century. The emergentists thought that at certain critical thresholds of the evolutionary process, non-physical attributes naturally emerged; without necessarily indicating the existence of a new substance (the emergentists were not dualists), these attributes are involved in the causal history of the system, in such a way that both physical and non-physical factors must now be taken into account to describe the situation. Emergent properties are considered to be basic, in the sense that no explanation is proposed either for their origin, or for the form that the forces associated with them take. Their existence must be accepted, in the words of one of the proponents of this view, "with the 'natural piety' of the investigator. It admits no explanation."[64]

---

62. See pp. 35f. above.

63. Bachelard, *Rationalisme appliqué*, speaks of "regional rationalisms."

64. Alexander, *Space, Time and Deity*, 46f. Other classic works on emergentism were Morgan, *Emergent Evolution*; and Broad, *Mind and Place* (Horgan, "From Supervenience to Superdupervenience," 557f.).

The non-reductionist perspective of this view is in agreement with what we have seen in creationism. But the concept of emergence needs to be defined more clearly, before one can say if it adequately explains the multiplicity of creation. In fact, the term can cover quite different understandings: some think that the emergent properties genuinely give rise to new, non-physical forces, while for others they are only irreplaceable for epistemological reasons, since a microphysical explanation is too complex.[65] From a creationist perspective, one important question is whether one grants emergent properties an absolute underived status, such that they become quasi-divine (as the phrase "natural piety" might suggest). Similarly, we should make sure that emergence does not imply a fragmented view of reality, to ensure that reality is sufficiently unified. Only when we have a detailed explanation of emergence that answers these questions, can we decide whether the concept is relevant for explaining the plurality of reality, a plurality that is united by its common origin in the creative act.

UNIFIED PLURALITY

If creationism tends to expect a universal order *and* rejects reductionist aspirations, we must try to understand how the natural order can be universal, without any science being able to describe it exhaustively. Theological and philosophical considerations together make it easier to jointly accept these two consequences of the biblical worldview. As concerns theology, we can bring into play the theme of the incomprehensibility of God's works. This theme occurs frequently in Old Testament texts that mention nature (for example, Ps 139:6, 17–18; Isa 40:12–14; Jer 31:37; 33:22). These in no way justify a radically skeptical attitude: as God's image, humanity shares with its Creator the privilege of knowledge. However, this theme goes against the presumption of omniscience. Only God can know the natural order in an exhaustive way, since he is its Creator. Humanity, on the other hand, must approach it by means of different scientific practices. Since we live in a world that we did not ourselves create, we must resist the arrogant quest for a "theory of everything." No human procedure can claim to exhaust the richness of reality.

---

65. Clayton, *Mind and Emergence*, 9ff., speaks in this context of "strong" and "weak" emergence.

On the philosophical side, let us recall a theme that risks being eclipsed by the reductionist hopes of certain scientists and philosophers: modern science, at its beginnings, was characterized by a renouncing of Greek science's ambition to describe the *essence* of things. This kind of science possessed only one possible description of a being; it sought to formulate *the* true definition: "The idea of a science, for an ancient Greek, was not only the idea of a science of x but the idea of the complete science of x. There could be only one science of a given thing: for unless it grasped the essence of the thing it was not a science of it, and one thing had only one essence. When that was discovered, all the 'properties' of the thing could be deduced."[66]

Modern science, since its origins, has been more humble and gives itself a more limited goal: to describe certain "affections" of objects, by adopting a specific point of view (kinematic, for example, in Galileo's famous inclined plane experiments). It is thus ironic that some seek to absolutize scientific knowledge obtained precisely by means of the rigorous application of a limited point of view. This is why Evandro Agazzi has no problem castigating "reductionism as the negation of the scientific spirit."[67]

Nancy Cartwright makes an illuminating contribution in this context (despite her not accepting the universality of the natural order): the fact that a theory exhaustively describes a certain set of phenomena, without making use of elements outside that set, does not imply that the only things that exist are contained in that set; the predictive closure of a theory is not the same as universality.[68] For example, there are concepts in biology, and even more so in psychology, which elude any kind of definition in terms of physico-chemical properties. To insist that such a reductionist program be possible does not make one a more "scientific" biologist or psychologist. In contrast, a physicist will expect of his or her theory (in its domain of validity, that is, phenomena that admit physical description) that any deviation from a theoretical description can itself be described by the same theory. We can therefore understand different scientific practices as being different projections of our multidimensional reality. Each captures a specific aspect of the created order, and

---

66. Collingwood, *New Leviathan*, 253.

67. Agazzi, "Reductionism as Negation," 1–29. On the deliberately limited nature of the modern scientific method, see ibid., 5, 7.

68. Cartwright, *Dappled World*, 33.

only a consideration of the different points of view can do justice to the plurality of reality.

Why then does reductionism (especially in its physicalist form) exert such a strong pull on a good many philosophers and scientists today? To answer this question, we must first recognize the practical benefits of reductionist programs: our intellectual understanding and our technological mastery increase each time a reduction is successful. Nevertheless, we can hardly limit ourselves to such utilitarian considerations, since reductionism, as an absolutization of a domain of knowledge, is more than a trivial generalization of a procedure that has borne (partial) fruit in the past. It corresponds to a recurring answer that human thinking has formulated when faced with multiplicity: in the quest for unity, it is tempting to reduce the many to the One, by eliminating differences.[69] We can interpret this as the search for an immanent *ersatz* of the unity that is grounded in the Creator. Even if we have lost sight of multiplicity's transcendent roots, our nostalgia for unity remains. Rather than seeking it in God, one turns to reality, which one no longer considers to be created, and establishes a unifying principle within it. But "by seeking itself and its absolute origin in one of these aspects [of experience], the thinking *I* turns to the absolutization of the relative."[70] On the other hand, those who find multiplicity's union not in creation but in the Creator, are able to welcome all of reality's multiform richness, without imposing a reductionist view on it.[71]

Nancy Cartwright's dappled world is an example of the other kind of answer that autonomous human thinking can give when faced with the experience of multiplicity. This second type of response is antithetical to the reductionist claim: rather than absolutizing one aspect of reality, it exalts the plurality of experience. Cartwright reacts against "fundamentalism," that is, against any system that makes one type of phenomena the basis of reality. Instead, she adopts a fragmented worldview, which requires a radical break from the quest for unity.[72] Thus, she proposes a naturalist version of anti-reductionism, which is distinguished from its creationist equivalent not only by its religious underpinnings, but also by the exact form that it takes. Cartwright makes use

---

69. Agazzi, "Reductionism as Negation," 1.
70. Dooyeweerd, *Twilight of Western Thought*, 27.
71. Van Til, *Christian Theory of Knowledge*, 50s; Petcher, "Science and Belief," 259.
72. Cartwright, *Dappled World*, 23, 31. Cf. p. 64 above.

of a dimension of radical disorder not unlike the Greek idea of matter, to justify her pluralism.[73] The creationist version of anti-reductionism has no need of an irrational principle to make its multifaceted view of reality work. It can accommodate different scientific practices as limited, yet legitimate, projections of the relationships between human beings and reality. The difference is that human knowledge is placed in the context of divine knowledge, such that partial knowledge can still be genuinely true. This wider perspective means one can abandon any pretension to omniscience and be satisfied with one's finite condition without ceding to irrationalism, since God knows perfectly those dimensions of reality that lie beyond the grasp of the human intellect, and he guarantees their rational nature.[74]

It follows from this that the relationship between creationism and science is a complex one. The exact description of natural phenomena fits neatly into a worldview inspired by the Bible. Believing that the world is the creation of a wise and faithful God is a strong motivation to seek a natural order above and beyond what has already been discovered; creationism thus provides justification for the universality of the lawful order as a regulating principle in science. It is even likely that the Judeo-Christian worldview positively contributed to the emergence of the new scientific method at the start of the modern era. That said, we by no means absolutize scientific practice (let alone one discipline in particular); a believer must not forget that the possibility of applying mathematics to nature is but one part of faith in God.[75] In particular, acknowledging the incomprehensibility of God's works means we are obliged to accept the limitations of any scientific description. It is even possible that areas of disorder persistently remain in what we perceive of the natural order. We can not decide *a priori* the degree of order that God has implanted; the Creator's freedom requires the empirical approach not only as regards the formulation of laws of nature, but also as regards their domain of validity.

---

73. Cartwright, *Laws of Physics Lie*, 128; Cartwright, *Dappled World*, 58. Cf. Jaeger, *Lois de la nature*, 249f.

74. Van Til, *Survey of Christian Epistemology*, 200, and Van Til, *Christian Theory of Knowledge*, 17, 26, 135. See pp. 97f. below.

75. Collingwood, *Essay on Metaphysics*, 257, criticizes the logical positivists for committing this error.

CREATION AND CHANCE

We have seen that the idea of creation does not necessarily exclude all appearances of disorder in the description of natural phenomena. It is nevertheless true that creationism leads us to resist the irrational tendency, which underlies the vision of Cartwright (and which is reminiscent of Greek science's unintelligibility of matter). It follows that the way we view the possible disorder in nature will not be the same. We have already seen that creationism upholds, in contrast to the dappled world model, the universality of the legal order as a regulative principle of scientific practice. In addition, creationism provides a different assessment of chance, a topic that has been of particular importance ever since quantum mechanics introduced irreducible probabilistic descriptions at the most fundamental level of theories in physics. Chance also plays a key role in the neo-Darwinian reconstruction of the origin of species: novelty appears according to random genetic mutations.

The concept of chance is a decidedly difficult notion to work with. Several different understandings of it overlap in these discussions: that which has no causal link to what precedes, that which is unpredictable, that which has no apparent order. In any case, we must resist the mythologizing of chance: it is neither an efficient cause, which produces events, nor a creative principle, able to bring forth a new entity. We must therefore reject the temptation to attribute an action to chance; it cannot be invoked in order to account for an event that would otherwise remain unexplained. This is reflected, in the theistic view, by the fact that Fortune has no place there: chance is not an autonomous principle of chaos that might constitute an enemy of the creational order. Biblical texts that speak of the *ḥōq* that the Creator's will imposes on the sea are of particular significance here. The sea, in the mythology of Israel's neighbors, symbolized the chaos that threatened to engulf the humans' habitat. To say that the sea is subject to the divine *ḥōq* amounts to affirming that nothing escapes God's determination. The meaning of the Hebrew word is twofold: depending on the context, it can refer to the limit or border, or the law or rule. In some passages, the second meaning is clearly in view (Jer 31:35–36; Job 38:10, Prov 8:29).[76] It follows that chaos is not only delimited by God's sovereignty; it is entirely subject to it. There remains no zone of influence inside which chaos can do as it pleases.

---

76. Jaeger, *Laws of Nature*, 150–53; 163–68.

We cannot, however, conclude from this a deterministic natural order, like that dreamed of by mechanistic philosophers, inspired by Newtonian physics. For determination by God's sovereign will is not the same thing as the determinism of scientific laws. Concluding the second from the first would be to confuse primary and secondary causes. The book of Proverbs specifically insists on God's control over random events: "The lot is cast into the lap; its every decision comes from the Lord" (Prov 16:33). It follows from this that providential control over events may take various forms: "The God of biblical theism is beholden to none to account for his creative agency. If he freely wills into being a succession of events in which one half of the sub-microscopic details at any time are unspecified by their precursors, this would involve no inconsistency with his character, still less with his sovereignty, as portrayed in the Bible."[77]

It is interesting that John Calvin, who has often been criticized for having a deterministic view of reality, does not see his doctrine of predestination as excluding accidental events. Granted, he professes with St. Augustine that "the will of God is necessity, and that every thing is necessary which he has willed; just as those things will certainly happen which he has foreseen."[78] But one should not conclude from this that events are rigidly determined; many events appear random to us, despite the fact that God directs them. For one must distinguish between providential control and the necessity inherent in causal series: "That which God has determined, though it must come to pass, is not, however, precisely, or in its own nature, necessary."[79] Of course, he cannot accept the idea of a chaotic principle, independent of God, and he rejects the idea of the "wheel of *fortune*": it is not chance which presides over the course of history, but the divine counsel. But God can will accidental events as *accidental*; in this way, Calvin includes chance as part of the divine decree: "In regard to supernatural events, though these are occurring every day, how few are there who ascribe them to the ruling providence of God—how many who imagine that they are casual results produced by the blind evolutions of the wheel of chance? Even when, under the

---

77. MacKay, *Science, Chance and Providence*, 30.

78. Calvin, *Institutes* III, XXIII, 8, 232, based on Augustine, *On Genesis*, book VI, chap. XV.

79. Calvin, *Institutes* I, XVI, 9, 181.

guidance and direction of these events, we are in a manner forced to the contemplation of God."[80]

Not only are accidents of history part of the divine plan; Calvin also takes care to demarcate his position from a determinism that would subject everything that happens to an inflexible necessity, inherent in the natural course of events: "Those who would cast obloquy on this doctrine [of providence], calumniate it as the dogma of the Stoics concerning fate ... We do not admit the term Fate ... For we do not with the Stoics imagine a necessity consisting of a perpetual chain of causes, and a kind of involved series contained in nature, but we hold that God is the disposer and ruler of all things,—that from the remotest eternity, according to his own wisdom, he decreed what he was to do, and now by his power executes what he decreed."[81]

What allows us to avoid Stoic determinism is that, on one hand, the intervention of the sovereign Lord is not on the same level as the natural order; he is not an immanent cause, but the transcendent Creator who sustains, in his wisdom, the course of nature and history. On the other hand, his providential action participates in his personal nature; it is in no way a "blind" determinism, such as that postulated by, for example, mechanistic philosophy.

We have already seen a consequence of this: the bipartite human condition—body and mind—is not paradoxical. There is no antithesis between human freedom and the natural order, if one understands that the latter results from a free act; the natural order is fundamentally open to the exercise of freedom. It follows, in turn, that the encounter with the world should not be limited to a single method. The constitutive duality of human beings suggests a multifaceted reality, and so scientific practice inspired by creationism will be multiform.

This refusal of reductionism implies that we do not need to bring in chance to explain the novelty that arises over the course of time. The first creation story in Genesis suggests (and the current evolutionary reconstruction does not disprove) that new orders of existence have made their entry on the world's stage during its history. Any reductionist program must ultimately deny the novelty of these forms of being; they have merely a surface appearance of novelty if, for example, the biological domain is no more than a consequence of physicochemical laws. Chance is then

80. Ibid., I, V, 11, 59.
81. Ibid., I, XVI, 8, 179.

invoked to explain how what appears to be new could have come about, despite its determination by previous forms of existence. In this way, chance takes on a quasi-mythological form, when, for example, Jacques Monod believes "that chance *alone* is at the source of every innovation, of all creation in the biosphere," and believes that it is a definitive reason to reject any kind of teleological action.[82] For any system that makes human reason the measure of all things has difficulty finding a place for novelty, and with it, for the experience of time and of history. One is often left, in an entirely transparent rationalistic system, with no more than unexplained individuality and absolute chance to account for the historical dimension of reality; as a result, such a system finds itself paradoxically pushed towards irrationalism.[83]

Creationism has absolutely no need of such loopholes and refuses to make chance an autonomous principle, which would ultimately amount to divinizing it. The antithesis of chance and divine action is simply not acceptable; similarly, the reductionist claim distorts the perception of scientific data. The novelty of life and of free human action does not cause any problems for the biblical worldview. Even if in the past these things did not yet exist, they are not in tension with "inferior" forms of existence; for everything that is created is a result of the will of a personal and living God. Thus it is not necessary to bring in chance as an antinomial principle in order to explain the emergence of life and consciousness. In any case, such an "explanation" confuses contingency and chance: one does not explain historical evolution by establishing the absence of cause and effect (effective or predictable, as the case may be). A similar confusion would be to think that a free act must be understood according to the modalities of indeterminism specific to a decision based on the toss of a coin. A responsible act has it own particular logic, which cannot be reduced to physics alone. But it is inadequate (and not even that relevant) to resort to an indeterministic or incomplete scientific description. Affirming that an act is free is not primarily saying something about its indetermination by physical causes, but rather expressing the conviction that it accomplishes the will of the agent.

---

82. Monod, *Chance and Necessity*, 112.

83. Van Til, *Christian Theory of Knowledge*, 166, 168, 256; Popper, *The Open Universe*, sections 18, 21f., 26.

QUANTUM INDETERMINISM

In quantum theory we are faced with an idea of chance that is both fundamental to our physical understanding of the world, and very controversial; it is therefore imperative that we consider its implications for the role that chance plays in a created world. Since its beginnings, quantum theory has intrigued many by the role that probabilistic predictions play in it. In general, the behavior of a microscopic system is not predictable; only statistical predictions are possible. Thus, quantum mechanics specifies the average time taken for a radioactive atom to decay, but the exact moment when it decays is unpredictable.

The probabilistic nature of quantum mechanics is highly counterintuitive, given how different it is from our common experience based on contact with medium-sized objects, sandwiched between the atomic level and the vast distances of the universe. There have been (and still are) numerous attempts to understand the strangeness of the quantum world, and a plethora of interpretations, some of them conflicting, have been proposed.[84] In the context of our study, it is worthwhile to draw out two approaches that allow for a connection to the Greek idea of matter; they specifically ask to what extent developments in twentieth-century physics might challenge the critique of this idea, a critique which creationism upholds.

Werner Heisenberg himself explicitly stated the connection between the probabilistic nature of quantum mechanics and the Greek concept of matter, with its idea of *potentia*; he thereby tried to give meaning to the attribution of a state vector to an individual quantum system. While the probability theorems of this theory allow us to accurately predict the behavior of a sufficiently large group of identical quantum objects, the wave function of an individual quantum system would describe its potential to produce certain effects when one performs the appropriate measurements. This *potentia* thus constitutes an intermediate level of reality, between quantum systems and the observation of certain effects when a measurement is taken. It provides the medium for the change that a measurement causes in a quantum system. In this way, it plays a

---

84. For a classification of the different interpretations, see e.g., Bitbol, *Mécanique quantique*, chap. 3–5, and Mittelstaedt, *Interpretation of Quantum Mechanics*, 1–18, 41–46.

role similar to the matter, which, for Aristotle, is the substrate that accommodates changes.[85]

However, this analogy is misleading. In quantum mechanics, the concept of probability only applies to groups of systems rather than individual systems; in particular, no measurement exists for the supposed attribute that would be the probability of an individual system. Moreover, the wave function contains all the information about the state of the system (on the condition that it is pure). We can describe this wave function without using probability, simply by writing the state vector with respect to any orthonormal basis. The *potentia* that Heisenberg postulated cannot therefore constitute an additional level of reality, in addition to the objective properties of the system. Recent results have indeed shown that quantum mechanics' probabilistic predictions derive, without any additional postulates, from the description of individual quantum systems, using the wave function, which as we have seen can be expressed in a non-probabilistic way, and the assumption that the objective properties of the system can be obtained by measurement with certainty.[86] It is therefore impossible to consider that the probabilistic nature of quantum theory, when it deals with sets of systems, refers to an intermediate level of reality, the so-called *potentia*.

A second connection between quantum theory and the Greek concept of matter emerges in the debate about the possible incompleteness of quantum mechanics. The debate was started by the seminal paper by Albert Einstein, Boris Podolsky, and Nathan Rosen, which revealed, for the first time, the non-local correlations that quantum mechanics predicts between two systems that have previously interacted.[87] This consequence of the formalism appeared so unacceptable to Einstein that he concludes that quantum theory only provides a partial description of reality, and that a more fundamental realm must lie outside it. A new and decisive stage in the debate was reached with the work of J. S. Bell. The latter succeeded in showing that the probabilistic nature of quantum predictions

---

85. Heisenberg, "Plancksche Entdeckung," 135–48 (quoted by Mittelstaedt, *Interpretation of Quantum Mechanics*, 62) and *Physics and Philosophy*, chap. IX. Karl Popper made a similar proposal, but his concept of "propensity" is meant to explain the attribution of probabilities to individual systems in general, not just in quantum mechanics (Popper, *World of Propensities*, 1–26).

86. Mittelstaedt, *Interpretation of Quantum Mechanics*, 47–57; for the critique of Heisenberg's proposal, see ibid., 62–64.

87. Einstein et al., "Quantum-Mechanical Description," 777–80.

is not restricted to the limits of our knowledge; it leads to contradictory results if one postulates that quantum theory is only a partial description of a hidden reality.[88]

This result cautions against trying to see the probabilistic nature of quantum mechanics as an indication of its incompleteness. Quantum theory in itself bears no sign pointing to a deeper reality of which it provides only a partial description. Thus, there is no reason to interpret the strangeness of the microscopic world as an indication of the limits of mathematical description. As much as for Galilean physics, modern physics is driven by the belief that mathematical descriptions apply to our "lowly" world; there is no question of merely approximate instantiations of mathematical forms that only belong in the world of Ideas. One should also note that quantum mechanics' probabilistic predictions are governed by precise (not just approximative) mathematical laws. As we have seen, (complex) mathematical considerations even allow us to deduce statistical structures from the non-probabilistic mathematical description of individual quantum systems. It is, therefore, wrong to imagine that another level of reality might be hiding behind the atomic world, where mathematical description would be impossible. Quite the opposite: quantum mechanics describes an effectual order, even if this order reveals features that go against common sense. We should not really be that surprised; our common sense has its source in the world of macroscopic objects, and the shift to the atomic world does not come naturally.

These considerations show that the presumption of order that arises from the idea of creation is not undermined by quantum mechanics. In particular, the creationist perspective is not prey to the fundamental motive that led Einstein to view the indeterminacy of quantum theory as a sign of its incompleteness: in a strictly deterministic system, like that of Spinoza, the only possible source of indeterminate events is our ignorance: "A thing can in no respect be called contingent, save in relation to the imperfection of our knowledge."[89] On the contrary, the biblical view emphasizes the contingency of the natural order, since it depends on the free act of creation. Of course, we are not in any way suggesting that theism could have foreseen an indeterministic microscopic order. The

---

88. The result is specifically valid for local hidden variable theories; it does not rule out strictly deterministic theories of a non-local nature (Bitbol, *Mécanique quantique*, 341–64).

89. Spinoza, *Ethics*, First part, scholium I of the prop. XXXIII, 18.

biblical worldview highlights precisely the freedom of the creative act; we should not therefore try to deduce the shape the created order might take from theological arguments. Nevertheless, creationism makes room for chance, without abandoning a scientific description of nature, and thus has no trouble accepting quantum theory's indeterminacy.

Similarly, we should avoid the idea of quantum indeterminacy being the privileged place for divine intervention.[90] This idea fails to correctly distinguish between physical and theological categories, and so is unsatisfying as much for the scientist as it is for the believer. Trying to fit divine action into the gaps in the scientific description clearly shows a confusion of primary and secondary causes: God is not an additional causal factor alongside the entities that populate the world. His action is therefore not in competition with the established natural order; it is manifested just as much in his providential sustaining as it is by a miracle, should one occur. Looking for "gaps" in the picture which science gives us, and invoking God to explain them, is more deistic than theistic: a solid understanding of creation allows us to reject any kind of idea of a "God of the gaps."

In addition to this theological objection, which by itself is decisive, it should be emphasized that the alleged gap does not exist. Bell's work (which has now been largely verified experimentally) has precisely shown that quantum mechanics rules out any kind of "additional" determination of quantum events.[91] Nothing in quantum theory requires any further theological causality. Or, to say it more carefully: there is no more need for divine action in the strange world of quanta, than there is in the more familiar physics of the seventeenth century. In both frameworks, it would be wrong to situate the Creator's action in any gaps in the scientific description. Rather, he sustains the whole of the natural order and ensures its openness to other modes of interaction than simply that of the objectifying examination that characterizes the scientific process.

---

90. As does, for example, Pollard, *Chance and Providence*, quoted (and critiqued) by Polkinghorne, "Metaphysics of Divine Action," 152. Polkinghorne prefers to resort to the unpredictability of chaotic systems (ibid., 153f)—a proposal which is guilty of a similar confusion (despite his denial of this in Polkinghorne, *Science and Theology*, 89).

91. Mittelstaedt, "Bedeutung physikalischer Erkenntnisse," 140f.; Van Fraassen, "Charybdis of Realism," 108–13. Dowe, "Chance and Providence," 16, asserts that God can play the role of "hidden variable" since he can act non-locally and that the Bell inequalities only forbid local hidden variables. This observation once again confuses physical causality with divine action.

four

The Relational Nature of Knowledge

> That is why knowledge that occurs in this space cannot be interpreted by any defective case but solely by the highest, adequate, and fully valid one, that is by the meeting of another person. For this is not a special case of knowledge beside others, but that which gives direction to all other cases of intellectual or sense knowledge which are below it, because they are inferior in depth of meaning; they all are, at least inchoatively, forms of meeting and letting meet, and thus of the being-for-another of the world's creatures.
>
> —Hans Urs von Balthasar, *The God Question and Modern Man*

THE WORLD AS TEXT

Not only does creationism suggest certain characteristics of the lawful order of nature—that it is stable, rational, and multifaceted—it also implies a particular view of humankind's knowledge of this natural order. Admittedly, trinitarian theism does not provide an answer to every possible question in epistemology. Expecting a religious worldview to furnish a complete philosophical theory would be to confuse the domains of theology and philosophy. The same prudence is called for in epistemology as for ontology: creationism will lead us toward some options and away from others, without resolving the whole field of philosophical inquiry.

Nevertheless, creationism has particular implications for the epistemological position that one adopts. Our task is, therefore, to identify the main tendencies, so as to better understand how the creationist worldview fits with scientific practice, which aims to understand the natural order.

No discussion of this subject can ignore the theme of the *logos*, a highly influential concept in early Christian thinking. This key notion sets the course of discussions about the nature of knowledge, right from the start of patristic theology, and has its origin in the Scriptures themselves, which use the metaphor of the word in relation to the structure of the world. Right at the beginning of the Bible, in the first chapter of Genesis, the word brings forth an ordered creation: "And God said, 'Let there be light,' and there was light . . ." Ten times in the narrative, the author refers to the creative word. Other Bible texts show the same idea. Thus, the psalmist celebrates God's word in creation: "By the word of the LORD the heavens were made, and by the breath of his mouth all their host [i.e., the stars]" (Ps 33:6).[1]

The creative word is at the center of one of the most significant New Testament contributions to the doctrine of creation: its authors attribute creation, and more specifically the providential sustaining of the world, to the second person of the Trinity. The prologue of John's Gospel echoes the first creation narrative in Genesis, by giving Christ the title of *logos*.[2] The anonymous author of the Epistle to the Hebrews states that the Son, the final revelation of the Father, sustains "all things by his powerful word" (Heb 1:3).

It follows that truth is the correspondence between thought or word and the structure of reality. Human beings do not live in a world that they have created themselves or which is lacking in form. They must "adjust" their minds in accordance with the order that they have already received as a "given." Their knowledge act is always secondary to the creative act that has shaped the environment in which they find themselves. In this way, creationism denounces as illusory both empiricism (of a Humean sort) and Kant's revised version of it: both hold that the material of our experience is not in-formed, even if they differ over the relationship

---

1. Berkouwer, *General Revelation*, 128f., notes that nowhere in the nature psalms do we find any tension between God's word at work in nature and the revelation given to Israel in the law.

2. See pp. 59f. above.

between the knower and the absence of external order. While empiricism is content simply to state this absence, in Kantianism the task of ordering the world falls to the human understanding and this, ultimately, means the Creator is replaced by the human mind, which imposes its categories on reality.[3] But if God's word structures creation, we do not live "in a world governed by no laws except those we create ourselves";[4] humanity is therefore not the Creator, but only the "finite reinterpreter"[5] of the world's order. Humankind is faced with "the gift [of being] that marks the *exteriority* of the provenance . . . The theologian must remain 'realistic' insofar as the created order cannot truthfully appear except via a *mediation of being*, a mediation that indicates that the created order possesses its own solidity *and* that it exists to point to a free self-positing which alone gives it this solidity, and its thickness, its reality."[6]

Because of the given nature of the world's structure, creationism leads to an epistemology that honors, in its principal orientation, the standard definition of truth as correspondence with facts—the venerable *adaequatio rei et intellectus* of scholastic discussions.[7] However, in light of the *logos* theme, we realize that the traditional view is incomplete. True knowledge is not simply found in the correspondence between thought and facts, but comes from an agreement between thought and thought: a human being knows when his or her mind grasps the structure of reality, created by God's word: "Facts themselves are God's thoughts realized and made manifest in time. The evidence of the senses and of reason can only be conceived of from this viewpoint as a revelation from God."[8]

From this perspective, the universe is one that speaks,[9] and the world, a text. Jacques Derrida's slogan: "There is nothing outside of the

---

3. Van Til, *Common Grace and Gospel*, 5, and Van Til, "Kant or Christ," 134f., 138. See p. 160ff. below, for a more in-depth discussion of Kant's philosophy of science.

4. Van Fraassen, "World of Empiricism," 123.

5. Van Til, *Survey of Christian Epistemology*, 203.

6. Gisel, *Création*, 170 (the author uses the term "realist" in the context of the dispute over universals).

7. Blocher, "Qu'est-ce que la vérité?," 7–13, 38–46, shows that this is the primary meaning of truth in the Bible, even if this statement requires some qualifications, something we will come to shortly.

8. Lecerf, *Dogmatique réformée*, vol. 1, 154; cf. ibid., 138, 284.

9. This metaphor is borrowed from private correspondence with Charles Harper, dated 25 April, 2003.

text,"[10] comes to mind; but the affirmation takes on a radically different meaning to that intended by Derrida. No, there are no facts without interpretation, one never reaches an experiential foundation that is not mediated by speech. But, to extend the metaphor: we read the text in the author's *presence*; the text is not unintelligible, nor is it open to all possible (de)constructions. The world has a definite order that is accessible to rational investigation.

This view of knowledge allows us to deal with a common critique leveled at realism: how can one compare facts and their interpretation (in thought or speech), given that these constitute two very different categories? How does one relate a linguistic (or propositional) entity to the factual element to which it is supposed to correspond? Creation by the *logos* can do justice to this objection, since it acknowledges the interpreted nature of any fact. "Factual" reality never exists in its raw state; it is always already in-formed by the divine word. Human reason is not therefore confronted with a foreign kind of experiential substance: "The world of the senses is not opposed to the intelligible. The world of the senses is intelligible by constitution."[11] Thus, there is no reason for a dichotomy between fact and thought (or speech); the notion of knowledge one obtains from creationism only admits (a kind of) idealism, inasmuch as it accepts that all order is grounded in the mind of God.[12]

At the same time, such an understanding avoids the unraveling of knowledge that threatens idealism in its usual form. The interpretation of facts which knowledge leads to is not that of the human knower, nor that of a suitably-defined community. Humankind is always directed back to the supreme interpretation of the natural order, sanctioned by the authority of the Creator himself. We thereby avoid both skepticism and relativism, since the divine interpretation of facts reveals, and even constitutes, their essence; both in terms of knowledge, and in practice, we are not in a situation where "anything goes."

---

10. "*Il n'y a pas de hors-texte.*" (Derrida, *Of Grammatology*, 158).

11. Tresmontant, *Etudes de métaphysique biblique*, 8.

12. Van Til, *Common Grace and Gospel*, 64, calls God our "concrete universal," thus bringing out the idea that the solution to the problem of knowledge is found in God, in whom thought and being are "coterminous."

THE INCOMPREHENSIBILITY OF GOD AS THE CONTEXT FOR KNOWLEDGE

Creationism not only rejects empiricism's formless experience, it also opposes rationalism's overestimation of human reason: neither "the brute facts of empiricism," nor "abstract principles of rationalism" have any place in a resolutely theistic epistemology.[13] Acknowledging that the world receives its structure from the creative act inevitably means situating human knowledge itself inside the created realm. Human beings are part of the created order, an order that both encompasses and transcends us at the same time. The world's structure is therefore not totally transparent to human reason; theology must, in accordance with the Bible, confess not only the incomprehensibility of God, but also that of his works (Ps 139:5–6, 17–18; Eccl 3:11; Isa 40:13).[14] It is first and foremost the Creator who understands the world's "text." The Lord's knowledge then constitutes the framework inside which human knowledge is located. In the words of Cornelius Van Til, we are called to think God's thoughts after him: "God . . . must be thought of as being determinative of the objects of knowledge. In other words, he must . . . be thought of as the only ultimate interpreter, and man must be thought of as a finite reinterpreter."[15]

As a result, human beings must accept that they can only *partially* grasp reality: they can never know, in a comprehensive way, either God, the world, or themselves. Similarly, human knowledge is inherently provisional: when we acknowledge that we are creatures, we accept that our knowledge has a great deal of room for improvement. As we discover creation's order from the inside, rather than looking at it "from above," we proceed by successive exploration of delimited sections of reality. We can never attain the ultimate truth about the world, but must always progress in our understanding of reality.[16]

What may at first appear as a humbling of human knowledge actually proves to be profoundly liberating on closer examination: the honest recognition of the derivative nature of human thought frees us from the rationalist obligation of exhaustive knowledge, which will forever

---

13. Ibid., 52; cf. 45.
14. Cf. Kaiser, *Creational Theology and History*, 21f., 25.
15. Van Til, *Survey of Christian Epistemology*, 203.
16. O'Donovan, *Resurrection and Moral Order*, 79.

remain beyond our means. Since human knowledge sits in the wider context of divine knowledge, it can be fragmentary *and* entirely reliable, since God's total knowledge of reality guarantees the truth of partial knowledge. There is therefore no longer any need to understand the whole structure of the world in order to have access to true knowledge: "*If one does not make human knowledge wholly dependent upon the original self-knowledge and consequent revelation of God to man, then man will have to seek knowledge within himself as the final reference point . . .* Then he will have to hold that if he cannot attain to such an exhaustive understanding of reality, he has no *true* knowledge of anything at all. Either man must then know everything or he knows nothing. This is the dilemma that confronts every form of non-Christian epistemology."[17]

It is precisely divine incomprehensibility that allows us to hold together both the authentic truth, and the fragmentary nature, of knowledge: humankind can accept that its understanding of the world will always be partial, without lapsing into irrationalism, precisely because God transcends the world. For only when the human subject acknowledges his immersion in a reality that transcends him can he abandon the pretension of total knowledge, while relying on the omniscience of the Creator. God knows perfectly the part of reality that eludes human knowledge, and ensures its orderliness.

Given the famous role that Descartes gives to human thought (and to doubt, especially), it is remarkable that in his work we see a similar immersion of humanity's self-knowledge in divine incomprehensibility: "I clearly understand that there is more reality in an infinite substance than in a finite one, and hence that my perception of the infinite, that is God, is in some way prior to my perception of the finite, that is myself. For how could I understand that I doubted or desired—that is, lacked something—and that I was not wholly perfect, unless there were in me some idea of a more perfect being which enabled me to recognize my own defects by comparison?"[18]

---

17. Van Til, *Christian Theory of Knowledge*, 17.

18. Descartes, *Meditations on First Philosophy*, Third meditation, 31. By referring to Descartes I am not overlooking the differences that remain between his system and what I believe to be a coherent theistic conception of knowledge. In particular, the difference between finite and infinite does not correspond exactly to the distinction between Creator and creature. Moreover, one might ask whether Descartes has a tendency to replace God with the *idea* that we have of him.

Human beings can only know themselves as subjects with reference to the idea of a perfect Being. Since finite human reason cannot contain the Infinite, the Infinite is necessarily incomprehensible; but this incomprehensibility does not lead to ignorance. Quite the contrary: God, for Descartes, presents himself to the mind as the most vivid idea, since it encompasses all others, exceeding them all in its reality and solidity: "Whatever I clearly and distinctly perceive as being real and true, and implying any perfection, is wholly contained in [this idea]."[19]

Accepting, without remorse, the partial nature of all human knowledge brings us to the more modest (and hence more feasible) aim of modern science: the latter abandoned the ideal of complete knowledge, which dominated, in large measure, the science of antiquity. The aim was no longer to describe the essence of things, but their behavior under well-defined experimental conditions—this reining-in of aspirations to omniscience is without doubt one reason for the startling successes of the new scientific method from the seventeenth century onwards.[20] As we have seen, the limited goal of the new scientific approach also avoids the pressure of reductionism: since the various sciences only describe one aspect of nature from one particular viewpoint, they should not pretend to exhaust all of reality's richness. One can thus grant each one its own validity, as long as one accepts that the human subject has but partial access to reality. Different fragmentary "snapshots" can thereby complement each other to enrich our understanding of nature.[21]

The limit imposed on human knowledge by the incomprehensibility of divine works has very different consequences to those caused by a limit of immanent origin. We have already seen this when comparing creationism's rejection of reductionism with Nancy Cartwright's dappled world.[22] The derivative nature of human knowledge leads us to declare it partial and provisional, without having to resort to a principle of disorder. Situating human knowledge in the broader framework of divine incomprehensibility precisely allows us to avoid rationalism without falling into irrationalism, since God knows completely the aspects of reality that are out of our intellectual reach, and he maintains sovereign control over them.

19. Ibid., 32; cf. Marion, "Raison formelle de l'infini," 113.
20. Cf. Heisenberg, *Physics and Philosophy*, 73–75; cf. also p. 83 above.
21. Cf. pp. 83–85 above.
22. Cf. pp. 84f. above.

In earlier times, irrationalism found support in the Greek idea of matter—a perspective that can be detected, in fact, as an undercurrent in Cartwright's work.[23] For Plato, what is accessible to the senses is not the object of knowledge; since the intellect can only apprehend that which is eternal, our historically-evolving world eludes human reason. Timaeus' "likely story"[24] declares, right from the outset, the opposition between rationality and observation: "That which is apprehended by intelligence and reason is always in the same state; but that which is conceived by opinion with the help of sensation and without reason, is always in a process of becoming and perishing and never really is."[25] A similar opposition is found in Thomas Aquinas' writing: "Forms are actually intelligible only insofar as they are separated from matter and material conditions . . . It is, therefore, necessary that every substance capable of intellectual understanding be completely free of matter such that it have no matter as part of itself, nor be like a form impressed on matter."[26] He underlines that "all matter impedes intelligibility" and not "only corporeal matter."[27]

It is not difficult to see how such a view is in tension with a scientific method based on observation and experiment. The experimental method of the new philosophy of nature, which took shape in the seventeenth century, is based on the belief that the world of the senses, the material world, as it is, is the object of rational knowledge. On this point it agrees with the creationist worldview: since everything that exists is the work of a wise and orderly God, nothing is fundamentally unintelligible. In such a conception, "the real is solid food for the intellect. It is in no way inert, insignificant, foreign to the intellect, or unable to be assimilated. There is no 'matter' in the sense of 'thing which resists the intellect,' utter garbage for the mind."[28]

It is also quite possible that the lack of a broader context in which to situate human knowledge was partly responsible for the dichotomy in Greek philosophy between what is accessible to the senses, and what is accessible to the intellect. If divine incomprehensibility does not

23. Cf. p. 64 above.
24. Plato, *Timaeus* 29d.
25. Ibid., 27d–28a (italics mine); cf. ibid., 51d–52a.
26. Aquinas, *On Being and Essence*, 52.
27. Ibid. Cf. Aquinas, *Summa theologiae* Ia, q. 12, art. 4; and ibid., q. 14, art. 1.
28. Tresmontant, *Etudes de métaphysique biblique*, 220.

provide the context in which knowledge can be fragmentary *and* true, we are obliged to try and find a guarantor of rationality within human knowledge itself. Hence the temptation to confuse true knowledge with complete knowledge, and to make intelligibility dependent on the availability of an entirely transparent logical system. Van Til discerns in this the root of the dilemma that autonomous thinking is faced with: "Man must . . . virtually reduce the facts that confront him to logical relations; the 'thingness' of each thing must give up its individuality in order that it may be known; to be known, a thing or fact must be *wholly* known."[29] When this happens, a thing's individuality can only be recovered at the expense of its intelligibility; contingency, and with it historical development, elude rational understanding. When, however, we realize our dependence on divine omniscience, which encompasses our partial knowledge, we are freed from the dichotomy of observation set against intellectual understanding, and the world, in its singularity, is opened up to rational exploration.

THE NOETIC EFFECTS OF SIN

The boundary on human knowledge constituted by the incomprehensibility of divine works should not be confused with another source of limitation, which, unlike the matter-form dichotomy, is fully part of the biblical view of reality. Human knowledge is not only that of a creature, but of a *fallen* creature. The epistemology that one develops from the Bible's teaching cannot ignore this important element of biblical anthropology that understands human beings to be sinful. Although the Christian tradition (with the exception of the Augustinian movement) has tended to minimize the noetic effects of sin, the unity of the human being is such that we cannot dissociate cognition from the other faculties, to the point where it is unaffected by sin. The Apostle Paul makes a link between a defiled conscience and a defiled mind (Titus 1:15); not only are sinners ignorant of the life of God, but their understanding is darkened (Eph 4:18). In fact, we do not even need to resort to these biblical affirmations to realize that misguided motives hinder the reception of truth. History, alas, provides sufficient examples where people have used—apparently, in all sincerity—twisted ideologies to justify the worst of crimes.

---

29. Van Til, *Christian Theory of Knowledge*, 15.

The Bible's story of the fall (Gen 3), and the conclusions we can draw from it concerning our knowledge of the world, played a role in seventeenth-century discussions about philosophy of science. The Protestant Reformation had favored, a century before, a literal interpretation of the Bible, and had revived the Augustinian tradition; the two factors combined to bring renewed attention to the doctrine of original sin. Catholic circles were not immune from this influence, especially given their own Augustinian revival in the Jansenism of Port-Royal. Different philosophical movements invoked differing conceptions of the fall. Behind the Cartesians' rationalist optimism one discerns a limited view of sin's effects on reason. In this perspective it is, of course, necessary to eliminate the causes of error by an increased vigilance, but this discipline primarily intends to restore the hierarchy between reason, senses, and passions, which was disrupted by the fall. In contrast, the empiricists' skepticism stems from their strong belief in the devastating consequences of sin, which only a long and rigorous experimental examination can, to some extent, overcome. On both sides, the expressed aim was to restore the knowledge that Adam had in Eden—a goal that the Royal Society explicitly included in its program when it was founded in 1660.[30]

When one tries to integrate the noetic effects of sin into one's epistemology, one must inevitably distance oneself from any form of naïve realism: neither the impressions of the senses, nor reason's spontaneous ideas give an infallible picture of the reality. The fact of sin makes us acknowledge the possibility (the reality, even) of error, and thereby highlights the active role that the subject plays—for better or for worse—in the construction of knowledge. The shape of reality does not simply imprint itself on humans' minds, the latter being merely receptors; the fact that error is possible assumes that the knower participates in the development of knowledge. The presence of sin therefore requires us to monitor closely the processes by which knowledge is constructed. Depending on one's view of the noetic effects of sin, this monitoring takes on different forms: for Cartesians, rigorous reasoning, for empiricists, painstaking experimentation in a community setting, or even, for alchemists, a godly life. In any case, the fall's disruption of the perception of the natural order (and possibly of the order itself) provided, in the seventeenth century, a convenient argument against an Aristotelian

---

30. Harrison, "Original Sin and Knowledge," 239-51, 257-59. Cf. Harrison, *Fall of Man, passim*.

philosophy of science; the latter relied too much on common sense and direct observation of nature, thereby neglecting the complications of the scientific enterprise, owing to sin.[31]

As important as the doctrine of sin is for epistemology, one must nevertheless remember that sin remains secondary: it is always a disruption of creation and thus parasitic on it. Even though the Bible communicates a very strong belief in evil, it is in no way dualistic. Evil—of which sin is the form most often mentioned in Scripture—is not an autonomous principle, able to claim any independence with respect to the creative act. It is always, according to the time-worn definition, the deprivation of something good. It follows that evil remains (mysteriously) subject to God's sovereignty and cannot destroy either the created order or humankind's partial ability to understand the latter. Sin implies, of course, that besides being limited, human knowledge is partly wrong. It must, therefore, remain open not only to being refined and deepened, but also to being revised. Nevertheless, sin does not invalidate the action of the *logos*, both in the world and in humanity: "The universe, though fractured and broken, displays the fact that its brokenness is the brokenness of order and not merely unordered chaos. Thus it remains accessible to knowledge in part."[32] Interpreting the world's text has become more difficult, but not by any means impossible. The rigors of the scientific method are one way to "rescue" knowledge in a fallen world. However, their successes should not blind us to the fact that the ideal of comprehensive knowledge is not part of the creational order, but belongs to the perversion of sin. Wanting to control the whole of reality—either in deed, or in thought—is nothing other than sinful human pride. We should not therefore pit comprehensive knowledge against limited knowledge, but rather, partial knowledge against false knowledge. While creationism keeps us from skepticism, it in no way encourages pretentious aspirations to complete and exhaustive knowledge.[33]

---

31. Harrison, "Original Sin and Knowledge," 251, 254, 256.
32. O'Donovan, *Resurrection and Moral Order*, 88.
33. Cf. Geertsema, "Faith and Science," 295f.

THE PERSONAL NATURE OF KNOWLEDGE[34]

Understanding the world as revelation and, in consequence, human knowledge as response to the divine *logos*, helps bring back into focus one idea that the classical tradition (in both philosophy of science and theology) has tended to neglect, but which has recently started to gain the attention that it deserves: the notion that knowledge does not exist in the abstract, it is always possessed by a subject. It would be fatal to disregard the personal dimension of all knowledge and treat it as a mere imperfection that we would like to leave behind. There is no knowledge without someone to do the knowing.

Logical positivism, which dominated the first half of the twentieth century, is paradigmatic of philosophical approaches that seek to establish impersonal knowledge. The complete formalization of knowledge thus became an ideal that was ardently sought and yet remained inaccessible. Admittedly, science can only prosper when those doing it respect the high standards of intersubjective rationality. Personal taste must not influence the results of scientific practice. But the historical research of Thomas Kuhn, Paul Feyerabend, and others has shown that scientific research does not proceed by simple induction from neutrally-observed "facts." Firstly, in focusing on a particular research problem, the scientist (or his laboratory) makes an existential commitment. Secondly, no formal process relieves him or her of the responsibility of choosing to pursue one line of investigation and abandoning another: "To select good questions for investigation is the mark of scientific talent, and any theory of inductive inference in which this talent plays no part is a *Hamlet* without the prince."[35] Moreover, scientists often compare the experience of finding the right solution to an "enlightenment" that cannot be completely put into words. Even when new theories are found, they are often accepted despite the lack of sufficient experimental evidence, based on criteria that are certainly effective but near-impossible to formalize, such as their rational "beauty" or theoretical unification.[36] The Copernican Revolution is a superb example of this: throughout the

---

34. This section develops the central part of Jaeger, "Cosmic Order," 47–51.

35. Polanyi, *Personal Knowledge*, 30.

36. For the function of such rational virtues in Einstein's scientific practice and philosophy of science, see Jaeger, *Croire et connaître*, 35–37, 109–14.

sixteenth century, there was no experimental result able to differentiate between the geocentric and heliocentric hypotheses.[37]

Interpreting the natural order by means of the *logos* links in with the observation of the centrality of the personal dimension in the quest for knowledge, including scientific knowledge. For the idea of *logos* sees the cosmic order in terms of personal categories. Already in the Hebrew Bible, the God who speaks the creative word reveals himself as having personal attributes. Creation is not an impersonal emanation from the divine nature, as it is in the pantheistic worldview. It is the free act of the transcendent Lord who chooses to call the universe into existence. The New Testament underlines the personal nature of the cosmic order when it connects the latter to the *Logos* who is the Son of God. The doctrine of the Trinity affirms the full personhood of the Son when it speaks of one God in three persons: the Son exists eternally in loving communion with the Father and the Spirit. The doctrine of the incarnation depends on personhood: the *Logos* became a man, "when the time had come" (literally "in the fullness of time," Gal 4:4), and thus took on the nature that, in the visible creation, most bears the signs of personhood. Systematic theology traditionally teaches that Christ's human nature is anhypostatic: the person of Jesus Christ is precisely the person of the eternal *Logos*, emphasizing once again the personal nature of the Word that sustains the world (Col 1:16; Heb 1:3).

This is why interpreting the natural order in terms of the divine Word doesn't place scientific knowledge and personal involvement in opposition, something that has often influenced thinking about science since at least the time of the Enlightenment. The human factor has a place in the realm of scientific research; for nature, being the work of the personal Creator, requires human beings for its exploration, who are themselves fully involved as persons. There is therefore no reason at all to deny the personal dimension of knowledge. Scientists bring to their work different aspects of their being: their existential interests, their intuition, their faith-based assumptions. Any science that tried to exclude the personal dimension would not only be less human; it would also be ill-suited to the object of its research: being of personal origin, the natural order eludes all methods that aim to be impersonal. A human dimension is inherent in all knowledge, even in the "hardest" of sciences. This is not a flaw, as positivism imagines. On the contrary, this dimension is

---

37. Kuhn, *The Copernican Revolution, passim*; Polanyi, "Science and Reality," 177–96.

an essential part of what the scientific study of nature must be. There is no other way of grasping our created reality in all its fullness.

When we accept the personal character of all knowledge, we must also let go of the idea that the scientific method (even in its plurality) grants us privileged access to reality. Of course, this is not to belittle the incredible complexity of the new insights that science's rigorous investigation has procured for us. But we must resist the idea that the natural sciences, and physics in particular, are the paradigm that should guide our exploration of the whole of reality. Since theism believes that the ultimate reality is personal, it encourages us to find the paradigm for knowledge in the empathetic relationship between two people. The latter exercises our knowledge capabilities more fully than the investigation of matter and inanimate forces. It is when we interact with another person that the personal nature of the knowledge act is seen most clearly, such that it becomes an opportunity for a higher form of knowledge.

It is true that no human knowledge is impersonal, or strictly objective. But the measure of subjectivity varies according to the modalities of the encounter: "Facts about living things are more highly personal than the facts of the inanimate world. Moreover, as we ascend to higher manifestations of life, we have to exercise ever more personal faculties—involving a more far-reaching participation of the knower."[38] When we discover, in the encounter between individuals, the paradigm for knowledge, we do not thereby deny the relevance of the scientific method. But the latter is shown to be the reduction of a more complex process of knowledge; its simplifying rigor is the price we pay for its effectiveness. We can compare the scientific method to a projection from a multidimensional space onto a plane: although very useful in its domain, an objectifying investigation only captures certain aspects of a reality that goes deeper than science can imagine.

The hierarchy of knowledge—from the study of inanimate nature to the encounter between two people—provides an additional argument against reductionism. The consequences of this are twofold: first in terms of the relationship between different scientific disciplines, and also with respect to the status of human activities that are outside the scientific domain. In the former case, one way that the various sciences are distinguished from each other is by the degree to which they include the personal dimension, and therefore one kind of science cannot be

---

38. Polanyi, *Personal Knowledge*, 347.

reduced to another. We cannot hope to deduce psychology from biology, or biology from physics. This doesn't mean that nothing is gained from the applying the methods of a more "fundamental" science to another field of inquiry. But we cannot hope to exhaust the field of investigation by this type of reductionist research project. The hierarchy of knowledge works in the opposite direction. It is the empathic encounter between two people that sets the standard for our human exploration of reality; the hard sciences are but a diminished projection, which, despite all its usefulness, cannot claim to be supreme.

As regards the second consequence, acknowledging the personal dimension of every knowledge act prevents us from opposing science on one side, and art, religion, and philosophy on the other. A theistic epistemology agrees at this point with the post-Kantian attempts to overcome the antithesis of science and art, which we see in Kant's work. According to his *Critique of Judgment* (1790), the transcendental subject *mimics* knowledge in aesthetic judgment: imagination and understanding freely agree on it, without the constraint of concepts and laws; for beauty relates to what is subjective, in the act of perception, unrelated to the object. In aesthetic pleasure, "we act ... as if we knew, but ... we don't know anything."[39]

Almost immediately after the publication of Kant's critical program, philosophers sought to bring science and art closer together, taking advantage of some of the insinuations in Kant's work itself. Among the earliest is Wilhelm von Humboldt (1767–1835), an influential humanist and reformer of higher education in Germany. An expert in many languages, he draws attention to a symbolic dimension in the use of language, which is also indispensable for science. Similarly, the physician, physiologist, and physicist Hermann von Helmholtz (1821–94) acknowledges, in his later writing, the "artistic inference" at work in scientific practice, since perception already presupposes an interpretative phase (largely unconscious), one level up from the "atoms" of sensation provided by the sensory nerves. For Helmholtz, scientific knowledge is symbolic; that is, it need bear no resemblance whatsoever to reality. It suffices to postulate a nomological similarity between our system of signs and the structure of the world.[40] The neo-Kantian Ernst Cassirer (1874–1945) finds in Helmholtz the inspiration for his "symbolic forms":

39. Sherringham, *Philosophie esthétique*, 172.
40. Helmholtz, "The Facts of Perception," 366–408.

he sees science as a symbolic language system, alongside other systems like art, myth, and religion. Continuing in this vein, several key figures in quantum mechanics—including Heisenberg and Bohr—believed that twentieth-century physics' discoveries invalidated the Kantian distinction between schematism and symbolism. Science itself operates in abstract spaces (Hilbert space, in the case of quantum theory), and scientific concepts are of a symbolic nature and do not "stick" to objects insofar as the very idea of permanent objects has become problematic. Science cannot therefore claim special status and is, like art, a strategy by which humankind tries to find its bearings in the world.

Of course, these post-Kantian attempts to overcome the critical dichotomy between science and art assume a conceptual framework substantially different from the personalistic epistemology sketched out in these pages. One should not by any means confuse these two approaches or claim that they support each other. However, the similarities are not accidental, for we see a rapprochement of science and other human activities, without one being reduced to the other, using quite different angles of attack. This fact alone undermines the rhetoric of some of scientism's adherents, who would like to convince the public that we have proven (preferably by scientific methods!) that science is *the* preferred mode, or even the *only* mode, of knowledge. Greater attention to the sciences' methods and results invalidate such a reductionist view of human activities. The view we have adopted here can satisfactorily explain them: seeing the *Logos*' work in the orderliness of the universe frees us from the totalitarian exploitation of science, while guaranteeing that scientific research has a suitable realm of validity.[41]

SITUATED KNOWLEDGE

When one accepts the fully human nature of knowledge, we touch on another leitmotif present in recent philosophical writing: every knowledge act is situated, there is no "view from nowhere."[42] Different schools of thought express this theme, each with their own particular nuances. Martin Heidegger (1889–1976) emphasizes the finite boundary within

---

41. On the agreement between creationism and several fundamental assumptions of science (the intelligibility of the natural order, the empirical approach), see Jaeger, *Philosophie chrétienne des sciences*, chap. 3.

42. The suggestive title of Thomas Nagel's book, *The View from Nowhere*.

which all human *Dasein* is situated, since it is circumscribed by the void of death. Only within this finite limit can things make any sense, and so all knowledge lies within the hermeneutical circle: it is always developed from the starting point of an existing understanding. Pre-suppositions (theoretical and pre-theoretical) are therefore not a defect to be eliminated; quite the opposite: no knowledge is possible without these *a priori* elements. Unlike Kant, however, the *a priori* is not of a fixed and unique nature; it depends on the contingent situation in which knowledge is constructed, and evolves in a reciprocity with the interpretations to which it gives access. Hans-Georg Gadamer (1900–2002) builds on Heidegger's hermeneutical circle to underline the essential role of received traditions in the development of knowledge.[43]

The historical research of Kuhn, Feyerabend, and others, has established the *fact* of the overwhelming influence of sociocultural conditions and the prejudices of research communities. The "sociology of knowledge," from the 1970s onwards, has affirmed their *right* to have that role: knowledge only exists in a political and historical context; knowledge cannot be considered independently of the situation in which it originated. Before this, the novel analysis of the knowledge act proposed by Michael Polanyi (1891–1976) had brought to light the foundational nature of belief systems. Extending the Augustinian "if you will not believe, you shall not understand" (*nisi credideritis, non intelligetis*) "we must now recognize belief once more as the source of all knowledge. Tacit assent and intellectual passions, the sharing of an idiom and of a cultural heritage, affiliation to a like-minded community: such are the impulses which shape our vision of the nature of things on which we rely for our mastery of things. No intelligence, however critical or original, can operate outside such a fiduciary framework."[44]

Creationism's conception of knowledge is in agreement with the fundamental belief that unites these different approaches: since human knowledge is that of a *creature*, it assumes by its very nature a particular perspective. Human beings are situated inside the created order and cannot extract themselves from it to reach an Archimedean point that would allow them to survey the whole of reality. A human being always observes the world *from somewhere*.

---

43. Gadamer, *Truth and Method*, 277–85. Cf. Westphal, "Hermeneutics as Epistemology," 420.

44. Polanyi, *Personal Knowledge*, 266.

This "localization," which is appropriate for the creature's knowledge, comes in different forms. To start with, human beings are quite literally localized in space and in time. In the way that it recounts historical events, the Bible agrees with our common sense, which situates human existence spatiotemporally. But above and beyond this incorporating of pre-scientific experience, space and time acquire theological meaning, for salvation history is worked out in specific places and at specific times. The cross—redemption's focal point—illustrates the structure common to all salvation events: the reconciling of God and humankind does not take place in a mythical spiritual world, outside of space and time. It takes place—in a very literal sense!—on a hill outside Jerusalem, of which tradition has preserved the name, and during a Passover celebration, under the government of Pontius Pilate. The fact that the Apostles' Creed includes the name of the Roman procurator in its brief summary of the Christian faith shows, from the very start, the importance that Christians placed on salvation's rootedness in history.

We can, however, widen the idea of the "localization" of knowledge: its positioning in time and space goes hand in hand with its insertion in a communal history; for the "place" that a human being occupies can be defined (perhaps first and foremost) by his or her relationships with other human beings. An individual's knowledge is always developed in response to an inherited conceptual framework, that of ideas and knowledge transmitted during education. The corporal rootedness of a human being's knowledge is paired with the fact that his or her dependence on historical context is not solely limited to ideas. Creationism can thus accept the importance of social, political, and economic conditions that work in historiography of science has uncovered.

The strategic position that genealogies occupy in Scripture indicates the importance of humanity's rootedness in a communal history. From the creation stories onwards, genealogies punctuate the narrative of salvation history (Gen 4:17–22; 5:3–32; 10; etc.), so much so that they annoy many a contemporary reader who does not grasp their significance. Similarly, two Gospels include a genealogy of Christ (Matt 1:1–17; Luke 3:23–38); the insistence with which the New Testament writers call him "son of David" shows that even the incarnate Son participates in collective solidarity. The communal nature of knowledge also justifies the emphasis that both Testaments place on the traditions received from privileged witnesses and on the transmission of the faith to future generations (Deut 6:7; Ps 78:3f; 1 Cor 11:2; Jude 3).

The historical rootedness of human beings, which the Scriptures bring to the fore, resonates with the contemporary rejection of the "point of view from nowhere." However, in the creationist perspective, the situated nature of knowledge takes on a particular shade that is not found (for good reason) in the "secular" epistemological outlines: the place that a being has in the world is only secondary; it does not have the power to determine him completely. The creature is primarily defined by the creative act; its interactions with the world are subordinate to its relationship with God. It follows that knowledge not only depends on historical and cultural conditions, but first and foremost on the individual's religious orientation and the community to which he or she belongs. Thus the belief system, which is the context for all knowledge, fundamentally depends on one's attitude to the Creator: *faith*, in its true sense, precedes the knowledge act. This foundational role of faith was emphasized in the Augustinian tradition; we find it again in *credo, ut intelligam* ("I believe in order to understand") of Anselm of Canterbury (1033–1109). Abraham Kuyper built a complete epistemology on the strength of this insight, by insisting on the universal role of the "faith function" that directs any rational endeavor. Such recognition of the primacy of faith is a translation, into epistemological language, of the Hebrew wisdom literature's old maxim: "The fear of the LORD is the principle [or beginning] of wisdom" (Ps 111:10; Prov 1:7; see Job 28:28).

THE RELATIONAL DIMENSION OF CREATION

We can detect, underneath knowledge's rootedness in history, an aspect that is fundamental for the creationist view, to which classical conceptions have not always done justice: creatures are, in their very essence, relational, because it is their relationship with the Creator that confers existence on them. Recognizing this dependence on the transcendent foundation in turn implies horizontal networks of relationship; Leibniz's monads are profoundly alien to the creationist view (despite his theistic intentions). The conviction that the presence of otherness in the creation reflects the distinction between Creator and creature is especially found in Scripture's teaching about sexual differentiation among humankind: the relationship between man and woman serves as an illustration of God's relationship to his creation (Rom 1:22–27; Eph 5:31f.). But the principle seems to hold more generally: the creature is not alone, but with others, since it does not exist by itself, but in relationship with the Creator.

It seems possible to link the relational nature of creation to the mystery of the Trinity itself. This connection finds New Testament support in the parallel that the Apostle Paul draws between the otherness of man and woman, and the intra-trinitarian relation between the Father and the Son (1 Cor 11:3). The "being-with" aspect that creatures possess seems to reflect the relational nature of the ultimate reality.[45] For unlike unitary monotheisms, the biblical view does not present the divine essence in solitary uniqueness, it sees it as structured by the relations between Father, Son, and Spirit.

In the view developed here, the relationship between the knower and the object of knowledge is not a problem. Human beings do not stand over against an environment from which they are isolated. They are part of the created order that they have a vocation to understand. Thus, they know the world insofar as they participate in it.[46] At the same time, the creative act ensures their own solidity; there is no confusion between the subject and the world, which would blur the distinction and thereby jeopardize the possibility of any real knowledge. Indeed, the concept of creation allows us to hold together the relational dimension *and* the objective existence of the creature. We thereby avoid both the absolutizing of the distinction between subject and object, seen in classical realism, and their confusion, which we find in pantheism. The former isolates the subject from the world and thus makes any real communication inherently problematic; the latter loses the experience of otherness, which is essential to the encounter that knowledge procures.

By founding the horizontal network of relationships on the "vertical" relationship with the Creator, creationism escapes the skeptical and relativist temptations that endanger any conception that fully recognizes the situated character of knowledge. The reason is that local perspectives are not ultimate; they sit within the perfect knowledge of reality that the Creator possesses. In this way, we avoid the fragmentation of knowledge that poses a threat to all immanent explanations. Similarly,

---

45. The term "relational nature" should be understood here in its strongest sense: "Trinitarian relations do not have a subject in which they are inherent, but exist as *subsistent* relations" (Bartmann, *Précis de théologie dogmatique*, 240).

46. O'Donovan, *Resurrection and Moral Order*, 79.

we are guaranteed that any one perspective can be translated into another, making it possible to communicate even when starting from different points of view. Admittedly, because of the incomprehensible nature of the encompassing reality, human beings do not necessarily have at their disposal the comprehensive methods needed to accomplish this translation from one viewpoint to another. But what is perhaps not *de facto* possible remains so *de jure*. In this way, the wider context in which creationism places human knowledge protects it against relativism, while fully recognizing the influence of historical and cultural conditions on knowledge. It therefore encourages an attitude distinct from both classical realism and "post"-modern relativism: it is able to exploit the richness of complementary perspectives, while keeping the unity of knowledge as a guiding principle for its acquisition. This is why it does not shirk the idea of building a *system* of thought, without going so far as to absolutize such a system.

Since creationism detects a relational dimension to reality, it is able to take on board some of the criticisms that have been leveled at the representational theory of truth. One such criticism is based on the Copenhagen school's interpretation of quantum mechanics, which emphasizes the participatory nature of the new physics theory. Niels Bohr (1885–1962) states, for example, that "we are here reminded of the old wisdom that . . . we are as well actors as spectators in the great drama of existence."[47] Similarly, Heisenberg says that "when we speak of the picture of nature in the exact science of our age, we do not mean a picture of nature so much as a *picture of our relationships with nature*."[48]

The Copenhagen interpretation is far from being unanimously accepted by experts in quantum mechanics; it rather seems that when it comes to the quantum revolution, there are (almost) as many different interpretations are there are philosophers of science working on the subject. It would therefore be ill advised for us to try to settle the debate here in favor of one of them. But assuming that Bohr and Heisenberg's interpretation were right, how would the creationist view fit with it? Given that we have seen how such a worldview suggests an objective natural order, one must resist idealism, a direction in which the Copenhagen interpretation has often been developed. Experiments at the atomic level do not just bring to light structures that human activity (practical and

---

47. Bohr, "Atomic Physics and International Cooperation," 134.
48. Heisenberg, *Physicist's Conception of Nature*, 29.

theoretical) have introduced there. The quantum physicist encounters, just as much as does his classical colleague, the resistance of a reality that is outside himself and which, as a result, may contradict his models. The stubborn realism of most experimental physicists is clear evidence of this aspect of their work.

At the same time, creationism does not isolate the knower from the object to be known, which would, in effect, set in opposition the twin elements of the epistemological relationship. In this way, creationism seems consistent with an understanding of "quantum mechanics as a contextual predictive schema."[49] Admittedly, this is not to suggest that a clearer perception of the relational dimension of creation would have accelerated progress in quantum mechanics. Creationism precisely emphasizes the contingency of the natural order and encourages the (relative) independence of the various fields of knowledge. In this worldview we should not expect that theories in physics be derivable from theological or philosophical beliefs. The relational aspect of creation nevertheless shows that a (moderately) contextualistic interpretation of quantum mechanics is not at odds with creationism. But unlike the Eastern religions, with which some have been tempted to compare the new perspective in physics, the theistic view preserves the face-to-face juxtaposition of the knower and the reality to be explored. It therefore finds itself in agreement with the experience of otherness that occurs when one encounters the bizarre life form that is contemporary physics.

THE FREEDOM OF KNOWLEDGE

The conception of knowledge outlined here holds together features that other approaches consider antinomial: it is *both* realistic *and* relational, objective *and* personal. This balance corresponds to a very specific conception of the freedom of the knower, which is made possible by reference to the transcendent foundation of reality. There are different aspects to this freedom, and they appear most clearly when we compare this approach to other explanations of humanity's place in the world.

Firstly, because of the multidimensional view that creationism favors, human freedom eludes any scientific determination that believes itself to be exhaustive. The Bible says that humans are created "as God's

---

49. The title of the second chapter of Bitbol, *Mécanique quantique*, 141.

image,"⁵⁰ which emphasizes their special status. Although the first chapter of Genesis depicts their creation on the same day as that of land animals—thereby underlining their solidarity with the animal kingdom—their privileged relationship with the Creator rules out any transposition to the human sphere of conceptual tools adapted to the non-human part of creation. Without necessarily coming from a Christian perspective, many philosophers have insisted in particular that rationality presupposes the free exercise of human faculties, which lies beyond the laws of physics or chemistry. Thus Descartes stresses that "*a critical grasp of truth, and a proper assessment of an argument, must be a free voluntary action.*"[51] Popper agrees with him on this point: if human reason were entirely determined by the physicochemical laws, how would it be able to arrive at conclusions that were also true?[52]

There is no need to develop this belief in the direction taken by Descartes: his dualism of substances—extended and thinking—is not the only anthropology that upholds freedom of thought with respect to scientific determinations. Thomas Aquinas interprets the soul as the form of the material body, which allows him to maintain the duality, while accepting that the mind is realized in a material substrate.[53] Some contemporary philosophers of science even attempt to develop non-dualistic but non-reductionistic anthropologies, in order to honor Scripture's teaching that humankind is created in God's image.[54]

Secondly, conceptions that render the subject passive in the knowledge act are equally harmful to the knower's freedom, as creationism describes it. It is the privilege of the creature, which is God's image, not to receive knowledge in the way that melted wax receives the seal's pattern. Although part of the created order, humanity transcends it, so as to be able to have a conscious relationship with the Creator. Human

50. For this translation, see pp. 32f. above.

51. Popper, *Open Universe*, 81, referring to Descartes, *Principles of Philosophy*, I, 36-39.

52. Popper, *Open Universe*, 84. Thinking along similar lines, Lewis, *Abolition of Man*, 45, believes that the replacement of moral rules by scientific determinations would signify the end of humanity; those who would attempt to make this transition are not "bad men. They are not men at all. Stepping outside the *Tao*, they have stepped in the void."

53. Stump, "Non-Cartesian Substance Dualism," 505-31.

54. Murphy, "Supervenience and Downward Efficacy," 147-64; Van Inwagen, "Dualism and Materialism," 475-88. One recalls Donald Davidson's "anomalous monism," which combines physicalism and non-reductionism, even though his motivation certainly doesn't come from Christian anthropology.

knowledge is not, therefore, merely reception; the human mind constructs and develops knowledge. That one can tell a lie is proof of this: when lying one *claims* something that one knows to be at odds with reality.[55]

Different philosophers have stressed the active role played by the knower. To give but one well-known example: Einstein's almost visceral realism did not stop him from highlighting the mind's creative activity in the construction of scientific theories. He knew that it is impossible to deduce the laws of physics from experimental results using a formalizable method: "There is no logical path to these laws; only intuition, resting on sympathetic understanding of experience, can reach them."[56] The concepts and principles that form the basis of scientific theories are "free inventions of the human intellect, which cannot be justified either by the nature of that intellect or in any other fashion *a priori*. These fundamental concepts . . . form the essential part of a theory, which reason cannot touch."[57] The fact that free constructions of the human mind can give order to experimental data is the "miracle" of knowledge that Einstein admits unequivocally: "What will always be incomprehensible about the world is its comprehensibility."[58]

When we acknowledge the active role of the knower, we can no longer be satisfied with coarse realism, which sees the human mind as merely a mirror of reality. But the supposed passivity of the human mind can take more subtle forms, which are hardly any more satisfactory. Contemporary "naturalized" philosophers of science provide an example of an approach where the subject ends up being absorbed by the object, since the former is a function of the natural order. If the knower "emerges" from the natural world, he or she is no longer juxtaposed face-to-face with the reality that is to be known. Of course, Einstein's astonishment at the intelligibility of the world no longer has any place in such a perspective, since reason is not truly able to detach itself from nature. But this comes at high price. First, the subject's own solidity is lost; in consequence, it is not clear what the mind's freedom is based on

---

55. Blocher, "Qu'est-ce que la vérité?," 47.
56. Einstein, "Principles of Research," 226.
57. Einstein, "Method of Theoretical Physics," 272.
58. Einstein writes in German, "Das ewig Unbegreifliche an der Welt ist ihre Begreiflichkeit" (Einstein, "Physik und Realität," 315). Einstein's realism is strongly linked to this sense of wonder that he expresses. We can only be surprised at the order that human beings can find in the world of experiments if this order is, in its very nature, independent of humanity.

with respect to the environment from which it is supposed to emerge. Science's history has witnessed many tentative false starts, dead ends, and unexpected breakthroughs that have accompanied the development of knowledge, even in the "hard" sciences; the distance between knower and object of knowledge that these suggest is hard to conceive in such naturalized perspectives. More fundamentally, no knowledge is left that is worthy of the name. All that remains is a *simulacrum* of knowledge, which may perhaps help us find our bearings in the world, but the experience of otherness, which is fundamental to knowledge, has vanished.

Over against epistemologies that reduce the subject to a passive role, creationism maintains the tension between the knower and the world to be known. This tension is not a sign of unresolved antinomy; it is highly constructive, for it is the place where a true encounter becomes possible. The fact that this tension does not degenerate into sterile opposition comes from the very heart of the creationist view: the natural order and the human subject both have their origin in the creative act. Thus they are not foreign to one another; authentic communication can be built on their common source. Since the difference between the Creator and the creature is constitutive for reality, the relationship between humanity and the world is fundamentally not a problem: being God's "vicars," human beings experience, in the knowledge act, a reflection of foundational alterity.

In addition to this stands the fact that the personal dimension is not secondary, for everything that exists is the result of a free act performed by a personal Creator. Thus the project of the naturalized philosopher of science loses its relevance: why would we want to explain the knower, by means of a reality that is devoid of this personal dimension? The personal, the "subjective" aspect, is always *already there*. So the structuring action of human consciousness can be fully acknowledged, without the complicity between reason and nature becoming incomprehensible. There is no need to deny the freedom of the human mind in the knowledge act, to reduce the intellect's work to a passive receiving of reality's order, be it given (as in classical realism) or emergent. Rather, reality is "steeped," in its very essence, in the personal dimension. Creationism thus allows us to hold together the mind's creative activity and the understanding of an objective order, because the knower is "at home" in a created world.

Just as strongly as it resists the dissolution of the subject, the creationist perspective also rejects Hume's empiricism and Kant's idealism, which both contain the belief that humans are faced with the formless raw material of experience. We can detect here the abandoning of the objective element, at least in its orderly dimension. Granted, both conceptions dissolve the "miracle of knowledge," since the objective element loses its solidity faced with the subject. But they set themselves the unenviable task of explaining scientific practice without postulating any kind of lawfulness in nature. It is true that Kantianism acknowledges the role (believing it to be constitutive) that the mind's faculties play in the development of knowledge. In this way, unlike Hume's empiricism, it has an ordering element. But how can we ensure that theoretical activity applies to experience, if there is no correspondence to it in the world of phenomena? Thus Kant sees that the categories of the understanding *must* apply to perceptions, but it is doubtful whether his system ensures that they *can*. The fact that he introduces the imagination as an intermediate faculty between the senses and understanding hides the problem rather than solving it. "Kant's fundamental question, 'How is natural science possible?' thus led him to build numerous bridges to cross from the mind that thinks to the reality that is, but it is still a complete mystery as to the nature of the water flowing under these bridges."[59]

Since in the biblical view, humankind is faced with an ordered reality, our freedom is not "the ecstasy of freedom in a world governed by no laws except those we create ourselves."[60] The knower does not imprint his mind's structures onto the formless raw material of experience—whether these structures be *a priori* and universal, as in Kant, or *a posteriori* and relative to the historical context, as in the different versions of neo-Kantianism. Ultimately, the very status of human knowledge is at stake: is it autonomous or secondary? Kantianism contains the hidden assumption that human beings only know what they themselves have produced. Hence the requirement that knowledge not concern "things in themselves," but "things as objects of possible experience," so that they conform to the structures that the mind itself has introduced.[61] But from the biblical perspective, human beings are not ultimate, and neither is their knowledge. Thus, human subjects do not draw knowledge out of themselves; they are faced with the created order, from which they develop their knowledge, knowledge that is by definition derivative.

59. Brun, *Vagabonds de l'Occident*, 115f.
60. Van Fraassen, "World of Empiricism," 123.
61. Kant, *Prolegomena*, § 17; cf. § 11, 14, 56.

The fact that knowers find their freedom in the encounter with an outside world that is "given" to them, translates into philosophical terms the idea of freedom, which was brought to the fore by Augustine and his heirs. In this context, freedom does not mean independence, rejection of hegemony, and the absence of imposed laws, as in the humanist ideals of the Enlightenment. Quite the contrary, this freedom is lived out in joyfully accepted dependence on the Creator. Not only does this freedom agree to submit to the divine order, it also finds therein the only context in which it can exist. What would be alienating in relation to another creature becomes the very source of freedom in the context of a relationship with the Creator: divine action does not hinder the creature's fulfillment, but provides it with an indispensable foundation. "Coup d'état freedom"[62] is but an illusion: by rejecting the structured framework that results from creation, human beings destroy their only possible framework for life.

Historically, Augustine brought this concept of freedom to bear in his debate with Pelagius. It allowed him to affirm that God's sovereign election does not abolish the voluntary adherence to salvation: "If God has mercy, we also will, for the power to will is given with the mercy itself."[63] Not only "without his calling we cannot even will,"[64] but also "true liberty" is found, for Augustine, in obedience to the divine command, which is only possible by the work of grace.[65] Concerning the final state in which the believer cannot even sin any more, he writes, "[Man's] will will be much freer, because he will then have no power whatever to serve sin."[66] In Augustine's intuition (used by Calvin, among others), we find ourselves once again faced with the mystery of creation: God does not need to "stand back" to grant the world space to be free. Quite the contrary: the creative act, extended by God's providential care, gives the creature full integrity, which harmoniously combines with complete dependence on the transcendent foundation.

As regards knowledge, we come back to the Gospel saying: "The truth shall set you free" (John 8:32). Adherence to what is pro-posed does not annihilate freedom; instead the latter finds there the only place

---

62. Lecerf, *Dogmatique réformée*, vol. 1, 62.
63. Augustine, *To Simplician—On Various Questions*, book 1, question 2, 394.
64. Ibid., 395.
65. Augustine, *Enchiridion* IX, 30, 63; cf. ibid., XXVI, 101f, 124–25.
66. Ibid., XXVIII, 105, 127–28.

where it can be exercised. The subject's creative activity does not manipulate formless material; the order of reality is rather the opportunity, the indispensable context, that allows the mind's structuring work. "Our ordering depends on God's to provide the condition for its freedom. It is free because it has a given order to respond to in attention or disregard, in conformity or disconformity, with obedience or rebellion."[67] Creationism thus leads us to affirm both the given order of reality and the subject's free activity in the construction of knowledge. Only the interaction of these two elements makes the knowledge act productive. The fact that it can be an encounter, and not just a juxtaposition, depends on the transcendent foundation of all that exists: their common origin in God affords a complicity between humankind and the world, without their having to give up the ordered solidity which both possess.

In particular, such a view allows to articulate the moral responsibility of the knowledge act without the addition of an irrational principle. One need not oppose rational constraints and personal freedom in order to take knowledge's moral dimension into account. On this point, creationism is at odds with the "voluntarist" epistemology proposed by Bas Van Fraassen: for him, personal responsibility comes into play at exactly the point where rational constraints on knowledge come to an end. He thus considers that more traditional epistemologies, in which certain knowledge rules (induction, inference to the best explanation, etc.) "determine a uniquely correct belief (neither too strong nor too weak) on the basis of the given evidence," are "a flight from personal responsibility."[68] When van Fraassen comments on Pascal's wager, he is overjoyed to discover that it is an example of a responsible decision without rational constraints, since in his interpretation, the wager excludes neither of the two possible actions as rational. In this way, "choice and its responsibility never slip from our shoulders; no recipe for rational behavior can remove them."[69]

In the creationist view, however, there is simply no reason for the dichotomy between rational rules and epistemic responsibility. Since the construction of knowledge is a fully human activity—personal, relational, and free—when engaging in it we both exercise our *will* and are

---

67. O'Donovan, *Resurrection and Moral Order*, 36f.

68. Van Fraassen, "Constructive Empiricism Now," 162.

69. Van Fraassen, *Empirical Stance*, 100, which comments Pascal, *Pensées*. no. 233 (Brunschvicg ordering), 114. Cf. Jaeger, *Lois de la nature*, 298–301, 312–14, 329.

responsible for our choices. But as Augustine saw it, our freedom consists precisely in the voluntary adherence to the truth that the Word of God sets before us. It does not presuppose a world without structure, nor reasoning without rules. Rather, the subject's responsibility is to embrace the shape of reality, laid down by the creative act, and their knowing is no less rational by virtue of its freedom.

Analyzing the knower's freedom shows, perhaps more clearly than any other aspect of the epistemology outlined here, the primordial importance of the personal nature of ultimate reality, which theism affirms. Since human beings are immersed in a context whose ultimate determination can be described in personal categories, their freedom can be affirmed to a point where other conceptions lead only to contradictions. Their knowledge is a response to a pre-ordered environment, yet is developed in a creative and innovative process. Humankind confronts the world that is to be known, while maintaining a dynamic relationship with it. It is a matter of moral responsibility, while at the same time, our thoughts follow the contours of reality.

Moreover, the fact that the creature has its existential foundation in the Creator himself makes it possible to admit immanent dependencies, without ending up with determinism; for internal connections are only penultimate. Thus the human mind can be grounded in a physical body, without the laws that govern matter exhaustively determining the workings of reason. In the same way, human beings are influenced by their historical and cultural context, while keeping enough personal freedom to ensure their responsibility. Since the founding principle of existence is nothing less—or, rather, no one less—than the transcendent Creator, immanent determinations, being impersonal to a greater or lesser extent, cannot destroy the freedom laid down in the act of creation. For "a finite personality could function in none other than a completely personalistic atmosphere, and such an atmosphere can be supplied to him only if his existence depends entirely upon the exhaustive personality of God."[70] As the apostolic saying succinctly puts is, "where the Spirit of the Lord is, there is freedom" (2 Cor 3:17).

---

70. Van Til, *Survey of Christian Epistemology*, 97.

five

Explaining the Natural Order

> If . . . God exists . . . , everything, absolutely everything, derives its meaning from him, including the movement by which we might acknowledge him, including the word "proof" itself by which we name this movement.
> —Georges Morel, *Problèmes actuels de religion*, 1968

THE PHYSICO-THEOLOGICAL PROOF

One final step needs to be taken to conclude this description of nature's laws from a creation perspective. We have seen the outworkings of this worldview, both in terms of its expectations of the order itself, and those concerning the knowledge of this order. It remains for us to clarify how the idea of creation casts light on the explanation of the world's orderly nature. Such efforts at explanation are, by nature, meta-physical—in the etymological sense of the word: they are not simply content to describe the natural order in its factuality, but seek to provide it with a foundation that justifies its existence.

Natural theology has traditionally given the status of proof to the chain of argument that starts from the world's order and arrives at its transcendent cause. This "physico-theological" proof (of which the "teleological" proof, which relates the order to its goal, is a variant) is one of the standard proofs of the existence of God. Thomas Aquinas' five ways are, without a doubt, the most well-known effort to rigorously formulate how the world's order, or even its mere existence, prove that God exists: the movement of beings in the world requires a first mover, put in motion by no other; a thing's existence indicates an efficient first cause; contingent events must be based on a necessary being; the hierarchy of beings culminates in a perfect being; and the purpose displayed by many unintelligent beings requires an intelligent being that directs them to their ends.[1]

The fact that the physico-theological proof was proposed as proof of God's existence does not relieve us of the task of assessing its relevance and consequences in the context of creationism. For simply stating that a proof's conclusion is true is not sufficient to establish its validity. The physico-theological proof achieves the result the theist wants: the affirmation of God's existence. But this fact in itself does not yet show whether the path taken to get there is suitable or not. It follows that the question of the proof's validity arises even *within* the vision adopted here, and requires that we examine it closely. However, we should not forget the intended goal: the aim is not apologetics, showing to what extent the world's order suggests a transcendent foundation, without assuming the idea of creation. It was, of course, with the aim of convincing unbelievers that theistic proofs were developed, but our project is more modest: to study the question of what explanation of the natural order fits the creationist worldview.

Three observations are important in this context. Firstly, creationism does acknowledge that the world's order indicates a Creator; the creature's structured existence can only truly be explained by the act of creation. Thus, we must unequivocally affirm the validity of the physico-theological proof's fundamental belief: God's action explains the lawfulness of nature, and it provides the only explanation of it that is correct, that is, which agrees with the facts. This first observation might seem, at first sight, totally lacking in interest for us: after all, why bother insisting that the creative act can be concluded from the world's order, if we have already assumed a theistic view? The emphasis is, however, worthwhile, when we realize that criticism of the proofs of God's existence has not been limited to non-Christian writers; many theologians have joined in, ever since Hume and Kant served to discredit theistic proofs in the eyes

---

1. Aquinas, *Summa theologiae* Ia, q. 2, art. 3.

of modern philosophy. The existentialist philosopher Søren Kierkegaard (1813–55), whose influence on contemporary theology has been considerable, even saw these proofs as the invention of another Judas, betraying Christ with the "kiss . . . of stupidity."[2] Over against the current trend, which exalts the riskiness of faith in the absence of rational proof, creationism firmly maintains that inferring God's existence from lawfulness of nature is indeed valid.

Secondly, it is nevertheless wise to qualify the weight that we grant to the physico-theological proof's *specific formulations*. In this regard, Aquinas' five ways can serve as a warning: they crucially depend on the conceptual framework of Aristotelian philosophy, which we have found to be in contradiction with the biblical view at several key points. Our critique primarily focused on the hierarchy of beings: if one rejects such an approach to reality, it is obvious that one can no longer find God at the top of the pyramid of beings. But some of the other four ways also prove to be dependent on Aristotle's philosophy when we examine them more closely. Regarding the notion of movement, for example, there is little in common with the way modern physics considers motion. Even the designation of God as the "unmoved Mover," i.e., the pure act, fits better with the philosophy of Aristotle—which remains pagan, despite Aquinas' best efforts to baptize it—than with the biblical image of the living God.[3]

The Thomist five ways therefore warn us of the danger of adding foreign elements to the creationist view, when we seek to condense into a proof the conviction that creation explains the lawfulness of nature. In fact, the idea of creation itself imposes a certain reticence on us as concerns such a proof's precision. For even if creation as a concept implies the belief in the world's structured nature, the Creator's freedom prevents us from deducing the "how" of this order from theological considerations alone. Determining of the precise contours of nature's laws is therefore the job of the empirical sciences. Given the provisional nature of all scientific knowledge, theology is taking a risk if it introduces particular elements of order in its reasoning. That does not mean it is always forbidden: the possibility of dialogue with the scientists of one's day comes at the cost of using their categories, which will probably become obsolete at a later date. But the theologian must be aware of

2. Kierkegaard, *Sickness unto Death*, 71.
3. Cf. pp. 26–31 above.

the source of these contributions, and distinguish them from the core of his conceptual framework. Thus, the physico-theological proof will take as its starting point the very fact that there *is* a natural order, rather than a particular aspect of this order that the empirical sciences have discovered.

Thirdly and finally, creationism obliges us to denounce the claim to neutral rationality, which has often accompanied the use of theistic proofs. The First Vatican Council (1869–70) condemned as heretical the assertion that "the One true God, our Creator and Lord, cannot be known with certainty with the *natural* light of human reason through the things that are created."[4] The physico-theological proof is an exercise of reason, without reference to faith. Underlying it is the belief that "there is a twofold order of knowledge . . . We know at the one level by natural reason, at the other level by divine faith."[5] The encyclical *Fides et Ratio* (dated 14 September, 1998) expresses the same view when it compares faith and reason to the "two wings on which the human spirit rises to the contemplation of truth."[6]

It is not just recent trends in philosophy of science that undermine this kind of separation between faith and reason, highlighting as they do the omnipresence of existential presuppositions in any system of knowledge. The exaltation of natural reason also seems blind to the majestic "In the beginning, God" (Gen 1:1). Since God is the foundation of everything that exists, we should find his primacy in the domain of knowledge. The writers of the Old Testament wisdom books thus call the fear of God the "first principle of knowledge,"[7] "beginning of knowledge"—or as one French Bible translation puts it, the "ABC of wisdom"[8] (Prov 1:7). If God is the One that Scripture shows us—self-sufficient, transcendent, and source of all reality—no "neutral" fact is imaginable. Everything must be interpreted with respect to the Creator, for only dependence on him can confer to the creature its existence and

---

4. "Deum unum et verum, creatorem et Dominium nostrum, per ea, quae facta sunt, *naturali* rationis humanae lumine certo cognosci non posse" (Denzinger and Schönmetzer, *Enchiridion Symbolorum*, par. 3026, 593. English translation from Neuner and Dupuis, "Christian Faith," 41; italics mine).

5. Declaration of the First Vatican Council, quoted by John Paul II, *Fides et ratio*, § 9.

6. John Paul II, *Fides et ratio*, § 1.

7. Scott, *Proverbs, Ecclesiastes*, 33, provides this translation.

8. Alliance Biblique Universelle, *Bible en français courant*, 995.

its meaning: "If God is self-sufficient, he alone is self-explanatory. And if he alone is self-explanatory, then he must be the final reference point in all human predication. He is then like the sun from which all lights on earth derive the power of illumination. You do not use a candle in order to search for the sun. The idea of a candle is derived from the sun. So the very idea of any fact in the universe is that it is derivative."[9]

Therefore, setting God's existence on one side, even in an *ad hominem* argument, deforms the way we perceive reality. God is not just the conclusion of the explanation of the natural order; he must be its starting point. The radical dependence of all human knowledge has two aspects to it: the natural order is not recognized for what it really is, and human reasoning is ultimately unintelligible, unless we admit the idea of transcendence. As Auguste Lecerf puts it: "God alone makes reason's authority intelligible to reason."[10]

By neglecting the radical way in which knowledge is rooted in God, the way the physico-theological proof has traditionally been used has left it vulnerable to the Kantian critique: the transcendent Being is not found at the end of any immanent causal chain. God is not the first (or last) element in a series that lies within the world. Even if such an argument were to succeed, it would not prove God's existence, but only that of an immanent god—which, incidentally, would be nowhere near sufficient to halt the regression induced by the repeated request for explanation. Of course, the critical use of reason leads to a recognition of the limits of human deductions: humanity can work out that there is no immanent explanation for the natural order. But turning this negative affirmation into a positive one would be going beyond the limits of what reasoning based on immanence can attain.[11]

Only by taking transcendence into account, from the very outset of one's reasoning, can one overcome the Kantian critique while heeding its warning. If we do not pretend to confine the natural order and our knowledge capabilities to the horizontal dimension, it is justified to infer from the existence of an orderly world that God exists. The Kantian

9. Van Til, *Christian Theory of Knowledge*, 12.
10. Lecerf, *Dogmatique réformée*, 265.
11. Kant, *Prolegomena*, § 57–60, 129–31, 139, 142, 144. Kant, however, insists that we do not invent ["erdichten"] the necessary Being, when we seek to base the contingent world on God (ibid., § 59, 142; cf. § 53, 123). This fact is reminiscent of his assertion of the existence of the *Ding an sich*; Kant did not take agnosticism to its logical extreme, even though his name is often invoked in support of the latter.

critique no longer applies, for we are not starting from immanent reality in order to deduce the existence of the transcendent Being. As the world and humankind are created, they are rooted in the deity. Human reason is not overstepping its limits when it mentions God; in a radical sense, it is always talking about God.[12] For the "natural light" of reason is but a suicidal abstraction; any exercise of reason happens within the context of creation. Ultimately, there is no such thing as purely immanent reality: *everything* bears witness to the Creator, who alone is the source of all that exists.

As we cannot exclude faith from the exercise of reason, it is not surprising that, in fact, we only come across creationism in those places where the biblical revelation is known. As valid as theistic proofs may be *within* the Judeo-Christian worldview, no "natural" light has ever given rise to the idea of an absolute and unique Person, on whom the existence of the entire universe is based, without the influence of Scripture.[13] This observation is consistent with the essentially negative way that the Apostle Paul uses the evidence of creation, in the well-known passage in his Epistle to the Romans. It is true that God's invisible perfections, "that is to say, his eternal power and his divinity, can be seen, since the creation of the world, when one reflects on his works." But the sinner refuses to acknowledge him. He has the proof right in front of him—Paul even says that the sinner *knows* God. And yet, he "holds the truth captive in unrighteousness" and does not draw the necessary practical conclusions, namely, worship and obedience to the Lord (Rom 1:18–21). Given the existential consequences, we cannot reason in a detached way about the existence of God. Even though the physico-theological proof is valid, it is still only acknowledged by those who are willing to submit to it. Since it relates to the deity, who both sustains and transcends humanity, one can only receive it by faith.

---

12. Pannenberg, *Systematic Theology*, 345, n. 14, argues that all language is rooted in religious themes (referring to Cassirer, *Philosophie der symbolischen Formen*, 71–107). He emphasizes that the scope of Kant's critique is limited to proofs that only involve the idea of God as a conclusion, whereas it is the foundation of all knowledge possessed by finite beings (Pannenberg, *Systematic Theology*, 352f).

13. Cf. Gilson, *Spirit of Mediaeval Philosophy*, 43, 59f., 72ff.

A PROBABILISTIC NATURAL THEOLOGY: RICHARD SWINBURNE

Aquinas' five ways are doubtlessly the most well known form of the physico-theological proof, but they are far from being the only one. Two versions in particular deserve our attention, since they make use of the argument in the context of the contemporary philosophical debate about laws of nature. Looking closely at these proposals will bring out more clearly what forms natural theology can (and cannot) take today, if it is to be faithful to the doctrine of creation.

Richard Swinburne (born 1934), Emeritus Professor of the Philosophy of the Christian Religion for over twenty-five years at Oxford, has developed a series of cumulative arguments for the existence of God. His treatment of the subject is impressive in its magnitude, its precision, and its determination to take into account the latest developments in science and philosophy. One element of his approach is the inference of God's existence from the laws of nature (which Swinburne lists, somewhat unusually, under "teleological arguments").[14] While the delicate intricacies of his argument deserve to be studied, it suffices here to outline the general structure of his approach in order to discern to what extent it is in harmony with its intent: proving the existence of God.

In constructing his natural theology, Swinburne opts for an original approach. He believes that the standard theistic proofs are not valid if read as deductive arguments; they are better taken as *a posteriori* inductive considerations, which have probabilistic weight, without going so far as to prove, with complete certainty, the existence of God.[15] So it seems to him "fairly clear that no argument from temporal order, whether Aquinas's fifth way or any other argument, can be a good deductive argument . . . Although the existence of order may be good evidence of a designer, it is surely compatible with the non-existence of one—it is hardly a logically necessary truth that all order is brought about by a person."[16] It follows that his line of argument, if conclusive, only demonstrates a certain probability of theism. Other competing views are not ruled out, even if they are less likely. More specifically, Swinburne tries to show that theism is more probable than naturalism, since the latter is currently its most popular rival.

---

14. Swinburne, *Existence of God*, chap. 8.
15. More precisely, he employs Bayes' formalism of confirmation (ibid., 66–72).
16. Ibid., 155.

We need go no further to realize that such an approach does not sit happily with the creationist perspective adopted here. For in order to say that theism is more probable that naturalism, one must concede that naturalism be *possible*. But from what standpoint can Swinburne make such an assertion? One would need to find common ground shared by both worldviews, from which one could compare the relative probabilities of theism and naturalism. But if one accepts creatures' radical dependence on God, there is no such common ground. The world as seen by the naturalist is not the same as that of the theist. One is self-explanatory, the other, created. From the creationist perspective, the naturalist is wrong, even as concerns those aspects of his knowledge that relate to nature: "If the Creator is not known, then the creation is not known *as creation* . . . [When this happens,] the order of reality is not truly known at all. Order cannot be perceived piece by piece, but only as a whole. A form that is conceived incompletely must be perceived wrongly."[17] Similarly, the naturalist cannot accept even the *possibility* of a transcendent Creator, for such a being cannot coexist with the world as the naturalist sees it. It is misguided to think that we could take as our starting point, in the argumentative approach, one particular aspect of the world (especially its ordered structure) that the believer and the atheist see in the same way.

It is, therefore, no surprise to see that Swinburne, despite the language employed (and, undoubtedly, despite his best intentions) adopts a definition of God that lacks the full transcendent weight of the church's traditional creeds. But to realize that this has happened, one must go beneath the surface-level of the definition chosen: "A personal being without a body (that is to say, a spirit), which, of necessity, is eternal, perfectly free, omnipotent, omniscient, perfectly good, and creator of all things."[18] Although the words are traditional, their meaning is not: all the divine attributes must be interpreted in a univocal way; Aquinas' insistence that human language only applies to God analogically has no place in Swinburne's rational theology. The difference is clearly seen in the concept of eternity, which for Swinburne is simply temporal existence with neither beginning nor end. But the same is true for all the other attributes: Swinburne's God is not incomprehensible. It is, therefore, highly significant that he is considered as "one part of

---

17. O'Donovan, *Resurrection and Moral Order*, 88.
18. Swinburne, *Existence of God*, 7.

the universe";[19] transcendence gets lost in the attempt to prove God's existence to the naturalist. Therefore, we understand the standpoint from which Swinburne compares the relative probabilities of theism and naturalism: it is a naturalism that remains agnostic about the existence of a super-intelligent, super-powerful, and perfectly moral agent. But theism is not just "naturalism + god." Swinburne's version of the theistic arguments actually proves to be self-defeating—and this serves as a particularly clear illustration of the Kantian warning: an immanent chain of argument can never reach transcendence.

It is thus highly revealing when Swinburne write that he "use[s] 'God' as the name of the person picked out by [the] description"[20] given above—as if God could be pigeon-holed by a system of definitions that one has come up with without reference to him. The experience of the sovereign Lord, on the contrary, led the Apostle Paul to perceive the opposite: it is from the "Father that everything of paternal authority,[21] in heaven and on earth, receives its name" (Eph 3:15). But for Swinburne, the laws of logic (and even those of morality) occupy a higher position than God. Though he affirms, with Christian tradition, that God possesses his characteristics necessarily,[22] it is only in the sense of Saul Kripke's rigid designators: since one has defined God as a being who is personal, omnipotent, omniscient, etc., he is such essentially: "Having these properties is essential to being the kind of being that God is."[23]

As to the assertion that God exists necessarily, it means only that his existence "is a brute fact that is inexplicable." But one should not be fooled by this: God is well and truly, for Swinburne, "a logically contingent being";[24] we are a very, very long way from Van Til's idea that

---

19. Richard Swinburne, plenary discussion during the conference, "The Origin of the Laws of Nature and the Existence of God," Ecole normale supérieure, Paris, 30 April, 2004.

20. Swinburne, *Existence of God*, 7.

21. In Greek *patria*, "family" (in the widest sense), "race," "people." My translation tries to conserve the word's etymological proximity with *pater*, "father."

22. Swinburne includes the fact of being the Creator of the world among the attributes that necessarily apply to God (Swinburne, *Existence of God*, 96). To preserve the freedom of the creative act, we must read into this assertion a conditional necessity: God is necessarily the Creator of the word *if* the latter exists.

23. Ibid., 95.

24. Ibid., 96.

God, in his transcendence, is the source of all probability.[25] Of course, from the moment one recognizes the fundamental role that God has, not only in the order of existence, but also in that of modality, one can no longer assign a probability to his existence. Without Him, any modal assertion collapses. This is why any true theist should not even wish for Swinburne's probabilistic apologetics to succeed: for if it did, it would have proved *ipso facto* that God is not the *absolute* foundation implied by the concept of creation.

Since Swinburne's general approach does not adequately consider the faith frameworks in which all thinking takes place—whether theistic, naturalistic, or otherwise—one should not be surprised to find a similar short-sightedness with regard to other elements in his reasoning. To give but two examples: firstly, his approach makes use of, in a crucial way, the need for explanation. To be fair, Swinburne pays attention to the problems related to it. He devotes no less than three chapters of his magnum opus, *The Existence of God*,[26] to this question. But one's impression, when reading them, is that he is not aware of the role that basic beliefs play in determining the kind of explanations that are required, and that are satisfactory. And yet "it is inconceivable that a notion such as explanation could fail to depend crucially upon one's most general picture of the world and its ways."[27] When, for example, Swinburne rejects the Humean conception of laws of nature, with the argument that it does not explain the regularities observed,[28] one must remember that the philosopher of science who works within this tradition does not claim to explain the appearance of order. Now, one can be convinced that such a philosopher is wrong in giving up the search for explanation but it is fanciful to think that he might agree with our belief in the opposite direction, without *ipso facto* abandoning his thought (and perhaps even life) framework. The request for an explanation that Swinburne proposes is not a neutral consideration, shared by the opposing parties in the debate. The only way a Humean could accept it would be by changing his philosophical position.

Secondly, the same observation applies to the way that Swinburne uses the criterion of simplicity. The use of this criterion is already made

---

25. Van Til, *Survey of Christian Epistemology*, 107, quoted above pp. 17f.
26. Swinburne, *Existence of God*, chaps. 2–4.
27. Railton, "Explanation and Metaphysical Controversy," 221.
28. Swinburne, *Existence of God*, 30, 160.

problematic by the difficulty of defining exactly what one means by simplicity. While it is true that many attempts have been made to define simplicity in an objective way, none of them is really convincing when applied to a sufficiently large domain of theoretical construction in the sciences.[29] Moreover, simplicity seems to harbor an irreducible residue of subjectivity: "Simplicity, as applied to tasks, is at least a triadic relation; a sentence of the form '… is simpler than _____' is always elliptical for sentences of the form '… is simpler than _____ for ***.'"[30]

Even more problematic is Swinburne's belief that simplicity is a reliable guide towards the truth. Why should one accept his certainty that (all else being equal), "the simpler a theory, the more probable it is"?[31] We can easily understand why scientists prefer simple theories: handling more complicated theories requires more work. But on what grounds can we say that our preference directs us towards the *truth*? The computational difficulties that humans have are no doubt trivial from nature's point of view. The basic assumptions that one adopts thus influence, in a decisive manner, the significance that we are willing to grant to simplicity.

It would be useful to examine Swinburne's argument in more depth, but the above already shows how his natural theology sits with respect to creationism. Let us bring out, in conclusion, one final point: Swinburne takes great care to include the fruit of recent philosophical discussion in his version of what he calls the "teleological" argument. He discusses, in particular, three approaches:[32] Humean analysis, represented by David Lewis,[33] laws as relations between universals, as proposed by David Armstrong,[34] and the approach based on causal powers, that Rom Harré

---

29. Hesse, "Simplicity," 446–48, presents some of these attempts; Sober, "Simplicity (in Scientific Theories)," 780–83, complements her article, with respect to more recent approaches.

30. Carroll, *Laws of Nature*, 49. Swinburne, *Existence of God*, 53, defines what he means by simplicity, but his definition is a long way from answering all the philosophical concerns raised by this concept.

31. Swinburne, *Existence of God*, 53.

32. Ibid., 29–35, 160–62.

33. Lewis, *Counterfactuals*, 73, and Lewis, "Theory of Universals," 41–43. Cf. Jaeger, *Lois de la nature*, chap. 3.

34. Armstrong, *Law of Nature*, 75–191; Armstrong, *States of Affairs*, 220–62. Cf. Jaeger, *Lois de la nature*, chap. 2.

and E. H. Madden have revived.[35] It is probably no coincidence that neither Nancy Cartwright nor Bas Van Fraassen get a mention. Their skeptical approaches question (for quite different reasons) the idea that it is necessary, or even useful, to postulate an underlying universal order in order to explain the success of the natural sciences.[36] An in-depth dialog with their respective arguments would no doubt highlight the inevitable role that worldview plays, given the extent to which their work is at odds with the general framework of Swinburne's natural theology. But the latter is probably too spellbound by the myth of neutral reason to feel the challenge that such skeptical approaches constitute for any argument that tries to trace back from the natural order to its transcendent source. Swinburne's selection of explanations for laws of nature from among those currently on the market in philosophy of science seems to share the myopia that more generally characterizes his argument and which prevents him from grasping the radical distance between theism and any other explanation (or non-explanation) of the natural order.

AN ANALYTICAL NATURAL THEOLOGY: JOHN FOSTER

The second theistic line of argument which we will consider here comes from another Oxford scholar. John Foster (born 1941) first proposed his proof of the existence of God in an article published in 2001 entitled "Regularities, Laws of Nature and the Existence of God," and later devoted a monograph to the subject, *The Divine Lawmaker: Lectures on Induction, Laws of Nature, and the Existence of God*.[37] He constructs the physico-theological argument as an inference to the best explanation:[38] the existence of God provides the best explanation for observed uniformity of nature and the role that the latter plays in our inductive practices. More specifically, Foster develops his theistic proof in four steps: first he introduces the puzzle of induction, of which David Hume provides the

---

35. Harré, *Laws of Nature*, passim.

36. Cartwright, *Dappled World*, 1ff., 23ff.; Van Fraassen, *Laws and Symmetry*, chaps. II–VIII.

37. Foster, "Regularities, Laws and God," 145–61; Foster, *Divine Lawmaker*. See ibid., 160, n. 1, for the fact that the article mentioned is where Foster develops this line of argument for the first time.

38. The validity of such inferences is a bone of contention between philosophers of science, and this is true generally, not just in the specific context of theistic arguments. For a defense of this argumentative strategy, see Lipton, *Best Explanation*, passim; for a critique, Van Fraassen, *Laws and Symmetry*, chap. VI.

classic formulation in his *Enquiry Concerning Human Understanding*.[39] Next, Foster defends the "nomological-explanatory solution" of this problem: the observed regularity allows one to infer, as the best explanation, the (objective) existence of a law, which in turn guarantees the inductive inference of the same regularity in the future.[40] Thirdly, he tries to show that no naturalist theory of the concept of law is satisfactory; in particular, it seems difficult, impossible even, to understand in a naturalist context so-called "natural" necessity, which sits between the strict necessity of logic and pure contingency. Finally, Foster proposes "a God of the relevant (broadly Judaeo-Christian) type" as the solution to the puzzle of natural necessity.[41]

Foster's outline shares with other natural theologies the belief that the natural order requires, for its explanation, the postulate that God exists. However, it employs a novel argumentative strategy, which justifies the adjective "analytical": by analogy with the methods of conceptual analysis of analytic philosophy, the *concept* of law plays a predominant role in Foster's proof of the existence of God. In fact, the crux of his argument is the assertion that this concept does not make sense without the theistic postulate.[42]

Rather than following Foster's argument step by step, let us note a few salient points: along with many in the field of analytical philosophy, Foster seems wedded to the myth that reason is neutral. Not only does he rely on a clear distinction between *a priori* and *a posteriori*,[43] he also maintains that his analysis is done in an "ideologically neutral spirit," while criticizing empiricists for using "preconceived philosophical theory about what kinds of thing we can make sense of."[44] In particular, he thinks that it is possible to put aside one's religious beliefs, and "judge things on their philosophical merits alone."[45] It is, therefore, not surprising that Foster sees virtually no problem with the requirement for explanation that figures predominantly in his proof of God's existence. He does, it is true, stress that the refusal to seek an explanation for

39. Hume, *Enquiry Concerning Human Understanding*, § 4f.
40. Foster, *Divine Lawmaker*, 47–49.
41. Ibid., 2.
42. Ibid., 72, 78f.
43. Ibid., 82f.
44. Ibid., 80f.
45. Ibid., 127.

natural regularities does not place the empiricist in a state of conceptual contradiction. Nevertheless, the absence of a cause for such regularity would imply a "very strange ... situation, whose obtaining, if we knew of it, would warrant huge surprise." Foster concludes that "the rational expectation must be that this situation does not obtain"[46]—apparently without realizing the circularity of his argument. For the empiricist does not actually concede that the search for explanation is the rational strategy to adopt in a surprising situation; he instead shows a preference confronted with the "brute facts" of existence.

As God's existence comes as the conclusion of a philosophical argument that sees itself as neutral, we might expect that Foster's God be completely transparent to human reason. In fact, "the postulation of a *non-natural—supernatural—*personal agent" precisely avoids having to resort to an explanation of the natural order that would be "beyond our comprehension." Foster brings in God in order to satisfy the rational requirement to "at least *aim* to construct an explanation within the limits of our understanding."[47] It is only normal then that Foster has no problem subjecting God to conceptual considerations; the argument that he uses to demonstrate that God is inside time is very significant in this regard. He concludes—contrary to the traditional position—that divine eternity means infinite temporal existence, because, he says, "I do not think that we can make sense of the notion of a personal being existing outside time."[48] This argument presupposes that our concepts inform us in a valid way about the divine nature; Foster thus deploys, in the supernatural realm, the confidence typical of many analytic philosophers, who think that conceptual analyses are capable of revealing reality to us. In a more holistic approach, however, which doesn't take separation between *a priori* and *a posteriori* as a logical given, our experience of reality participates in the formation of our concepts. Therefore, there is no reason that an encounter with the deity might not oblige us to radically rethink the conceptual "boxes" we have drawn up from our experience of nature alone.

For Foster, in any case, the depths of the divine spirit are not unfathomable. Not only is he convinced that considerations of simplicity suffice for postulating a unique divine being, who is both creator and

---

46. Ibid., 62; cf. 43f.
47. Ibid., 121.
48. Ibid., 133.

legislator of the world;[49] he also believes that the methods of creation are open to rational investigation. He finds the "plausible reason" for creation in the divine goodness.[50] To keep the common-sense idea of dispositions, we can assume that God has established laws, by which the universe evolves from an initial state, rather than his directly creating all the details of its development.[51] Foster even goes as far as to think about "divine psychology." In so doing, he believes that "our knowledge of the mind of God [—acquired by philosophical reasoning alone!—] make[s] it rational to suppose that he would set a premium on nomological uniformity."[52] Faced with such confidence in human reason's ability to understand both the nature of the universe and that of its Creator, we are not surprised by Foster's Freudian slip when he writes that "the God whose existence we are now assuming *conforms* to the requirements of the theistic account."[53] The god to whom Foster's theistic proof leads is not the sovereign Lord, to whom all that exists owes its subsistence and without whom any exercise of human reason would be doomed to failure. It is no surprise that a rationalist argument leads us only to the philosophers' god. Regardless of whether Foster's proof is valid, it certainly does not deserve to be called "theistic." Believers interested in dialogue with skeptics would be better off looking for other avenues for discussion than that presented by this kind of analytic natural theology.

PANTHEISM'S DECLARATION OF MYSTERY

It is time for us to turn to worldviews other than theism that offer alternative explanations of the natural order. At the risk of oversimplifying, three major types can be distinguished: non-theistic religious worldviews, scientific explanations, and the empiricists' refusal of the need for explanation. Let us look at these three groups of rival options in turn, without forgetting the specific question of interest to us: our task is not to construct an apologetic that shows theism's superiority over opposing worldviews as regards the explanation of laws of nature. The aim is more modest: to examine how the various explanatory projects appear

---

49. Ibid., 129–31.
50. Ibid., 145.
51. Ibid., 169.
52. Ibid., 183.
53. Ibid., 183 (italics mine).

in light of the idea of creation. Of course, it is not enough to highlight the points of conflict between the various worldviews; this tension itself is why we speak of rival positions. But it can be productive to evaluate one explanatory system, from an opposing standpoint, right down to its basic presuppositions. The comparison can bring out more clearly the "shape" of the explanatory system, highlighting its field lines and identifying its underlying motivations that would otherwise remain hidden. Furthermore, the chosen perspective itself takes on clearer contours when faced with rival positions; it must be refined and clarified. In any case, thinking is situated, and it is pointless to seek the "view from nowhere," which might allow a neutral assessment of a proposed explanation. It is, of course, important to "bring to life" the system under consideration by placing oneself on its territory, to show how the world looks from this point of view. But it is also instructive to attempt a comparative assessment by adopting a contrasting perspective. In accordance with our aim, it is this second method that will take priority in our consideration of rival positions to theism (even if the first is not completely absent), since our study consciously assumes the idea of creation.

When we direct our attention to explanatory projects of a nontheistic religious nature[54] we observe a wide variety, even within this group. However, our task is made easier by the fact that pantheism is today the only candidate among them to receive a significant audience. In human history, polytheistic explanations of natural phenomena have played a considerable role, but the difficulties they have in justifying the universality of the natural order—or simply in inspiring research into it—are such that polytheism no longer needs to be seriously taken into account when attempting to explain the degree of structure that the sciences have found in the world.

Albert Einstein is a well-known example of an eminent scientist who adopted a pantheistic worldview to explain scientific practice. However, upon close examination his writings reveal the two main problems that

---

54. If we understand "religious" in a broad sense, we can include here approaches that give an aesthetic explanation of the natural order: the world is ordered, because what is ordered is more beautiful that what is not. Of course, such an argument relies on the assumption that beauty brings things into existence, which amounts to making beauty a creative principle. Since the latter is impersonal, one finds here a form of pantheism, even if the deity is described in aesthetic rather than explicitly religious terms. A similar consideration applies to the ethical explanation adopted by Leslie, *Universes*, 165, "ethical needs for the existence of things are in some cases creatively effective."

pantheism faces in this context (not to mention the added difficulty that it has finding a basis for ethics).[55] Since pantheism favors *the One* to explain the universality of the laws of nature, how do we maintain *the Many*, which also characterizes our experience of the world? This first problem leads to a second one: how can one understand knowledge in a perspective dominated by the unity of reality, when it arises from an encounter between the knower and the known, and therefore requires a certain *otherness*? This second difficulty is exacerbated by the fact that the ultimate principle of pantheism is impersonal: what place is there, then, for human intelligence, given that the latter is fundamentally personal in nature?

When one compares pantheism's explanation of the natural order with that proposed by creationism, we see that the difficulties arise precisely from the points of tension between two opposing conceptions of the deity: firstly, the personal dimension of human knowledge fits seamlessly into a worldview where the ultimate being is a personal one; also, a personal God allows for the One and the Many to be held in productive tension, without this tension degenerating into opposition. The doctrine of the Trinity speaks of one divine essence in three persons, such that the One and the Many are rooted together in the Godhead. But, as Saint Augustine clearly perceived, the distinction of persons is the only differentiation in God that is compatible with his uniqueness.[56] In rejecting the personhood of ultimate reality, pantheism, without proposing any alternative solution, cuts itself off from creationism's explanations both of the harmony between the One and the Many in the natural order, and of humankind's ability to understand the world.

Nevertheless, when we put ourselves in the pantheist's shoes, it is clear that the lack of explanation is consistent with the overall worldview. For the pantheist rejects the distinction between the world and the deity: they are, at most, two different aspects of one reality. It follows that the deity cannot be used to explain the existence or nature of the world, since he cannot be detached from it. Although the pantheist refuses materialism's monist worldview, his aim is not to reintroduce a

---

55. What follows is no more than a brief presentation of the problems encountered by the pantheistic view, since the explanation receives a fuller treatment in my study of Einstein's cosmic religion (Jaeger, *Croire et connaître*, 164–70).

56. Augustine, *The Trinity*, book V, V, 6. Bartmann, *Lehrbuch der Dogmatik*, vol. 1, § 55, quotes texts from the Greek church fathers, which prefigure Augustine's discernment.

hint of duality, but to affirm a different *posture* with respect to the world: he tries to maintain the experience of the *mysterium tremendum*, and resists the reductionist claims of scientism's endeavors.

In Einstein's writing one finds especially clear confirmations of this kind of religious motivation in pantheism. When asked about the existence of God, Einstein replied: "My religiosity consists in a humble admiration of the infinitely superior spirit that reveals itself in the little that we, with our weak and transitory understanding, can comprehend of reality."[57]

Einstein's scientific work inevitably takes on a religious dimension, because it allows him to enter into communion with the mystery at work in nature. In his letter of March 30, 1952, to his friend Maurice Solovine, Einstein thus distances himself from "positivists and the professional atheists who are elated because they feel that they have not only successfully rid the world of gods but 'bared the miracles'";[58] the miracle that Einstein is talking about is the intelligibility of the natural order.

In a pantheistic system, acknowledging the mystery goes together with the refusal of any explanation. In the same letter to Maurice Solovine, the aging physicist stresses this point: "Oddly enough, we must be satisfied to acknowledge the 'miracle' without there being any legitimate way for us to approach it. I am forced to add that just to keep you from thinking that—weakened by age—I have fallen pray to the parsons."[59]

This terse remark shows that Einstein clearly perceives the difference between his view and theism (which he alludes to by means of the somewhat ironic reference to "parsons"): a pantheist proposes no basis for the natural order. In fact, he should not even *try* to propose one, lest he invalidate the particularity of his position: to acknowledge the mystery of the world as being *ultimate*.

Pantheism's lack of explanation for the natural order thus appears very differently, depending on whether one places oneself inside this view, or evaluates it from creationism's standpoint. From the latter perspective, the pantheist cuts himself off from a transcendent foundation and in doing so forfeits the explanation of the world's orderly structure; but from inside the pantheistic view, this lack of explanation is essential to the position adopted. The relativity of one's attitude toward the

---

57. Text written on a letter dated August 5, 1927, in Einstein, *The Human Side*, 66.
58. Einstein, *Letters to Solovine*, 133.
59. Ibid.

lack of explanation once again highlights philosophy's inherently situated nature. Relativity does not, however, imply relativ*ism*: debate about the arguments is still worthwhile. Thus one can point out that the two problems that have been raised—the experience of plurality, and knowledge—are not just an issue for creationism, but apply equally within the pantheistic conceptual system. For they are features of reality, which the pantheist himself acknowledges, while being in tension with the principle of unity that dominates his view. Even if he refuses to *explain* the natural order, in accordance with his basic religious position, the pantheist must deal with the internal tensions of his worldview, which arise from the form this order takes—combining the One and the Many—and from its intelligibility.

SCIENTISM'S CLAIM TO EXPLAIN EVERYTHING

The second major type of system that seeks to explain laws of nature is based on the naturalistic view, which is reasonably widespread today among both philosophers and scientists: the disposition that seeks an explanation of the natural order within science itself. This approach is consistent with pantheism in its rejection of a transcendent foundation, even though it draws the opposite conclusion as concerns religion: naturalism sees itself as an areligious, even anti-religious, position. It seeks to eliminate the mystery that the pantheist and theist find in nature, by means of a complete description of the natural order in scientific categories.

Given the grandiose ambitions that some harbor in this area, it is worth reminding ourselves of the fragmentary state of our current scientific knowledge. Despite the triumphalism of some academics and many popular science authors, even the most basic task of unifying the different theories in physics remains a long way off. It is true that some see string theory as being a promising candidate for such a universal theory; we must, however, be honest about the fact that at the present time, nobody knows how to reconcile quantum mechanics with general relativity. We do not even have an adequate formulation of quantum mechanics that is invariant under Lorentz transformations, that is, which could be used for speeds comparable to the speed of light.[60]

Hopes for progress towards such a unified theory appear very fragile indeed when one realizes the huge gulf between the domain where

---

60. Quantum field theory is unable to provide such a formulation in a satisfactory way (cf. Cao, *Conceptual Foundations, passim*).

its effects should become significant, and that accessible to our current experimental techniques (the so-called Planck length is, for example, 10 19 times smaller than the size of a proton). This fact leaves the early universe as the only possible laboratory for direct experimental verification of quantum gravity—with the obvious difficulty that we cannot repeat the experiment, nor influence its initial conditions!

One might, of course, hope that a unified theory in physics might predict effects at scales more easily accessible to our observation. But it is likely that some fundamental principles will not be discovered solely on the basis of experiments limited to the macroscopic or quantum domains—the latter being huge compared to Planck dimensions. Trying to discover the unified theory in such a way could be compared to guessing the details of quantum mechanics by observing only the macroscopic world. It is, in fact, an impossible mission, for phenomena that occur on the level above are, for the most part, independent of the structural details of the level below.[61]

It goes without saying—although this point is often overlooked—that a theory unifying quantum mechanics and general relativity would still be a long way from the grand promises of a true "theory of everything." We already see within physics that there are emergent phenomena that resist explanation from first principles alone, and reductionist programs become yet more risky when we come to biology. "So the triumph of the reductionism of the Greeks is a pyrrhic victory: We have succeeded in reducing all of ordinary physical behaviour to a simple, correct Theory of Everything only to discover that it has revealed exactly nothing about many things of great importance."[62]

But the critique of "scientific" explanatory ambitions does not stop there. Even if one day there were a completely satisfactory "theory of everything," the form of laws of nature would still itself be a brute fact that remains unexplained: why is it this theory and not another that describes the world?[63] When naturalists want to avoid leaving this question unanswered their only option is to resort to considerations of a conceptual nature. If they are metaphysically inclined, they will have to show that the theory found is the only one that is logically possible. Hume himself

---

61. Laughlin and Pines, "Theory of Everything," 29f. Cf. Curiel, "Excesses of Quantum Gravity," S424–41.

62. Laughlin and Pines, "Theory of Everything," 28.

63. Weinberg, "Can Science Explain Everything?," 50.

contemplated this alternative to the theistic explanation of the natural order: "Is it not probable . . . that the whole economy of the universe is conducted by a like necessity [to that of the nature of numbers], though no human algebra can furnish a key which solves the difficulty? And instead of admiring the order of natural beings, may it not happen, that, could we penetrate into the intimate nature of bodies, we should clearly see why it was absolutely impossible they could ever admit of any other disposition?"[64]

Few, however, are willing to accept that science is a matter of mere logic: why should one think that one theory alone be logically consistent? Thus if the naturalist is of (neo-)Kantian inclination, it is enough for him to show that only this theory gives rise to an image of the world that corresponds to human cognition, or that allows for the practice of science. While it is possible to deduce classical and relativistic mechanics, and most of the basic structures of quantum mechanics (i.e., of Hilbert space) by using Kantian arguments,[65] there are other parts of contemporary science that, so far, have resisted this kind of deduction: we have no idea how to explain, for example, the universal constants (like the speed of light); we likewise do not know how one could deduce Einstein's equations, which form the basis of the elegant theory of general relativity.

In any case, scientism's ambitions oblige us to go further: even if we managed a logical, or pragmatic-epistemic, justification of the theory of everything (can we really see this happening?), the ultimate question would remain unanswered: why does something exist rather than nothing?[66] For the realist one can also add the second foundational mystery of modern science: why does mathematics apply to the real world? In its (neo-)Kantian version, the question becomes: why is science possible? Answering such questions is beyond the realms of any scientific theory.

To support this claim, let us consider two recent proposals that hope to explain laws of nature in a scientific manner. The first—the concept of "law without law"—is defended by the American physicist John Archibald Wheeler (1911–2008), who is renowned for his determination

---

64. Hume, *Dialogues concerning Natural Religion*, Ninth part, 168f.
65. Mittelstaedt, *Klassische Mechanik*, 18 50; Mittelstaedt, *Zeitbegriff in der Physik*, 41–77, 127–31; and Mittelstaedt, "Interpreting Quantum Mechanics," 281–90; Bitbol, "Transcendental Deduction," 253–80.
66. Omnès, *Interpretation of Quantum Mechanics*, 350–52.

to "inhabit" a theory's formalism to the point of exploring its most counter-intuitive implications.[67] As regards the laws of nature, he is not content simply to deduce them from one (or more) fundamental law(s), which remain unexplained; he wants to anchor the lawful structure of the world in something outside of those laws. The two candidates that Wheeler explores are, firstly, mathematics, and secondly, statistical processes, which show no order at the microscopic level. From a combination of these two elements, he hopes to construct the lawful architecture of physics: "Every law of physics, to the extent that it is not pure tautology or mathematical identity, must be at bottom statistical and approximate in its predictions."[68]

The indeterministic world of quantum phenomena constitutes the realm of chance on which Wheeler tries to build his understanding of the world's lawful order: "I believe that everything is built higgledy-piggledy on the unpredictable outcome of billions upon billions of elementary quantum phenomena, and that the laws and initial conditions of physics arise out of this chaos by the action of a regulating principle, the discovery and proper formulation of which is the number one task of the coming . . . era of physics."[69] Whereas most place the laws of physics on a level in between logical necessity and logical contingency, Wheeler tries, by means of statistical methods, to understand them from the combination of these two extremes.

Even if we grant that the deduction Wheeler imagines is possible (nothing is less certain, given the current state of our knowledge), does it really provide the desired result of "law without law"? It may be true that neither mathematical laws, nor the chaos of multiple microscopic processes, belong to the realm of laws of nature. But to measure the success of the "law without law" project, one must remember its more general aim: provide a global explanation of the laws of nature. And here we must ask whether the deduction he proposes really fulfills the project's aims.

---

67. E.g., Wheeler and Ford, *Geons, Black Holes*, 237f., 253, concerning the "geon," a gravitational body composed exclusively of (electrodynamic or gravitational) fields; ibid., 257, concerning black holes and gravity waves.

68. Wheeler, "How Come the Quantum?," 314.

69. Wheeler, "Recognizing 'Law Without Law,'" 398.

Even if one accepts the analytical, and therefore obvious, nature of mathematics (as most do)[70] and one manages (despite most people's expectations) to retain, on the basis of logical arguments, one single mathematical structure as being the only possible description of our universe, the identification of a particular mathematical element with a specific part of physical reality amounts to experimentation and thus introduces a synthetic element that requires explanation.[71] Thus even if we managed to reduce the laws of physics to one mathematical structure, determined by logical arguments alone, we would *still* not have eliminated contingency from physics. As long as we try to explain every contingent element, the "law without law" project will fail, even under the most favorable conditions.

As concerns statistical processes, we see that they are no more promising in answering the question mentioned above. For the "law" of large numbers assumes at the very least the validity of mathematics to describe the emergence of structures from microscopic probabilistic processes. The element of contingency that mathematics carries when applied to physical reality therefore remains undiminished; the presence of numerous elementary factors is no help in this respect. Furthermore, no structure can arise from chaos without a "regulatory principle," and Wheeler himself admits as much: "No law springs unguided out of absolute chaos. It demands the guidance of a regulating principle."[72] Classical thermodynamics provides the best-known example: its laws emerge from the erratic movements of many particles. And yet, as David Deutsch writes, the "motion of molecules is not lawless, it is random. And randomness implies a probability distribution function, and that function, or the principle from which it

---

70. Willard Van Orman Quine is a notable exception, owing to his rejection of the distinction between analytical and synthetic propositions (Quine, "Two Dogmas of Empiricism," 20–46). Descartes is an example of an earlier author for whom the laws of logic demand an explanation (which he finds in God's creative activity).

71. Grene, editor's note, in Polanyi, *Knowing and Being*, 120; Deutsch, "Wheeler's 'Law Without Law,'" 587.

72. Wheeler, "Recognizing 'Law Without Law,'" 400; also ibid., 398. In this article, Wheeler studies four cases in which order emerges out of a large number of random events: Boltzmann's law, phenomena near a critical point, the random coupling of oscillators, and the "traveling salesman." In each case, Wheeler identifies the regulatory principle (ibid., 399–403). On can, however, discern a tendency to minimize the scope of contingent assumption which affect the calculations: for example, Wheeler has no problem with the application of mathematics to physical objects, nor does he consider some of the symmetry arguments employed to be part of the regulatory principle.

may be derived, is the missing underlying law."[73] Similarly, the behavior of a single elementary particle is, according to standard quantum mechanics, objectively undetermined, but nevertheless orderly, being described by the wave function. This fact allows for the emergence of a well-defined probability distribution for measurements in quantum mechanics, like the triggering of a photon counter. As a result, the probabilistic distribution of quantum phenomena is not, strictly speaking, a "law without law."[74]

The regulatory principle, which underlies the microscopic behavior, is a part of a lawful structure, and we return to the question of its foundation. Once again, one must choose between seeking a logically necessary deduction (which would place us in a vicious cycle) and accepting its empirical nature, which would introduce a flaw in the desired goal of a comprehensive explanation. Thus, the large numbers method cannot explain the lawful structure of our world by means of something outside of those laws. As Deutsch remarks, "in making a fundamental 'regulating principle' the new object of his search, Wheeler *ipso facto* abandons the search for 'law without law.' For a regulating principle is a law."[75]

The physicist Lee Smolin (born 1955) provides our second example of a global explanation of the laws of nature. His approach is comparable to that of Wheeler (on which he draws),[76] in terms of its speculative audacity and the all-inclusiveness of the proposed explanation; both require that science alone explain the lawful order of our world. But whereas Wheeler bases his approach on "nothing" (according to his "law without law"), Smolin's originality is to apply an evolutionary perspective to the laws of nature. In fact, Smolin tries to dispense with the idea of immutable laws, by deriving the laws that govern our universe from a process of cosmological evolution. By analogy with Darwin's theory of evolution, he suggests that "a great deal of the order and regularity we find in the physical world might have arisen just as the beauty of

---

73. Deutsch, "Wheeler's 'Law Without Law,'" 587.

74. One must qualify the assertion of Mittelstaedt, "Emergence of Statistical Laws," 265, when he writes, "A quantum mechanical probability law seems to emerge from objectively undetermined individual events as a 'law without law' in the sense of Wheeler." What Mittelstaedt shows is the more modest, but interesting, fact that one does not need Born's interpretation as an additional postulate. The description of quantum phenomena requires fewer structures than initially thought; to be more precise, quantum mechanics does not depend on a semantics which is external to the theory.

75. Deutsch, "Wheeler's 'Law Without Law,'" 587.

76. Smolin, "Cosmological Natural Selection," 706.

the living world came to be: through a process of self-organization, by means of which the world has evolved over time to become intricately structured."[77] The theory thus receives the revealing name "cosmological natural selection";[78] it is part of "a necessary process of liberation from the influences of this essentially religious view of the world,"[79] since Smolin believes that the idea of a creator God has in the past led to the idea of laws that are boundlessly valid.[80] His outline of cosmological evolution allows him to "describe a world that is whole unto itself, without any need of an external intelligence to serve as its inventor, organizer, or external observer."[81]

Given the current popularity of the idea of multiple universes in the field of cosmology, it is not surprising to see Smolin make use of such a scenario in order to flesh out his view. In line with Alan Guth and Stephen Hawking, he postulates that quantum effects prevent a gravitational singularity during the formation of a black hole; instead, the latter spawns a baby universe. Moreover, he postulates that the same physics theory describes both the parent universe and the new one. In particular, the temporal framework is conserved, but the natural "constants" undergo small changes during the reproductive process. Universes that maximize the number of black holes are thus those that produce the most offspring, for there is no equivalent to predatory animals in the case of cosmological evolution.[82] As the changes to the basic parameters are assumed to be small, a parent can pass on this advantage to its child universe. Thus, universes which maximize the number of black holes are more probable, and we must just happen to live in such a universe. In this way, the natural "constants" of our universe can be historically explained, in a way analogous to that proposed by Darwinism for the attributes of living beings: "The parameters of the standard model of elementary particle physics have the values we find them to [have] because these make the production of black holes much more likely than most other choices."[83]

---

77. Smolin, *Life of the Cosmos*, 16f.
78. Smolin, "Cosmological Natural Selection," 707.
79. Smolin, *Life of the Cosmos*, 242.
80. Ibid., 93f., 248.
81. Ibid., 242.
82. Ibid., 130.
83. Ibid., 119 (in italics); cf. 115–19, for the theory's postulates, and 129, for the importance of the postulate of small changes.

Let us put to one side the question of whether Smolin's evolutionary reconstruction is true or not.[84] For one must first evaluate the hypothesis relative to Smolin's wider aim: that of replacing the old idea of fixed laws of nature with a relational and historicist view. Seen from this perspective, what appeared to be a bold and revolutionary hypothesis now seems surprisingly conservative. Having the natural "constants" being subject to change is certainly a different way of seeing the world compared to the image presented by modern science. But the whole *structure* of the theory remains fixed. Even the strictest Platonist would gape in amazement were he to discover that a single theory was not only sufficient to describe our universe, but also to establish the existence of, and correctly describe a whole set of parallel universes (to which we would have, at best, very limited experimental access). Our hypothetical Platonist would be even more willing to accept the touch of historical contingency inherent in Smolin's proposal that his eternal "multiverse" satisfies the principle of plenitude: all possible universes will eventually come about, because "in eternity there is enough time for anything."[85] When Smolin talks of "processes that could have created or selected the laws that the universe would obey,"[86] one must not forget that this is a strictly limited phenomenon: the selection of universal constants that are valid for a universe. Contrary to what his rhetoric might suggest, his proposal does not contain any mechanism by which to generate the theoretical framework describing the "multiverse" or even, more modestly, the structural form of a universe's laws.[87]

Wheeler and Smolin are both perfect examples of the scientistic approach, which operates on the conviction that science, and only science, is qualified to explain everything. As audacious as their project is, their quest to explain everything by scientific methods proves to be an impossible mission. Neither Wheeler's "law without law" nor Smolin's evolutionary cosmology make good on their promise of providing, at this fundamental level, a scientific explanation for the laws of nature. Their failure serves as a sobering warning to anyone claiming to find a

84. Note, however, the very muted reception that Smolin's speculations received in cosmological circles: Rees, *Our Cosmic Habitat*, 177f.; Silk, "Holistic Cosmology," 26.

85. Smolin, *Life of the Cosmos*, 179; cf. 121.

86. Ibid., 20.

87. For a more thorough evaluation of Smolin's proposal, see Jaeger, "Lee Smolin," 372–86.

scientific foundation for the natural order. "Scientific" explanations of the natural order are therefore of strictly limited interest to us, at least insofar as their content is concern: they inevitably go beyond the limits of science in their attempt to provide an answer. Since such explanations restrict themselves to scientific methods and results, either they are inconsistent, or else they distort the scientific evidence—or, more often than not, both. However, what should get our attention is the mere fact that such all-encompassing explanatory projects exist: given that they are as desperate as they are erroneous, one should ask the question as to why some find them so appealing.

It is tempting to interpret these naturalist explanations as an indication of how difficult it is for human beings to accept unexplained brute facts. Totalitarian explanatory projects are thus faced with a dilemma: on one hand, they do not tolerate any contingent facts, which would remain unexplained; on the other, they refuse to "base" contingency on a necessary transcendent foundation. The only way left open to them is to eliminate contingency altogether. Those who pursue such a goal do not, in general, realize that the success in this area would mark the end of the science they so admire, for the empirical element that characterizes modern science would no longer have any place in a world which we can exhaustively describe.[88] As C. S. Lewis poetically expressed it:

> You cannot go on "explaining away" for ever: you will find that you have explained explanation itself away. You cannot go on "seeing through things" for ever. The whole point of seeing through something is to see something through it. It is good that the window should be transparent, because the street or garden beyond it is opaque. How if you saw through the garden too? It is no use trying to "see through" first principles. If you see through everything, then everything is transparent. But a wholly transparent world is an invisible world. To "see through" all things is the same as not to see.[89]

Science's heartbeat is the encounter with contingency; it flatlines if it claims to master contingency completely. Science is only of interest if it explores a world that "resists" it in its factual opacity. Exhaustively and exclusively capturing the natural order in scientific terms is equivalent to abolishing science. Thus all-encompassing explanatory projects are

---

88. Redhead, *From Physics to Metaphysics*, 68.
89. C. S. Lewis, *Abolition of Man*, 81.

by definition inconsistent: the "false consciousness" that Van Fraassen criticizes in materialism[90] is inherent to them: they disguise themselves as empirical hypotheses, but embody an attitude that persists despite shifts in the scientific paradigm. For they cannot help but delude themselves about the possibility of an immanent explanation: convincing others (or oneself) that an explanation that uses only science could account for all contingency. The inconsistency of such ambitions—which is evident even from their own standpoint—is brought into sharp relief when one considers them from a theistic perspective: the follower of scientism experiences the nostalgia of being rooted in a necessary foundation, but rejects transcendence. His posture, which wishes to be areligious, ends up, paradoxically, absolutizing science and the world that it seeks to describe. The Creator is thus replaced as explanatory foundation by a created thing. But science is not meant to provide ultimate explanations; if we try to extract them from it by force, we will only end up brutalizing science.

INTELLIGENT DESIGN AND THE "MULTIVERSE"

One particular misguided scientific explanation of contingency crops up so often in contemporary discussions about cosmology that its falsehood can go unnoticed: the dichotomy between multiple universes and intelligent design has dogged discussions about the anthropic principle.[91] Instead of attributing our universe's favorable conditions for life to a teleological act, some cosmologists try to explain them by resorting to the idea of multiple universes. According to them, many universes coexist without any causal interaction between them. Even if only a small fraction of them allow for the emergence of life we must find ourselves in such a universe for we could not exist elsewhere. The fact that our universe is favorable to life is thus totally unsurprising—such is the proposed explanation of the anthropic principle.[92] We find a forerunner of this argument in the atomism of antiquity: Lucretius believed that all possible configurations of atoms would come about in an eternal world

---

90. Van Fraassen, "Science, Materialism, False Consciousness," 149–81; Van Fraassen, *Empirical Stance*, 56ff.

91. For example (there are many others), North, "Principe Anthropique," 15f. It was Paul Shellard who first helped me to see the ill-founded nature of the dichotomy between multiverse and design (interview in Cambridge, 22 February, 2002).

92. For a summary presentation of the main scenarios currently being proposed, see Rees, *Our Cosmic Habitat*, 169ff.

(which, by virtue of its infinite duration, serves as a "multiverse"). The ordered state that we presently see should therefore also be repeated, in fact, an infinite number of times.[93]

Of course, the anthropic principle is not the only possible motivation for suggesting multiple universes: it is conceivable, for example, that certain experimental facts in our universe might suggest theories that predict the existence of other worlds.[94] Similarly, there are ways of responding to the anthropic principle that do not involve either teleological considerations or multiple universes. Many refuse, for instance, to be surprised that our world is favorable to life: if it were not, we would not be here to observe it. This answer to the anthropic principle is, however, not satisfactory, for the probability of an event remains unchanged by the mere fact that it occurs.[95] If one does not wish to be surprised that our world is favorable to life, it is more coherent to accept this as a brute fact: "The world is very unusual, but unusual things do occur by chance."[96] Another strategy is to challenge the principle itself: perhaps further investigation will show that biological life is not as severely restrictive of the choice of universal constants as most of the scientists studying this area currently believe.

But when one accepts the need for an explanation for the life-sustaining qualities of the universe, one must realize that multiple universes are of no help whatsoever—or more precisely, that only a particular kind of "multiverse" (a rather extravagant one) really constitutes an alternative to intelligent design. For even if the multiple universe scenario provides an explanation of the biophilic nature of *our* world, the need for explanation, in general, simply reappears at the next level up, that of the multiverse. Even if the life-supporting conditions of our universe no longer pose problems, the puzzle remains as to why the multiverse that exists contains (at least) one world that allows for life. Multiple-universe scenarios would only provide an alternative explanation to intelligent design if all possible multiverses (or a great many of

---

93. Lucretius, *De rerum natura* I, v. 1021–28, quoted by Clavier, *Théologie Naturelle*, 54. Hume, *Dialogues Concerning Natural Religion*, Eighth part, 145–54, refines the argument (cf. Hacking, "Inverse Gambler's Fallacy," 207f.).

94. Haarsma and Haarsma, "Neutrino Mass, Inflationary Cosmology," 160f.

95. Leslie, *Universes*, 9–14.

96. Hacking, "Inverse Gambler's Fallacy," 211.

them) contained at least one life-sustaining universe.[97] This is, however, far from being proven.

Most multiple-universe scenarios place themselves in the context of the "standard model," which leaves around twenty universal constants undetermined. For such a scenario to be pertinent, as an explanation of the biophilic nature of our universe, it must contain a selection of universes with varying values for the natural "constants," such that among these there is a biophilic universe. But if the anthropic principle is correct and the choice of these values is very restrictive, the probability of finding a biophilic universe within any multiverse remains low. The need to explain the conditions conducive to life remains, even after the introduction of multiple universes—just in a different form. The difficulty only disappears if all the possible multiverses (or at least a significant percentage of them) include universes corresponding to a wide range of universal constants, so that a biophilic universe will occur, with a significant degree of probability, within the limits set. But the wider one extends the range of universes included in a multiverse, the more difficult it becomes to imagine a mechanism that can generate these universes, within a given multiverse. One can still resort to the principle of plenitude: if *all* universes necessarily occur, the existence of ours is no longer a problem. This is actually the answer preferred by Brandon Carter, who coined the phrase "anthropic principle" in the first place.[98]

This hypothesis—which for most of us is already too extravagant—is, however, not yet extravagant enough to remove all cause for surprise at the life-sustaining character of our world. For it postulates the existence of all universes, *within* a given theory. But one can still ask the question: why is reality suitably described by a theory that includes a universe conducive to life? The explanatory regression will only come to a halt if all logically consistent theories included a biophilic world. In this case, the possibility of life would be a matter of pure logic—and most of us would be surprised by logic's rich potential: "If in the end mathematics alone wins us our one chance in 10^{229} we would have little

---

97. Earman, "SAP Also Rises," 315. In any case, the mystery will always remain as to why there is something rather than nothing. But the anthropic principle does not question existence as such, just one particularly salient characteristic of our world: its ability to sustain conscious life.

98. Hacking, "Inverse Gambler's Fallacy," 208, 210f.; Craig, "Teleological Argument," 144f.

choice but to become mystics."[99] But it's a safe bet that life is richer than logic. Why should we believe that all logically consistent worlds (or at least, a great many of them) could support life? Science fiction authors and philosophers of science have been busy inventing a whole heap of universes, not all of which are favorable to life. In fact, any model of an internally consistent theory of physics provides another example of a possible world. In many of them (the world of classical mechanics, for example), life is not possible.

One scenario remains which effectively provides an explanation for the anthropic principle: when we admit that *all* logically possible universes exist—without any restriction—then the existence of ours becomes trivial. Modal realism puts an end to the requirement for explanation that may arise from any contingent fact whatsoever, since this image of the world intends to eliminate contingency altogether. Of course, modal realism is not without its own conceptual problems. In fact, it is not even clear whether we can define it unambiguously: can we really speak of *all* possible worlds?[100] The modal realist might be tempted to defend himself by turning the difficulty back on the theist—the definition of God's omnipotence and omniscience could indeed pose a similar conceptual problem. But let those who seek a comprehensive scientific explanation be warned: the theist has never claimed to provide a complete logical definition of God. On the contrary, scientism's ambitions do not sit well with the "incomprehensibility" of the world—or rather the multiverse of all possible worlds. Accepting the mystery at the center of its worldview would indicate the failure of the scientistic project just as much as would the acknowledgment of an unexplained contingent fact.[101]

Let us not stop, however, at modal realism's problems of definition: it is the only kind of multiverse that can effectively satisfy the demand for explanation that arises, for many, from the anthropic principle (and indeed from any other remarkable aspect of our world). Should we therefore acknowledge modal realism as being the crowning achievement of the scientific project to explain everything? Smolin, himself a past master of multiple universes, believes that "to argue this way is not

---

99. Smolin, *Life of the Cosmos*, 56.

100. Forrest and Armstrong, "Argument Against Possible Worlds," 164–68; Lewis, *Plurality of Worlds*, 102f.; Nolan, "Recombination Unbound," 239–62.

101. Cf. Jaeger, *Lois de la Nature*, 165–83.

to reason, it is simply to give up looking for a rational explanation."[102] The fact that only the most exorbitant principle of plenitude can come close to satisfying the ambitions of the scientific project is hardly a ringing endorsement of modal realism; it is actually just a further indication of how outrageous it is to want to explain *everything* by scientific methods alone.

EMPIRICISM'S REFUSAL OF EXPLANATION

The failure of scientism's explanatory projects can only increase the attractiveness of the last major attitude toward the natural order that we will consider here: whereas the naturalist seeks to find an immanent justification for laws of nature, the empiricist[103] denies the need for an explanation. The two are united in their opposition to a religious interpretation of the world's order: the theist finds traces of the Creator, the pantheist worships the mystery of the world's intelligibility, but the naturalist and the empiricist refuse to abandon the scientific method in order to explain why our world has the structure it does. Yet the empiricist faces up to the impossibility of providing a scientific explanation for this fact. Rather than stubbornly pursuing misguided hopes, he is happy simply to state the existence of this order.

Although the empiricist does not see the natural order as having religious value, his posture is not necessarily anti-religious. Van Fraassen is one example of an empiricist (right down to the details of his religious attitude) who consciously makes room for religious belief.[104] But scientific activity is not the basis for a religious position (if there be one): they are two distinct areas that do not, fundamentally, require mutual illumination. Faith in God is not based on the order that the sciences describe; neither does it make that order intelligible. There is no longer any need to invoke God to explain the laws of nature when one is convinced there is nothing to explain. Despite his refusal to invest the world's structure with religious significance, the empiricist finds himself on similar ground to the pantheist: for the former, the order does not

---

102. Smolin, *Life of the Cosmos*, 55f.

103. In what follows, I use the term "empiricist" with a slightly different meaning to its habitual one. The core of the position I wish to describe is specifically the obstinate and generalized refusal to seek an explanation for contingent facts.

104. Van Fraassen, "Against Transcendental Empiricism," 312; Van Fraassen, *Empirical Stance*, 177f., 193; 251, n.1; 255, n. 32. Cf. Jaeger, "Bas Van Fraassen," 581–602.

need any explanation, for the latter, it is self-explanatory. In practice, it is easier to move from one approach to the other than one might think at first glance: the pantheist can revel so much in the absence of explanation, other than the natural order itself, that he plays down the aspect of mystery and approaches the empiricist's skepticism. The empiricist, on the other hand, may so insist on the refusal of any need for explanation that this refusal becomes reified and ends up taking on a quasi-religious status.[105] However, let us examine here empiricism in its "pure" form, which tries to keep to a simple refusal of the need for explanation.

Such refusal may take different practical forms. The clearest version remains the empiricism inspired by Hume: it goes no further than observing some regularities in the world, but rejects any need for explanation. Is someone surprised that all the countless electrons in the world have the same properties? He should not be. That's how our world is. Neither God, nor a law of nature, nor an Aristotelian essence is responsible for it. It's just a cosmic coincidence. Consistent Humeans "have reconciled themselves to, and embraced, the ultimately inexplicable *contingency* of the universe."[106]

Of course, more moderate forms exist: while still an empiricist, David Armstrong uses universals to account for the natural order, and Nancy Cartwright introduces the idea of capacities (close to Aristotelian natures), although she emphasizes more strongly than others the limits of order, just as contemporary science has shown.[107] Therefore, their accounts bring in additional resources to cope with the difficulties of the naïve Humean program that many consider to be insurmountable: if the regularities observed are not based on anything, how can one distinguish between accidental and nomological regularities, and how can one make counterfactual judgments? But the basic intuition remains unchanged: contingency does not need to be rooted in a necessary foundation. For neither Armstrong's universals nor Cartwright's capacities are necessary. It is empirical science's job to discover them; they are *a posteriori*.[108]

105. The "Middle Way" of Mahayana Buddhism shows how one can attribute a religious dimension to the position of skepticism (Nagarjuna, *Mulamadhyamakakarika*, passim).

106. Swartz, "Laws of Nature," § 7; Swartz, *Concept of Physical Law*, 204. James Clerk Maxwell, the founder of classic electrodynamics, used the regularity of subatomic particles as an argument in favor of the existence of God (Clavier, *Dieu sans barbe*, 76ff.).

107. Cf. pp. 64, 74–76 above.

108. Armstrong, *Law of Nature*, 83, and Armstrong, "Can a Naturalist Believe," 105f.; Cartwright, *Dappled World*, 81–83.

The fact that these two philosophers of science introduce an additional level of explanation in their respective accounts shows how difficult it is to not seek an explanation for contingent facts. One recalls in this regard Cartwright's belief that laws of nature are not intelligible without God: "I think that in the concept of law there is a little too much of God. We try to finesse the issue with possible worlds, fictive regularities, and *ceteris paribus* clauses. But in the end the concept of a law does not make sense without the supposition of a law-giver."[109]

But why should Aristotelian capacities be able to get by without God? The fact that the legal metaphor brings out more clearly the relationship to the Creator who establishes the laws of nature does not in any way alter the ontological status given to the natural order: the real choice is between the alternatives of self-sufficiency and dependence. If one does not want to accept as a brute fact that in a given situation, all electrons exhibit the same behavior, neither should one be happy to declare that each has the same capacity.[110] As John Wheeler put it: "No acceptable explanation for the miraculous identity of particles of the same type has ever been put forward. That identity must be regarded, not as a triviality, but as a central mystery of physics."[111] The difference between the empiricist's interpretation and that of the believer is not the shape that the natural order's description is given, but actually the status we give it: is the natural order self-sufficient, or does it require a transcendent foundation?[112]

THE PERMISSION TO ASK CERTAIN QUESTIONS

How does the empiricist's refusal to explain the natural order look when we shift to the creationist perspective? Viewed from this standpoint, such intellectual asceticism appears doubly problematic. Firstly, with respect to the most consistent version of empiricism, creationism sits uncomfortably with the Humean insistence on doing no more than observing natural regularities. Since God created the world to be orderly, the material that comes into contact with our senses is not formless. Thus, we are justified in distinguishing between what does happen and

109. Cartwright, "Natural Science 'Natural' Enough?," 299; cf. 75f. above.
110. Foster, *Divine Lawmaker*, 115; Kistler, "Laws, Exceptions and Tropes," 199, n. 18.
111. Wheeler, "End of Time," 305.
112. Brooke, "Natural Law," 94f.

what should happen. The genuine solidity of the created order allows one to make modal statements and formulate counterfactual judgments. But having rejected the naïve Humean understanding, the theist will be prudent in the choice he makes as concerns the formulation of that order—universals, capacities, underived modalities: the contingency of creation that he confesses will prevent him from deducing his philosophy of science on the basis of theological considerations alone.

Secondly and most importantly, creationism is diametrically opposed to the refusal to give a religious explanation of the natural order. Since the world is created, its lawfulness indicates a Creator. God is not only the ultimate explanation for this lawfulness, he is an entirely appropriate one. The refusal of an immanent explanation, characteristic of radical empiricism, becomes, from such a perspective, a sign: the preference for unexplained contingent facts can be understood when seen in connection to the opposition to a transcendent foundation. Incidentally, some empiricists themselves acknowledge a common motivation for both. Norman Swartz, who is an advocate of Humean analysis in its purest form, believes that "the theory that physical laws *govern* the world is the remnant of the ancient supernatural theory that God spake and Nature obeyed."[113] One must, therefore, treat laws as mere regularities, since "it is time . . . to adopt a thoroughly naturalistic philosophy of science, one which is not only purged of the hand of God, but is also purged of its unempirical latter-day surrogate, namely, nomological necessity."[114]

By resisting the transcendent explanation of the natural order, the empiricist is, of course, not just failing to take into account a mere additional causal factor, in continuity with that order. The Kantian critique of the physico-theological proof is valid: God is not at the beginning or the end of a homogeneous explanatory chain. Rather, the empiricist misses out on that which confers *consistency, coherence, and meaning* on nature's laws. He is like the observer who sees in an impressionist painting only a variety of colored dots, without recognizing the scene represented, nor the message it communicates.[115] The analytical philosopher Peter van Inwagen describes his conversion from a naturalistic point of

---

113. Swartz, "Neo-Humean Perspective," 69.

114. Swartz, "Laws of Nature," section "Naturalizing Philosophy."

115. This illustration develops a suggestion that Daniel Hillion made during a private discussion, 18 July, 2004.

view to a theistic worldview, in terms that evoke so precisely the difference between them that it is worth quoting his memory of it *in extenso*:

> I can remember having a picture of the cosmos, the physical universe, as a self-subsistent thing, something that is just *there* and requires no explanation. When I say "having a picture," I am trying to describe a state of mind that could be called up whenever I desired and was centered on a certain mental image. This mental image—it somehow represented the whole world—was associated with a felt conviction that what the image represented was self-subsistent. I can still call the image to mind (I *think* it's the same image), and it still represents the whole world, but it is now associated with a felt conviction that what it represents is *not* self-subsistent, that it must depend on something else, something that is not represented by any feature of the image, and must be, in some way that the experience leaves indeterminate, radically different in kind from what the image represents. Interestingly enough, there was a period of transition, a period during which I could move back and forth at will, in "duck-rabbit" fashion,[116] between experiencing the image as representing the world as self-subsistent and experiencing the image as representing the world as dependent . . . It is now impossible for me to represent the world to myself as anything but dependent.[117]

Self-subsistent or dependent—that is the issue at stake between the empiricist and the theist: is the world, in its factuality, the *terminus* of any explanation, or does it indicate a reality which transcends it and forms its foundation? The question that separates them is not primarily the acknowledgement of any particular feature of the world; it is the meaning of the whole, from which proceeds the interpretation of individual facts. Incidentally, the difference between these two ways of looking at the natural order is also apparent, in a similar form, in the way they handle miracles. For the theist, both the order and exceptions to it are a matter of divine action. The miracle, however, attracts our attention more, given its unusual nature, such that God's hand in it is seen more clearly. It therefore highlights the world's ontological dependence, which the repetition of natural regularities could lead us to forget. When one does not acknowledge God's action in the world, however, the most

---

116. Van Inwagen is referring here to the example of an ambiguous image that Ludwig Wittgenstein borrows from Joseph Jastrow: one can see, in the drawing, either a duck or a rabbit (Wittgenstein, *Philosophische Untersuchungen*, 1025)

117. Van Inwagen, "Quam dilecta," 35.

common reaction to miracles is to deny their occurrence. More subtly, one can, with Hume, state that from an epistemic point of view, there is no justification for believing that a miracle has occurred. But the empiricist position opens up another possibility, which comes very close to the key point of tension between this view and theism: if only we give up trying to explain what happens, we can accept even the most extraordinary fact, while depriving it of any significance whatsoever. Even faced with perfect historical proof for the virgin birth and the resurrection of Christ, an empiricist could respond: "Is it not wonderful . . . to see what strange things do happen in Reality. You seem to be a collector of oddities."[118] For once we get used to accepting contingency without seeking an explanation, no fact takes on any significance beyond the simple observation that it happened.

What distinguishes the theistic way of looking at the natural order from the empiricist's agnosticism, is ultimately the right to ask certain questions:

> What is at stake between the theist and the atheist? . . . It is about the legitimacy of a certain kind of question and about whether it can be right to set *a priori* limits to a capacity which is, as Aristotle says, potentially infinite; which being so, Thomas Aquinas adds, it is not going to be satisfied—that is to say, enjoy any question-stopping complacency in—even an infinite object. Deny that, and you do, for certain, deny God and you have got your atheism in one move. But in denying the legitimacy of the question you also deny intellect its nature . . . If you want to be an atheist, then, it is necessary only to find that *the world is* to be a platitudinously dull fact.[119]

Let us add that the theist not only maintains the legitimacy of humanity's "big" questions, but is moreover convinced that an answer exists. This answer is, of course, beyond our human capabilities; in this sense, creationism agrees with the Kantian critique, believing that natural theology is mistaken in giving itself the right to find God at the end

---

118. Van Til, *Christian Theory of Knowledge*, 297 (of course, Van Til does not acquiesce to this assertion).

119. Turner, "Atheist," 38f. Turner refers here to the debate broadcast on the radio between Bertrand Russell and Frederick C. Copleston, "Existence of God," 173f., in which Russell refuses to question the world's existence. Taking a negative theology approach, Turner focuses on the existence of the world, but his remark can be applied to the existence of order in the world.

of its argumentative chain. But that is not to say that faith in the Creator is irrational (or a-rational); reason discovers with delight that the world shines more brightly when we receive it as creation. Thus the empiricist's asceticism is not the only possible reaction to the fallacious presumptions of rational metaphysics. The inference from the natural order to God is valid when we accept it as a *gift*. Our own attempts cannot build a foundation—whether immanent or transcendent; the failure of scientistic projects and that of rationalist natural theologies serve to warn us of this. And yet agnostic skepticism is not the only way out: when human reason understands that it is surrounded by God's incomprehensibility, reason realizes it is faced with a Reality that transcends it and whom it is, by that very fact, invited to encounter.

THE EXPLANATION OF ORDER, *À LA* KANT

One novel attempt to explain the order described by the sciences is yet to be explored: Kant's philosophy of science and that of his neo-Kantian heirs both extends and goes beyond the empiricist's agnosticism. It proposes to explain this order by means of immanent factors alone, without committing scientism's errors. The refusal to resort to a transcendent foundation is fully assumed, and even justified, by a consideration of human cognitive faculties, which brings out the limits that are necessary for the latter to function properly. Kant tries to respond to Hume's skepticism, which threatens not only metaphysics, but also all scientific knowledge. In order to ensure that science is possible, Kant thus endeavors to put a strict limit on reason's claims. His aim is to establish an area within which knowledge can be guaranteed. Knowledge, according to Kant, arises from the union of sensations and concepts. From rationalism, he takes the idea that perceptions are blind without concepts; from empiricism, that concepts are empty without perceptions. But in contrast with rationalism, he refuses any kind of intellectual intuition;[120] as such, no rational metaphysics is possible. In contrast with empiricism, he establishes the existence of *a priori* synthetic judgments and, in doing so, the existence of necessary knowledge. Knowledge occurs when sensations, shaped by *a priori* forms of intuition (that is, space and time), are subsumed under the categories provided by the understanding. To use Aristotle's terms, the matter of knowledge comes from the senses

---

120. Kant, *Prolegomena*, § 13, remark II, 40.

(seen as pure receptivity in original Kantianism); the form is provided by the understanding, which is the creative and constructive faculty of human thought. It follows that the structures indicated by the sciences do not show a pre-structured nature:

> It is we therefore who carry into the phenomena which we call nature, order and regularity, nay, we should never find them in nature, if we ourselves, or the nature of our mind, had not originally placed them there . . .
>
> Although experience teaches us many laws, yet these are only particular determinations of higher laws, the highest of them . . . springing *a priori* from the understanding; not being derived from experience, but, on the contrary, imparting to the phenomena their regularity, and thus making experience possible. The understanding . . . is itself the lawgiver of nature, and without the understanding, nature, that is, a synthetical unity of the manifold of phenomena, according to rules, would be nowhere to be found.[121]

Thus, Kant not only accounts for the factuality of scientific knowledge, he also explains its necessity: whereas experiments only tell me about what is, and not what ought to be (on this point Kant remains faithful Hume), the phenomena *must* conform to the structures of the human mind, for otherwise it would be impossible to establish stable objects from the stream of sensory impressions: "Nature . . . in the *formal* sense, as the sum total of the rules to which all appearances must be subject if they are to be thought as connected in one experience, . . . is possible only by means of the constitution of our understanding, in accordance with which all these representations of sensibility are necessarily referred to one consciousness, and through which . . . experience is possible."[122]

In its neo-Kantian versions, the knower is relativized; he is constituted at the same time as his environment takes on structure. Thus, "Science is rather the stabilized byproduct of a dynamic reciprocal relation between reality as a whole and a special fraction of it. Defining this special fraction of reality qua subject is the reverse side of its actively extracting objectlike invariant clusters of phenomena."[123] The order that the sciences describe does not precede the knowledge act, but is

---

121. Kant, *Critique of Pure Reason*, 103.
122. Kant, *Prolegomena*, § 36, 70; cf. § 29, 63f.
123. Bitbol, "Cure for Metaphysical Illusions," 337.

constituted at the same instant that the subject and his rational faculties allow its understanding; it refers to the "resistances that emerge during the performance" of scientific practice.[124]

This is how the different Kantianisms are able to explain the "natural" order: the latter is not in the world, independently of us, but results from the knowledge act. Scientific lawfulness thereby finds an immanent justification, one that does not rely on the features of the world as such, but rather on our being-in-the-world. This is the reason why the Kantianisms are able to provide an immanent explanation of order without falling into scientism's error: they are not seeking a full explanation of the laws of nature among the results of science, because they do not reify the picture of the world that science gives us. At the same time, pre-Kantian metaphysics becomes obsolete: one would be wrong to infer God's existence from the natural order, since there is no order of *nature* which the physico-theological proof could take as its starting point. Kantian philosophies of science are thus characterized by a double rejection of transcendence. Not only do the structures of scientific theories not refer to the features of a *Ding an sich*, but also, science's lawfulness depends on the knower's action, and so no longer reveals the Creator's glory.

Although the different Kantianisms go beyond the mere observation of the natural order and offer an explanation for it, they nevertheless find themselves close to the empiricist position, in that they too accept a contingent aspect of reality without trying to root it in a necessary foundation. What is accepted as brute fact is thereby shifted: whereas the Humean empiricist acknowledges, without question, the regularities of phenomena, the Kantian takes science as his starting point. Admittedly, some have wanted to interpret Kantianism as proposing an explanation, even for the possibility of science. If the senses' data are radically formless and the human understanding and sensitivity give them a structure, should not we expect that our scientific theories are appropriate tools for the "world"? When one doesn't believe "that nature, outside of mathematical forms, is really something, and can say yes or no," the possibility of science is no longer a problem.[125]

---

124. Bitbol, "L'unité organique des opérateurs," 486. Cf. Bitbol, "Néo-pragmatisme et incommensurabilité," 203–34.

125. A line of argument developed by Alain, *Eléments de philosophie*, 145, quoted and commented on by Clavier, *Théologie naturelle*, 59.

Yet what continues to be striking, even from an idealistic or pragmatist view of science, is the *difficulty* of doing science: we are not free to propose whichever theory we please to describe phenomena; the things we observe do not just fit with any old model we might come up with. Philosophy of science must take into account reality's resistance, which the scientist constantly encounters in his or her daily work. Even if we do not admit that "the nature, out of mathematical forms, can say yes or no," *something* is capable of falsifying our theoretical models. In this context, it is of secondary importance whether this *something* is an aspect of the world, independent of the knowledge act, or if it involves our being-in-the-world. The difficulty of doing science indicates the existence of an effective order; the resistance that scientific work encounters would be unintelligible if reality were radically formless. Kant himself knew this, because he mentions the possibility of a chaotic world where sensations could not be organized into a coherent system; in such a world, science would not be possible:

> For the multiplicity and diversity of empirical laws could be so great that ... [it might never be possible] to bring these empirical laws themselves to the unity of kinship under a common principle, if ... the multiplicity and diversity of these laws, along with the natural forms corresponding to them, being infinitely great, were to present to us a raw chaotic aggregate and not the least trace of a system, even though we must presuppose such a system in accordance with transcendental laws.[126]

In addition, the subject himself is a bearer of structure. Formless sense data, which Kant takes from Hume, are just one side of this epistemology: the subject structuring activity, which is just as important, assumes that the subject is not pure formless matter. Kantianism, in its original version, held that the structure of the human mind is universal and fixed: although it would be wrong to equate Kant's position with innatism, the transcendental ego manifests very specific characteristics. And although the neo-Kantianisms abandoned their founder's *a-priorism*, acknowledging the fluidity of forms of knowledge does not abolish all structural elements. The stability, even relative stability, of certain forms cannot be understood without resorting to the subject-plus-world's predisposition to adopt them. Only a Feyerabendian relativism, for whom "anything goes," manages to get rid of all traces of order.

126. Kant, *Critique of Judgment*, 13; cf. Kant, *Critique of Pure Reason*, 2nd ed, xxxv.

Thus Kantianism cannot, either in its original form or in its "neo-" developments, get away from the observation that there is a certain contingent order, which science brings to light. This often gets forgotten —might it be because we live in a society in which the *possibility* of science is generally accepted as obvious? However, the fact that scientific practice is an unspoken assumption of our way of life by no means diminishes the contingency of its existence. Instead of starting from the world's order, the physico-theological proof may be adapted to the antirealistic strategy and start from the possibility of science, as long as it is recognized as contingent: the practice of science itself—the starting point of Kant's philosophy of science—thus constitutes the unexplained residue. If the Kantian does not wish to invest order—of the world or of our being-in-the-world—with a religious dimension, he must join his fellow empiricist in his opposition to the need for an explanation of contingency, even if what is considered a "brute" fact has changed.

While the absence of a transcendent explanation might, at first glance, appear to be a flaw, it is justified by the restricted nature of the area within which Kantianism thinks that understanding can legitimately be exercised: no knowledge can exist in relation to concepts that do not refer to a sensory experience. Of course, these are not arbitrary; Kant even says that we are "necessarily" led to them: reason's straining towards infinity inexorably draws us in their direction.[127] Furthermore, they play the role of regulatory ideas: reason's ideas—the soul, the world, and God—guide our search for knowledge's unity, just as the postulates of practical reason—the immortality of the soul, freedom, and the divine Legislator—are the assumptions for moral behavior. Nevertheless, they convey no knowledge whatsoever, as the famous adage goes: "I must . . . abolish knowledge, to make room for belief."[128] For Kant, knowledge only concerns phenomena; reality itself remains forever outside humanity's speculative power. As a result, any kind of natural theology is ruled out: human reason has no right to pronounce on ultimate reality. It follows that such a view consciously accepts unexplained contingency. Far from representing an annoying residue that must be repressed—as scientism tends to do—it becomes the symbol of human finitude: it proves that the knower cannot transgress the limits of that which is accessible to him. Thus, the epistemic restriction is a sign of humility, and lack of epistemic

---

127. Kant, *Prolegomena*, § 57, 102.
128. Kant, *Critique of Pure Reason*, "Preface to the Second Edition," xxxv.

closure is positively upheld: "Whereas [creation's] idea of a foundational origin tends to capture appearances in an illusory finitude, at the risk of banishing the open, the unknown, the infinite, to a transcendent figure or principle, [Kantism's] foundationless origin approach amounts to leaving this openness inhabit the whole of immanence."[129] Instead of a transcendent foundation, focus is placed on the self-organizing set of immanent factors, which are responsible for the emergence of the order that science observes. Human knowledge only concerns interdependence within the world; it has no access to the question of primitive, original dependence.

THE PRIVILEGE OF BEING SECONDARY

When one compares the Christian view to the different versions of Kantianism, it is worth remarking, first of all, that the theist can accommodate several themes that Kantianism brings to the fore. Firstly, the knower's constructive activity corresponds to the freedom of one who is created "as God's image."[130] In addition, the correlation between the structures of human cognitive faculties (or of scientific practice, in a pragmatic view) and scientific theories can be interpreted as a sign of the human mind's and nature's common origin in God. For this reason, the theist should not feel uncomfortable with the fact that one can indeed deduce some physical theories from the conditions of scientific practice.[131] Similarly, the theist can incorporate the fact that in contemporary physics theories, the concepts themselves are subordinate to the theory. In particular, measuring instruments are required to operate in accordance with the theory's data.[132] In special relativity, this constitutive circle is mirrored by the limited speed at which a signal can propagate (a signal of unlimited speed would allow us to instantly synchronize all clocks in the universe, thereby justifying the introduction of absolute time). In quantum mechanics, the requirement of self-consistency means that observation takes on a pivotal role, resulting in the famous measure "problem."[133]

---

129. Bitbol, "Origine et création," 16.
130. See pp. 115–17 above.
131. See p. 143 above.
132. Mittelstaedt, *Klassische Mechanik*, 13–18, and *Philosophical Problems of Modern Physics*, 35–36.
133. Bitbol, "Lois de la nature," 122.

Such reflexive characteristics in contemporary physics fit with the unified vision of reality that creationism proposes. Finally, the fact that in a Kantian view, the order shown up by science does not concern the world considered independently of the knower, but our being-in-the-world, is not an obstacle for physico-theological kind of argumentative strategy, because scientific practice remains a contingent fact.

The real conflict between the two perspectives, creationist and Kantian, comes about with respect to the distinction between knowledge and faith, which critical philosophy of science requires and which prohibits any knowledge of a transcendent foundation—even that of the *Ding an sich* lying behind the phenomena that science observes. This results in a very particular conception of knowledge: its object is not a reality that exists prior to the knowledge act, it is instead the human mind which itself provides knowledge's form. As Kant writes, "rules of the understanding are . . . *the very source of all truth*, that is, of the accordance of our cognition with objects, and on this ground, that they contain the basis of the possibility of experience."[134] Fundamentally, humans alone know what they themselves have created.

In contrast, the creationist perspective resolutely considers humankind to be *secondary*. Our knowledge concerns a reality of which we are not the origin and which receives its definition from elsewhere. Knowledge results from an encounter with the reality that transcends us: otherness is crucial for the knowledge act. Just as a genuine love relationship is enriched by one partner's resistance to the image the other has of him or her, knowledge is based on the solidness of reality. It is only by virtue of the fact that reality is *given* to me that my knowledge is pertinent. By the same token, this knowledge turns out to be authentically human: only God knows himself and the world in a perfectly transparent way, being the foundation of everything that exists. In contrast, humanity has a vocation to encounter a reality that it did not create, but which is offered to it as a place of life and of knowledge. In this way, the understanding does not impose its structures onto formless matter, but must align itself with the pre-existent order that is given to it. Creationism, therefore, adopts a view of knowledge more humble than that of the Kantian critique: humankind reigns in the "land of truth"[135] not as master, but as ambassador.

134. Kant, *Critique of Pure Reason*, 179f. (italics mine).
135. Ibid., 179.

This perspective may at first seem to belittle human capabilities. For the Christian opposes the Copernican revolution that Kant wishes to effect: the knower must align himself or herself with the object of knowledge, and not vice versa. However, taking second place is human reason's only effective antidote against the skepticism to which Kant's critique ultimately leads. When Kant compares "the land of truth" to "an island ... surrounded by a wide and stormy ocean, the region of illusion, where many a fog-bank, many an iceberg, seems to the mariner, on his voyage of discovery, a new country,"[136] we must not forget that the wide and stormy ocean encompasses everything that lies outside the strict realm of phenomena. All reality that exists independently of humanity forever remains beyond our cognitive grasp: "Beyond the sphere of phenomena, all is for us a mere void."[137] If Kant speaks of the *Ding an sich*, it is simply a way of designating the limits of human knowledge: "The conception of a noumenon is therefore merely a limitative conception and therefore only of negative use."[138]

While the creationist view is already at odds with Kantian skepticism as concerns our knowledge of the world, the contrast becomes quite striking when one turns to knowledge of God. At first glance, one might be tempted to reuse the "vast and stormy ocean" metaphor to describe divine incomprehensibility, since incomprehensibility denounces as erroneous the pretension of wanting to com-prehend[139] God; that is, to contain him within the limits of human reason. But incomprehensibility is not equal to unintelligibility, so it would be wrong to conclude that it is impossible to know God. Whereas the Kantian perspective prohibits cognitive access to anything that is not the object of sensory experience, for creationism, it is *God* who is incomprehensible: incomprehensibility is fully assumed by the Being who has conferred existence on us so that we might live in communion with him. Thus, the word "God" does not symbolize the limits of human reason; creationism leaves room for the pre-theoretical and universal nature of religious experience, which throughout human history has seen God not primarily as the culmination of a metaphysical argument (which for the Kantian is fallacious), but as a Reality who can be understood and encountered.

136. Ibid.
137. Ibid., 186.
138. Ibid., 186f.
139. Etymologically, "grasp together."

Let us dare to go one step further. Not only is it right to discredit the Kantian assumption that the intuition of the *senses* is the only source of knowledge (which rules out any experience of God), one should also question the empiricist legacy of this system, which gives the experience (of the individual) the job of assigning content to concepts. Kantianism on this point shares the selectivity of many modern epistemologies: despite the fact that in human education, teaching plays at least as great a role as personal experience, most theoretical models of human knowledge refuse to grant testimony and revelation their proper place. The fact that human beings are just as much (if not more) verbal creatures as they are sensing ones thereby goes unacknowledged. Why require that experience alone gives content to human ideas, given that language acquisition is largely dependent on hearing the speech of others? In agreement with this element of the human condition, the biblical view maintains the primacy of the *word* as concerns knowledge of the deity: not only the believer's words uttered in prayer, but first and foremost, the revelation that we listen to and that we obey; these are constitutive of humanity's relationship with transcendence.

From such a perspective, the religious element is not a problem; rather, it signals the very heart of humanity's vocation. Living in a world created by God and defining themselves in relation to their Creator, human beings find themselves the beneficiaries of the divine Word to which they must respond. Kantian asceticism, which leaves only sensory experience as the object of knowledge, therefore turns out to be unwarranted. For creationism, the island of knowledge, this "country of truth" is not confined to what our senses allow us see. Communication between the transcendent and the immanent remains possible, foundational, even, for the creature's reality.

Conclusion

The attitude farthest from creationism is undoubtedly narcissistic solipsism: encountering otherness is the fundamental experience for those whose thinking and life are centered on the difference between the Creator and the creature. Thus the movement of transcendence is primordial and determines the relationships that the theist has not only with God but also with the world: by analogy with the Creator who is distinct from the world, the subject finds himself face-to-face with nature, which he has a vocation to explore. Creationism resolutely chooses realism—realism as to the objective existence of the natural order, as to the possibility of knowing it, and also as concerns the transcendent foundation, from which the lawfulness of nature can be understood. Scientists, in their work, have a twofold experience of transcendence: firstly, the reality that they examine shows its own solidity by its resistance to experimental investigation and theoretical models. Secondly, the natural order points beyond itself—it testifies to him who established it; as the psalmist said, "The heavens declare the glory of God, and the firmament proclaims his handiwork. Each day tells the story to the next; each night gives knowledge of it to the next" (Ps 19:1).

In creationism, God's transcendence is paired with his immanence. "God is anything but an 'other!'"[1] In this way, the encounter does not harden into separation that would lead to opposition. The transcendent being maintains dynamic relationships with the created order; creationism

---

1. "*Dieu est tout-autre qu'un autre.*" The expression is from Father Jules Monchanin, quoted by Blocher, "Souveraineté et décision humaine," 7.

never degenerates into deism, where the natural order exists in isolation from its source. It follows that this realism is of a more relational—dare I say more human?—kind than tradition (both in philosophy and in theology) has often acknowledged. Firstly, creation is multifaceted, without its various beings differing by degrees of greater or lesser "reality." Secondly, the world contains determined structures, without reductionism or determinism. Finally, human knowledge is that of the creature: the subject comes into contact with reality, without dominating it. Human knowledge is a participation in the created order, and therefore situated and personal. This knowledge is truly free when it adopts, in the theories that are developed, the shape that reality reveals.

Thus the creationist understanding gives rise to a singular view of the natural order and of the knowledge that humanity can have of it. Its originality specifically comes to the fore when one considers the explanation that one can and should give for nature's lawfulness. For the contradictions observed between different worldviews concern the status of the order that the sciences describe: is it knowledge's ultimate reference? Pantheism, scientism, and empiricism all converge to answer in the affirmative. It is true that they differ as to the meaning they attach to the lawfulness of nature: pantheism attributes a religious significance, whereas scientism sees it as completely transparent to the scientific method, and empiricism takes it as a "brute" fact that does not allow for interpretation. However, by rejecting the transcendent foundation, these three approaches unite to declare the *world* as being the ultimate reality. For creationism, on the other hand, the world is never more than penultimate, being as it is the work of a sovereign Lord. Thus, we can adopt the realistic position without absolutizing it, meaning that creationism can harmoniously hold together aspects that other views oppose: objective order and non-reductionism, the exteriority of the world to be known and the personal involvement of the subject, metaphysical explanation of nature's laws and the finitude of human reason.

Disagreement about the status of the natural order is, therefore, necessarily paired with a difference of opinion about the status of human thought: one can resist the presumptuous errors of rational theology, which places human intelligence as the judge of ultimate realities, without forsaking the right to ask the big metaphysical questions—those concerning the beginning and the end of the world, the meaning of life, and the existence of God. Furthermore, we expect to understand the answers, even though (or precisely because) we have not invented them ourselves, but received them as a gift. Thus does human knowledge fit into the broader context of the divine mind, which will always remain beyond our understanding. Our knowledge is fully recognized as that of a creature: it remains limited, fragmented, and linked to a particular historical situation. And yet, despite its incompleteness, it can still be true, because God's perfect understanding of reality guarantees the consistency of the whole. In this way, we are freed from the vain pursuit of omniscience and may devote ourselves to our vocation: to explore reality, without succumbing to the illusion of a complete knowledge, which would confuse rational description and an exhaustive grasp of reality. From such a perspective, the practice of science is fully recognized. At the same time, we avoid reductionist and scientistic projects that wish to limit reality to the part of it that science enables us to see. Instead, it is far more fitting that we should put to work the full range of human activities, in order to encounter the breathtaking wealth of this world in which we live.

Bibliography

Adams, Marilyn McCord. *William Ockham*. Notre Dame: University of Notre Dame Press, 1987.
Adams, Robert Merrihew. *Leibniz: Determinist, Theist, Idealist*. Oxford: Oxford University Press, 1994.
Agazzi, Evandro. "Reductionism as Negation of the Scientific Spirit." In *The Problem of Reductionism in Science*, edited by Evandro Agazzi, 1–29. Dordrecht: Kluwer, 1991.
Alexander, Samuel. *Space, Time and Deity*. Gifford Lectures, 1916–18. New York: Humanities, 1920.
Alliance Biblique Universelle. *La Bible en français courant*. Rev. ed. Villiers-le-Bel, France: Société Biblique Française, 1997.
Aristotle. *Physics*. Translated by Robin Waterfield, edited by David Bostock. Oxford: Oxford University Press, 1999.
Armstrong, David M. "Can a Naturalist Believe in Universals?" In *Science in Reflection*, edited by Edna Ullmann-Margalit, Boston Studies in the Philosophy of Science 110. Dordrecht: Kluwer, 1988.
———. "Discussion: Reply to Van Fraassen." *Australasian Journal of Philosophy* 66 (1988) 224–29.
———. "Dispositions as Categorical States." In *Dispositions: A Debate*, edited by Tim Crane, 15–18. London: Routledge, 1996.
———. *What is a Law of Nature?* Cambridge: Cambridge University Press, 1983.
———. *A World of States of Affairs*. Cambridge: Cambridge University Press, 1997.
Augustine of Hippo. *The Augustine Catechism: The Enchiridion on Faith, Hope and Charity*. Edited by Boniface Ramsey and translated by Bruce Harbert. New York: New City, 2008.
———. *The City of God*. Translated by Marcus Dods. Peabody, MA: Hendrickson, 2009.
———. *The Confessions of Saint Augustine—Complete Thirteen Books*. Translated by Edward Bouverie Pusey. Rockville, MD: Arc Manor, 2008.
———. *Eighty-Three Different Questions*. The Fathers of the Church 70. Translated by David L. Mosher. Washington, DC: Catholic University of America Press, 2002.
———. *On Genesis*. The Works of Saint Augustine, part 1, vol. 4. Edited by John E. Rotelle and translated by Edmund Hill. New York: New City, 2002.

———. *The Retractations*. The Fathers of the Church 60. Translated by Mary Inez Bogan. Washington, DC: Catholic University of America Press, 1999.

———. *To Simplician—On Various Questions*. In *Augustine: Earlier Writings*, translated by John H. S. Burleigh, The Library of Christian Classics 6, 385–406. Philadelphia: Westminster, 1953.

———. *The Trinity*. The Works of Saint Augustine, part 1, vol. 5. Edited by John E. Rotelle and translated by Edmund Hill. New York: New City, 1991.

Bachelard, Gaston. *Le rationalisme appliqué*. 1949. 2nd ed. Paris: PUF, 1994.

Balthasar, Hans Urs von. *The God Question and Modern Man*. Translated by Hilda Graef. New York: Seabury, 1967.

Barr, James. *Biblical Words for Time*. Studies in Biblical Theology 33. 2nd ed. London: SCM, 1969.

Barth, Karl. *Church Dogmatics*, vol. I, part 1. Translated by Geoffrey William Bromley and Thomas F. Torrance. Edinburgh: T. & T. Clark, 1975.

Bartmann, Bernard. *Lehrbuch der Dogmatik*. 8th ed. 2 vols. Freiburg im Breisgau: Herder, 1932.

Basil of Caesarea, "On the Hexaemeron (I)." In *Exegetic Homilies*, Fathers of the Church 46, translated by Agnes Clare Way, 3–19. Washington: Catholic University of America Press, 1963.

Bavinck, Herman. *The Philosophy of Revelation*. Stone Lectures, Princeton Theological Seminary, 1908-9. Grand Rapids: Eerdmans, 1963.

Berkhof, Louis. *Systematic Theology*. 4th ed. Grand Rapids: Eerdmans, 1938.

Berkouwer, Gerrit C. *General Revelation*. Grand Rapids: Eerdmans, 1955.

Beuttler, Ulrich. "Das neuzeitliche Naturverständnis und seine Folgen." *Glaube und Denken* 15 (2002) 11–24.

Bilynskyj, Stephen S. *God, Nature and the Concept of Miracle*. PhD diss., University of Notre Dame, 1982.

Bitbol, Michel. "Le corps matériel et l'objet de la physique quantique." In *Qu'est-ce que la matière?: regards scientifiques et philosophiques*, edited by Françoise Monnoyeur, 187–211. Paris: Librairie générale française, 2000.

———. "A Cure for Metaphysical Illusions: Kant, Quantum Mechanics and the Madhyamaka." In *Buddhism and Science*, edited by B. A. Wallace, 325–61. New York: Columbia University Press, 2003.

———. "En quoi consiste la 'révolution quantique'?" *Revue internationale de systémique* 11 (1997) 215–39.

———. "Les lois de la nature: contingence ou nécessité." *Cahiers de Philosophie du Langage* 4 (2000) 101–49.

———. *Mécanique quantique: une introduction philosophique*. Paris: Flammarion, 1996.

———. "Néo-pragmatisme et incommensurabilité en physique." *Philosophia Scientiae* 8 (2004) 203–34.

———. "Origine et création." In *Les origines de la création*, Journée de la philosophie à l'Unesco 2002, edited by Guy Samama, 5–30. Paris: Unesco, 2004.

———. "Some Steps towards a Transcendental Deduction of Quantum Mechanics." *Philosophia Naturalis* 35 (1998) 253–73.

———. "L'unité organique des opérateurs de connaissance: la mécanique quantique, Kant, et le Madhyamaka." In *De la science à la philosophie: y a-t-il une unité de la connaissance?*, edited by Michel Cazenave, 470–501. Paris: Michel, 2005.

Blocher, Henri. "Divine Immutability." In *The Power and Weakness of God: Impassibility and Orthodoxy*, Third Edinburgh Conference in Christian Dogmatics, 1988, edited by Nigel M. de S. Cameron, 1–22. Edinburgh: Rutherford House, 1990.

———. "Immanence and Transcendence in Trinitarian Theology." In *The Trinity in a Pluralistic Age: Theological Essays on Culture and Religion*, edited by Kevin J. Vanhoozer, 104–23. Grand Rapids: Eerdmans, 1997.

———. *In the Beginning: The Opening Chapters of Genesis*. Translated by David G. Preston. Downers Grove, IL: InterVarsity, 1984.

———. *Prolégomènes: introduction à la théologie évangélique*. Rev. ed. Vaux-sur-Seine, France: Édifac, 2006.

———. "Qu'est-ce que la vérité?" *Hokhma* 12 (1979) 2–13, and *Hokhma* 13 (1980) 38–49.

———. "Souveraineté de Dieu et décision humaine." *Ichthus* 71 (1977) 2–9.

Boyle, Robert. *Christian Virtuoso: Shewing, that by Being Addicted to Experimental Philosophy, a Man is Rather Assisted than Indisposed to be a Good Christian*. In *The Works of Robert Boyle*, vol. 5, edited by Thomas Birch, 508–40. London: Johnston et al., 1772.

———. *A Free Enquiry into the Vulgarly Received Notion of Nature*. In *The Works of Robert Boyle*, vol. 5, edited by Thomas Birch, 158–254. London: Johnston et al., 1772.

———. *The Origin of Forms and Qualities According to the Corpuscular Philosophy*. In *Selected Philosophical Papers of Robert Boyle*, edited with introduction by Michael A. Stewart, 1–96. Indianapolis: Hackett, 1991.

———. *Some Considerations about the Reconcileableness of Reason and Religion*. In *The Works of Robert Boyle*, vol. 4, edited by Thomas Birch, 151–202. London: Johnston et al., 1772.

———. *The Works of Robert Boyle*. Edited by Thomas Birch. 6 vols. London: Johnston et al., 1772.

Brooke, John Hedley. "Natural Law in the Natural Sciences: The Origins of Modern Atheism?" *Science and Christian Belief* 4 (1992) 83–103.

———. "Religious Belief and the Natural Sciences: Mapping the Historical Landscape." In *Facets of Faith and Science*, vol. 1, edited by Jitse M. Van Der Meer, 1–26. Lanham, MD: University Press of America, 1996.

———. *Science and Religion: Some Historical Perspectives*. Cambridge: Cambridge University Press, 1991.

Brun, Jean. *Les vagabonds de l'Occident: l'expérience du voyage et la prison du moi*. Paris: Desclée, 1976.

Burkhardt, Helmut. *Einführung in die Ethik*. Vol. 1, *Grund und Norm sittlichen Handelns (Fundamentalethik)*. Giessen: Brunnen, 1996.

Calvin, John. *Institutes of the Christian Religion*. 2 vols. Translated by Henry Beveridge. Grand Rapids: Eerdmans, 1966.

———. *Sermons sur le livre de Iob*. Ioanis Calvini operae quae supersunt omnia 23, Brunswick, Germany: Schwetschke, 1887.

Cameron, Nigel M. de S., ed. *The Power and Weakness of God: Impassibility and Orthodoxy*. Third Edinburgh Conference in Christian Dogmatics, 1988. Edinburgh: Rutherford House, 1990.

Cao, Tian Yu. *Conceptual Foundations of Quantum Field Theory*. Cambridge: Cambridge University Press, 1999.

Carroll, John. *Laws of Nature*. Cambridge: Cambridge University Press, 1994.

Cartwright, Nancy. *The Dappled World: A Study of the Boundaries of Science*. Cambridge: Cambridge University Press, 1999.

———. *How the Laws of Physics Lie*. Oxford: Clarendon, 1983.

———. "Is Natural Science 'Natural' Enough? A Reply to Philip Allport." *Synthese* 94 (1993) 291–301.

———. *Nature's Capacities and Their Measurement*. Oxford: Clarendon, 1989.

———. "No God, No Laws." Online: http://personal.lse.ac.uk/cartwrig/PapersGeneral/NoGodNoLaws.pdf.

———. "Reply." In "Symposium on *The Dappled World*." *Philosophical Books* 43 (2002) 241–78.

Cassirer, Ernst. *The Individual and the Cosmos in Renaissance Philosophy*. Translated by Mario Domandi. Chicago: University of Chicago Press, 2010.

Chalmers, Alan F. "So the Laws of Physics Needn't Lie." *Australasian Journal of Philosophy* 71 (1993) 196–205.

———. *What Is This Thing Called Science?* 3rd ed. Buckingham, UK: Open University Press, 1999.

Chesterton, G. K. "The Blatchford Controversies." Part 2, "Why I Believe in Christianity." 1904. In *The Collected Works of G. K. Chesterton*, vol. 1, edited by David Dooley, 381–85. San Francisco: Ignatius, 1986.

Clavier, Paul. *Dieu sans barbe: vingt et une conversations instructives et amusantes sur la question très disputée de l'existence de Dieu*. Paris: Table Ronde, 2002.

———. *Qu'est-ce que la théologie naturelle?* Paris: Vrin, 2004.

Clayton, Philip. *Mind and Emergence*. Oxford: Oxford University Press, 2004.

Clouser, Roy. *Knowing with the Heart: Religious Experience and Belief in God*. Downers Grove, IL: InterVarsity, 1999.

———. "On the General Relation of Religion, Metaphysics, and Science." In *Facets of Faith and Science*, vol. 2, edited by Jitse M. Van der Meer, 57–80. Lanham, MD: University Press of America, 1996.

———. "A Sketch of Dooyeweerd's Philosophy of Science." In *Facets of Faith and Science*, vol. 2, edited by Jitse M. Van der Meer, 81–98. Lanham, MD: University Press of America, 1996.

Collingwood, Robin G. *An Essay on Metaphysics*. Oxford: Clarendon, 1940.

———. *The Idea of Nature*. Oxford: Clarendon, 1945.

———. *The New Leviathan: Or Man, Society, Civilization and Barbarism*. Oxford: Clarendon, 1942.

Collins, John C. *The God of Miracles: An Exegetical Examination of God's Action in the World*. Wheaton, IL: Crossway, 2000.

———. "Miqreh in 1 Samuel 6:9: 'Chance' or 'Event'?" *The Bible Translator* 51 (2000) 144–47.

Courtenay, William J. "Covenant and Causality in Pierre d'Ailly." *Speculum* 46 (1971) 94–119.

———. "The Dialectic of Divine Omnipotence." In *Covenant and Causality in Medieval Thought: Studies in Philosophy, Theology and Economic Practice*, article IV, 1–37. London: Variorum, 1984.

———. "The King and the Leaden Coin: The Economic Background of 'Sine qua non' Causality." *Traditio* 28 (1972) 185–209.

Craig, William Lane. "The Teleological Argument and the Anthropic Principle." In *The Logic of Rational Theism: Exploratory Essays*, edited by W. L. Craig and Mark S. McLeod, 127–53. Lewiston, NY: Mellen, 1990.

Craig, William Lane, and J. P. Moreland, eds. *Naturalism: A Critical Appraisal*. London: Routledge, 2000.

Curiel, Erik. "Against the Excesses of Quantum Gravity: A Plea for Modesty." *Philosophy of Science* 68 (Proceedings) (2001) S424–41.
Dales, Richard C. "The De-animation of the Heavens in the Middle Ages." *Journal of the History of Ideas* 41 (1980) 531–50.
Darwin, Charles. *On the Origin of Species by Means of Natural Selection: Or the Preservation of Favoured Races in the Struggle for Life*. New York: Appleton, 1869.
Davis, Edward B. "Christianity and Early Modern Science: The Foster Thesis Reconsidered." In *Evangelicals and Science in Historical Perspective*, edited by David N. Livingstone et al., 75–95. Oxford: Oxford University Press, 1999.
———. "Newton's Rejection of the 'Newtonian World View': The Role of Divine Will in Newton's Natural Philosophy." *Science and Christian Belief* 3 (1991) 103–17.
Denzinger, Heinrich, and Adolfus Schönmetzer, eds. *Enchiridion Symbolorum: Definitionum et Declarationum de Rebus Fidei et Morum*. 33rd ed. Freiburg im Breisgau: Herder, 1965.
Derrida, Jacques. *Of Grammatology*. Translated by Gayatri Chakravorty Spivak. Baltimore: John Hopkins University Press, 1998.
———. *Writing and Difference*. Edited and translated by Alan Bass. London: Routledge, 1978.
Descartes, René. *Discourse on Method and Meditations*. Translated by Elizabeth Sanderson Haldane and G. R. T. Ross. Mineola, NY: Dover, 2003.
———. *Meditations on First Philosophy: With Selections from the Objections and Replies*. Edited by John Cottingham. Cambridge: Cambridge University Press, 1996.
———. *The Philosophical Writings of Descartes*. 3 vols. Edited by John Cottingham et al. Cambridge: Cambridge University Press, 1991.
———. "The Treatise on Light." In *The World and Other Writings*. Cambridge Texts in the History of Philosophy. Edited by Stephen Gaukroger, 3–75. Cambridge: Cambridge University Press, 1998.
Deutsch, David. "On Wheeler's Notion of 'Law without Law' in Physics." In *Between Quantum and Cosmos: Studies and Essays in Honor of John Archibald Wheeler*, edited by Wojciech H. Zurek et al, 583–92.Princeton: Princeton University Press, 1988.
Dooyeweerd, Herman. *In the Twilight of Western Thought: Studies in the Pretended Autonomy of Philosophical Thought*. Nutley, NJ: Craig, 1975.
———. *A New Critique of Theoretical Thought*. 4 vols. 1935–36. Philipsburg, NJ: Presbyterian & Reformed, 1953–1958.
———. "La prétendue autonomie de la pensée philosophique. La base religieuse de la philosophie grecque, scolastique et humaniste. La nouvelle tâche d'une philosophie chrétienne." *Revue Réformée* 10.3 (1959) 3–76.
Dowe, Phil. "Chance and Providence." *Science and Christian Belief* 9 (1997) 3–20.
Duhem, Pierre. *Le système du monde: histoire des doctrines cosmologiques de Platon à Copernic*. 10 vols. Paris: Hermann, 1913–59.
Earman, John. "The SAP Also Rises: A Critical Examination of the Anthropic Principle." *American Philosophical Quarterly* 24 (1987) 307–17.
Eichrodt, Walter. *Theology of the Old Testament*. 2 vols. 1935. Old Testament Library. Translated by J. A. Baker. Philadelphia: Westminster, 1967.
Einstein, Albert. *The Human Side: New Glimpses from His Archives*. Edited by Helen Dukas and Banesh Hoffmann. Princeton: Princeton University Press, 1979.
———. "On the Method of Theoretical Physics." In *Ideas and Opinions*, edited by Carl Seeling, 270–76. New York: Crown, 1995.

---. "Physik und Realität." *Franklin Institute Journal* 221 (1936) 313–47, translated into English 349–82.

---. "Principles of Research." In *Ideas and Opinions*, edited by Carl Seeling, 224–27. New York: Crown, 1995.

Einstein, Albert, and Maurice Solovine. *Letters to Solovine:1906–1955*. New York: Carol, 1993.

Einstein, Albert, et al. "Can Quantum-Mechanical Description of Physical Reality Be Considered Complete?" *Physical Review* 47 (1935) 777–80.

Emery, Gilles. *La Trinité créatrice: Trinité et création dans les commentaires aux Sentences de Thomas d'Aquin et de ses précurseurs Albert le Grand et Bonaventure.* Paris: Vrin, 1995.

Force, James E. "The Nature of Newton's 'Holy Alliance' between Science and Religion." In *Rethinking the Scientific Revolution*, edited by Margaret Osler, 247–70. Cambridge: Cambridge University Press, 2000.

Forrest, Peter, and David M. Armstrong. "An Argument against David Lewis' Theory of Possible Worlds." *Australasian Journal of Philosophy* 62 (1984) 164–68.

Foster, John. *The Divine Lawmaker: Lectures on Induction, Laws of Nature, and the Existence of God.* Oxford: Clarendon, 2004.

---. "Regularities, Laws of Nature and the Existence of God." *Proceedings of the Aristotelian Society* 101 (2001) 145–61.

Foster, Michael B. "The Christian Doctrine of Creation and the Rise of Modern Natural Science." *Mind* 43 (1934) 446–68.

---. "Christian Theology and Modern Science of Nature (I)." *Mind* 44 (1935) 439–66.

---. "Christian Theology and Modern Science of Nature (II)." *Mind* 45 (1936) 1–27.

Funkenstein, Amos. *Theology and the Scientific Imagination from the Middle Ages to the Seventeenth Century.* Princeton: Princeton University Press, 1986.

Gadamer, Hans-Georg. *Truth and Method.* 2nd rev. ed. New York: Continuum, 1991.

Galileo. *Dialogue Concerning the Two Chief World Systems.* 1632. Translated by Stillman Drake. Berkeley, CA: University of California Press, 1967.

---. *Dialogues Concerning Two New Sciences.* 1638. Translated by Henry Crew and Alfonso de Salvio. New York: Dover, 1954.

Gay, John H. "Four Medieval Views of Creation." *Harvard Theological Review* 56 (1963) 243–73.

Geertsema, Henk G. "Faith and Science in Biblical Perspective: Human Responsibility before God." In *Facets of Faith and Science*, edited by Jitse M. Van der Meer, vol. 4, 285–312. Lanham, MD: University Press of America, 1996.

Gilson, Étienne. *History of Christian Philosophy in the Middle Ages.* Reprint. London: Sheed and Ward, 1980.

---. *The Spirit of Mediaeval Philosophy.* Gifford Lectures, 1931–32. 1932. Reprint. Notre Dame: University of Notre Dame Press, 1991.

Gisel, Pierre. *La création: essai sur la liberté et la nécessité, l'histoire et la loi, l'homme, le mal et Dieu.* 2nd ed. Geneva: Labor et Fides, 1987.

Grant, Edward. "The Condemnation of 1277, God's Absolute Power, and Physical Thought in the Late Middle Ages." *Viator* 10 (1979) 211–44.

Guerlac, Henry. "Theological Voluntarism and Biological Analogies in Newton's Physical Thought." *Journal of the History of Ideas* 44 (1983) 219–29.

Gunton, Colin. "The Trinity, Natural Theology, and a Theology of Nature." In *The Trinity in a Pluralistic Age: Theological Essays on Culture and Religion*, edited by Kevin J. Vanhoozer, 88–103. Grand Rapids: Eerdmans, 1997.

———. *The Triune Creator: A Historical and Systematic Study*. Edinburgh: Edinburgh University Press, 1998.

Haarsma, Loren D., and Deborah B. Haarsma. "Neutrino Mass, Inflationary Cosmology, and the Fine-Tuning Argument." *Perspectives on Science and Christian Faith* 50 (1998) 160–61.

Hacking, Ian. "The Inverse Gambler's Fallacy: The Arguments from Design. The Anthropic Principle Applied to Wheeler Universes." In *Readings in the Philosophy of Religion: An Analytic Approach*, edited by Baruch A. Brody, 202–12. Englewood Cliffs, NJ: Prentice Hall, 1992.

Hamilton, Victor P. *The Book of Genesis: Chapters 1–17*. New International Commentary of the Old Testament. Grand Rapids: Eerdmans, 1990.

Hampe, Michael. "Gesetz, Natur, Geltung—Historische Anmerkungen." In *Was sind und warum gelten Naturgesetze?*, edited by Peter Mittelstaedt and Gerhard Vollmer. *Philosophia Naturalis* 37 (2000) 241–53.

Harré, Rom. *Laws of Nature*. London: Duckworth, 1993.

Harris, R. Laird, et al., eds. *Theological Wordbook of the Old Testament*. 2 vols. Chicago: Moody, 1980.

Harrison, Peter. *The Bible, Protestantism, and the Rise of Natural Science*. Cambridge: Cambridge University Press, 1998.

———. *The Fall of Man and the Foundations of Science*. Cambridge: Cambridge University Press, 2007.

———. "Original Sin and the Problem of Knowledge in Early Modern Europe." *Journal of the History of Ideas* 63 (2002) 239–59.

Heidegger, Martin. *Being and Time: A Translation of Sein und Zeit*. Translated by Joan Stambaugh. Albany: State University of New York Press, 1996.

Heidemann, Dietmar H., and Kristina Engelhard, eds. *Warum Kant heute?: Systematische Bedeutung und Rezeption seiner Philosophie in der Gegenwart*. Berlin: de Gruyter, 2004.

Heisenberg, Werner. *Physics and Philosophy*. Gifford Lectures 1955/56. New York: Harper & Row, 1958.

Heisenberg, Werner. *The Physicist's Conception of Nature*. Translated by Arnold J. Pomerans. New York: Harcourt, Brace and World, 1958.

Helm, Paul. "The Impossibility of Divine Passibility." In *The Power and Weakness of God: Impassibility and Orthodoxy*. Third Edinburgh Conference in Christian Dogmatics, 1988, edited by Nigel M. de S. Cameron, 125–37. Edinburgh: Rutherford House, 1990.

Helmholtz, Hermann von. "The Facts of Perception." In *Selected Writings of Hermann von Helmholtz*, edited by Russell Kahl, 366–408. Middletown, CT: Wesleyan University Press, 1971.

Heslam, Peter. *Creating a Christian worldview: Abraham Kuyper's Lectures on Calvinism*. Grand Rapids: Eerdmans, 1998.

Hesse, Mary. "Simplicity." In *The Encyclopedia of Philosophy*, vol. 7, edited by Paul Edwards, 446–48. London: Collier Macmillan, 1967.

Hintikka, Jaakko. "A. O. Lovejoy on Plenitude in Aristotle." *Ajatus* 29 (1967) 5–11.

Hooykaas, Reijer. *Fact, Faith and Fiction in the Development of Science*. Gifford Lectures, University of St. Andrews, 1977. Dordrecht: Kluwer, 1999.

———. *Natural Law and Divine Miracle: A Historical-Critical Study of the Principle of Uniformity in Geology, Biology and Theology*. Leiden: Brill, 1959.

———. *Religion and the Rise of Modern Science*. Edinburgh: Scottish Academic Press, 1972.

Horgan, Terence. "From Supervenience to Superdupervenience: Meeting the Demands of a Material World." *Mind* 102 (1993) 555–86.

Hume, David. *Dialogues concerning Natural Religion*. In *Principal Writings on Religion, Including Dialogues concerning Natural Religion; and The Natural History of Religion*, edited by J. C. A. Gaskin. Oxford: Oxford University Press, 1993.

———. *An Enquiry concerning Human Understanding: A Critical Edition*. Edited by Tom L. Beauchamp. Oxford: Clarendon, 1998.

Hüttemann, Andreas. "Chaos und Naturgesetz—Cartesische Probleme." *Zeitschrift für Philosophische Forschung* 56 (2002) 517–44.

———. "Laws and Dispositions." *Philosophy of Science* 65 (1998) 121–35.

———, ed. *Kausalität und Naturgesetz in der frühen Neuzeit*. Stuttgart: Steiner, 2001.

Hyman, Arthur, et al., editors. *Philosophy in the Middle Ages: The Christian, Islamic, and Jewish Traditions*. Indianapolis: Hackett, 2010.

Irenaeus of Lyons. *On the Apostolic Preaching*. Translation and introduction by John Behr. Crestwood, NY: St Vladimir's Seminary Press, 1997.

Jaeger, Lydia. "Bas Van Fraassen on Religion and Knowledge: Is There a Third Way beyond Foundationalist Illusion and Bridled Irrationality?" *American Catholic Philosophy Quarterly* 80 (2006) 581–602.

———. "Cosmic Order and Divine Word." *Churchman* 118 (2004) 47–51.

———. "Dieu comme seule source de la connaissance—l'apologétique de Cornelius Van Til." *Théologie Évangélique* 1.3 (2002) 27–46.

———. "Diverses formes de nécessité dans l'Institution chrétienne." *Revue Réformée* 54 (2003) 54–69.

———. *Einstein, Polanyi and the Laws of Nature*. West Conshohocken, PA: Templeton, 2010.

———. "Lee Smolin: les lois issues de l'évolution." *Revue philosophique de Louvain* 106 (2008) 372–86.

———. *Lois de la nature et raisons du coeur: les convictions religieuses dans le débat épistémologique contemporain*. Berne: Lang, 2007.

———. *Pour une philosophie chrétienne des sciences*. Nogent-sur-Marne: Institut Biblique de Nogent, 2000.

———. "Le rapport entre la nature de Dieu et sa volonté dans l'Institution chrétienne." *Journal Européen de Théologie* 11 (2002) 109–18.

Jaki, Stanley L. *Science and Creation: From Eternal Cycles to an Oscillating Universe*. Edinburgh: Scottish Academic Press, 1974.

Jewish Publication Society. *JPS Hebrew-English Tanakh*. 2nd ed. Philadelphia: Jewish Publication Society, 1999.

John Paul II. *Fides et ratio*. 1998. No pages. Online: http://www.vatican.va/holy_father/john_paul_ii/encyclicals/documents/hf_jp-ii_enc_15101998_fides-et-ratio_en.html.

Jolley, Nicholas. *The Cambridge Companion to Leibniz*. Cambridge: Cambridge University Press, 1995.

Jüngel, Eberhard. *Gottes Sein ist im Werden: Verantwortliche Rede vom Sein Gottes bei Karl Barth*. Tübingen: Mohr, 1965.

Kaiser, Christopher B. *Creational Theology and the History of Physical Science: The Creationist Tradition from Basil to Bohr.* Leiden: Brill, 1997.

Kant, Immanuel. *Critique of the Power of Judgment.* The Cambridge Edition of the Works of Immanuel Kant in Translation. Edited by Paul Guyer and Eric Matthews. Cambridge: Cambridge University Press, 2001.

———. *Critique of Pure Reason: In Commemoration of the Centenary of Its First Publication.* Translated by Friedrich Max Müller. 2nd ed. New York: Macmillan, 1907.

———. *Critique of Pure Reason.* Bohn's Philosophical Library. Translated by John Miller Dow Meiklejohn. 2nd ed. London: Bohn, 1855.

———. *Prolegomena to Any Future Metaphysics that Will be Able to Come Forward as Science: With Selections from the Critique of Pure Reason.* Cambridge Texts in the History of Philosophy. Translated and edited by Gary Carl Hatfield. 2nd rev. ed. Cambridge: Cambridge University Press, 2004.

Kistler, Max. "Laws of Nature, Exceptions and Tropes." *Philosophia Scientiae* 7 (2003) 189–219.

Klaaren, Eugene M. *Religious Origins of Modern Science: Belief in Creation in Seventeenth-Century Thought.* Lanham, MD: University of America Press, 1985.

Knuuttila, Simo. *Modalities in Medieval Philosophy.* London: Routledge, 1993.

———. "Time and Creation in Augustine." In *The Cambridge Companion to Augustine*, edited by Eleonore Stump and Norman Kretzmann, 103–15. Cambridge: Cambridge University Press, 2001.

———. "Time and Modality in Scholasticism." In *Reforging the Great Chain of Being: Studies of the History of Modal Theories*, edited by Simo Knuuttila, 163–257. Dordrecht: Reidel, 1981.

Koyré, Alexandre. *Galileo Studies.* Translated by John Mepham. Atlantic Highlands, NJ: Humanities, 1978.

Kretzmann, Norman. *The Metaphysics of Creation: Aquinas's Natural Theology in Summa Contre Gentiles II*, Oxford: Clarendon, 1999.

Kripke, Saul A. *Naming and Necessity.* Rev. ed. Oxford: Blackwell, 1980.

Kuhn, Thomas S. *The Copernican Revolution: Planetary Astronomy in the Development of Western Thought.* Cambridge, MA: Harvard University Press, 1957.

———. *The Structure of Scientific Revolutions.* Chicago: University of Chicago Press, 1962.

Kuyper, Abraham. "Sphere Sovereignty." In *Abraham Kuyper: A Centennial Reader*, edited by James Bratt, 461–90. Grand Rapids: Eerdmans, 1998.

———. *Stone Lectures on Calvinism*, 1898. Grand Rapids: Eerdmans, 2002.

Langton, Douglas C. "Scotus and Possible Worlds." In *Knowledge and the Sciences in Medieval Philosophy.* Proceedings of the 8th International Congress of Medieval Philosophy, edited by Simo Knuuttila et al., vol. 2, 240–47. Helsinki: Luther-Agricola Society, 1990.

Laubier, Patrick de. *L'eschatologie.* Que sais-je? Paris: PUF, 1998.

Laughlin, Robert B. "Nobel Lecture: Fractional Quantization." *Reviews of Modern Physics* 71 (1999) 863–74.

Laughlin Robert B., and David Pines. "The Theory of Everything." *Proceedings of the National Academy of Sciences* 97 (2000) 28–31.

Lecerf, Auguste. *Introduction à la dogmatique réformée.* 2 vols. Paris: Editions "Je sers," 1931.

Lecourt, Dominique. "Loi (épistémologie)." In *Encyclopædia Universalis*, Corpus, 2nd ed., 1985, vol. 11, 203–6.

Leibniz, Gottfried Wilhelm. "Conversation avec Sténon sur la liberté." In *Discours de métaphysique et autres textes 1663–1689*. Translated with notes by Christiane Frémont. Paris: Flammarion, 2001.

———. "Discourse on Metaphysics." In *Philosophical Papers and Letters*, translated and edited, with an introduction by Leroy E. Loemker. 2nd ed. Dordrecht: Kluwer, 1989.

———. "On Contingency." In *The Shorter Leibniz Texts: A Collection of New Translations*, edited by Lloyd H. Strickland, 110–13. London: Continuum, 2006.

———. "On Freedom." In *Philosophical Papers and Letters*, translated and edited, with an introduction by Leroy E. Loemker. 2nd ed. Dordrecht: Kluwer, 1989.

———. "Specimen of Discoveries about Marvelous Secrets of a General Nature." In *Philosophical Writings*, edited by G. H. R. Parkinson and translated by Mary Morris and G. H. R. Parkinson, 75–86. London: Dent, 1973.

Leslie, John. *Universes*. London: Routledge, 1989.

Lewis, C. S. *The Abolition of Man: Or Reflections on Education with a Special Reference to the Teaching of English in the Upper Forms of Schools*. 2nd ed. London: Bles, 1946.

Lewis, David K. *Counterfactuals*. Oxford: Blackwell, 1973.

———. *On the Plurality of Worlds*. Oxford: Blackwell, 1986.

———. *Papers in Metaphysics and Epistemology*. Cambridge: Cambridge University Press, 1999.

Lipton, Peter. "All Else Being Equal." *Philosophy* 74 (1999) 155–68.

———. *Inference to the Best Explanation*. 2nd ed. London: Routledge, 2004.

Livingstone, David N. *Darwin's Forgotten Defenders: The Encounter between Evangelical Theology and Evolutionary Thought*. Edinburgh: Scottish Academic Press, 1987.

———. "Situating Evangelical Responses to Evolution." In *Evangelicals and Science in Historical Perspective*, edited by David N. Livingstone et al., 193–219. Oxford: Oxford University Press, 1999.

Locke, John. *Essays on the Law of Nature and Associated Writings*. 1664. Edited by Wolfgang Leyden. Oxford: Oxford University Press, 1954.

Lovejoy, Arthur O. *The Great Chain of Being: A Study of the History of an Idea*. William James Lectures, Harvard University, 1933. Cambridge: Harvard University Press, 1966.

Luther, Martin. "Lectures on Genesis." In vol. 1 of *Luther's Works*, American Edition. 55 vols. Edited by Jaroslav Pelikan and Helmut T. Lehmann. Philadelphia: Muehlenberg and Fortress, 1955–86.

Mackay, Donald. *Science, Chance and Providence*. Riddell Memorial Lectures, University of Newcastle-upon-Tyne, March 15–17, 1977. Oxford: Oxford University Press, 1978.

Maier, Anneliese. *Die Mechanisierung des Weltbilds im 17. Jahrhundert*. Leipzig: Meiner, 1938.

———. *Metaphysische Hintergründe der spätscholastischen Naturphilosophie*. Rome: di Storia e Letteratura, 1955.

Marion, Jean-Luc. "La raison formelle de l'infini." In *Christianisme: héritages et destins*, edited by Cyrille Michon, 109–32. Paris: Livre de Poche, 2002.

Maula, Erkka. "On Plato and Plenitude." *Ajatus* 29 (1967) 12–50.

McGrath, Alister, *A Scientific Theology*. 3 vols. Edinburgh: T. & T. Clark, 2001–2.

McTaggart, John McTaggart Ellis. *Some Dogmas of Religion*. 1909. Reprint. London: Arnold, 1930.

Melanchthon, Philipp. *Initia doctrinae physicae*. In *Opera quae supersunt omnia*, vol. 13, edited by Carl Gottlieb Bretschneider, 181–411. Halle: Schwetschke, 1846.

Mercer, Christia. *Leibniz's Metaphysics: Its Origins and Development*. Cambridge: Cambridge University Press, 2001.
Merton, Robert K. "Puritanism, Pietism and Science." In *Science and Religious Belief: A Selection of Recent Historical Studies*, edited by Colin A. Russell, 20–54. London: University of London Press, 1973.
Milton, John R. "The Origin and Development of the Concept of the 'Laws of Nature.'" *Archives Européennes de Sociologie* 22 (1981) 173–95.
Mittelstaedt, Peter. "The Emergence of Statistical Laws in Quantum Mechanics." In *New Developments on Fundamental Problems in Quantum Physics*, edited by Miguel Ferrero and Alwyn Van Der Merwe, 265–74. Dordrecht: Kluwer, 1997.
———. "Interpreting Quantum Mechanics—in the Light of Quantum Logic." In *Time, Quantum and Information*, edited by Lutz Castell and Otfried Ischebeck, 281–90. Heidelberg: Springer, 2003.
———. *The Interpretation of Quantum Mechanics and the Measurement Process*. Cambridge: Cambridge University Press, 1998.
———. *Klassische Mechanik*. Mannheim: Bibliographisches Institut, 1970.
———. *Philosophical Problems of Modern Physics*. Translated by Robert Cohn and John Stachel. Dordrecht: Reidel, 1975.
———. "Über die Bedeutung physikalischer Erkenntnisse für die Theologie." In *Evolution als Schöpfung? ein Streitgespräch zwischen Philosophen, Theologen und Naturwissenschaftlern*, edited by Paul Weingartner, 135–48. Stuttgart: Kohlhammer, 2001.
———. *Der Zeitbegriff in der Physik: physikalische und philosophische Untersuchungen zum Zeitbegriff in der klassischen und relativistischen Physik*. 3rd ed. Zurich: Bibliographisches Institut, 1989.
Monod, Jacques. *Chance and Necessity*. Translated by Austryn Wainhouse. New York: Knopf, 1971.
Morel, Georges. *Problèmes actuels de religion*. Recherches économiques et sociales. Paris: Aubier-Montaigne, 1968.
Morgan, John. "The Puritan Thesis Revisited." In *Evangelicals and Science in Historical Perspective*, edited by David N. Livingstone et al., 43–74. Oxford: Oxford University Press, 1999.
Murphy, Nancey. "Supervenience and the Downward Efficacy of the Mental: A Non-Reductive Physicalist Account of Human Action." In *Neuroscience and the Person: Scientific Perspectives on Divine Action*, edited by Robert J. Russell et al., 147–64. Vatican City: Vatican Observatory, 1999.
Nagarjuna. *Mulamadhyamakakarika of Nagarjuna: The Philosophy of the Middle Way*. Translated and edited by David J. Kalupahana. Delhi: Motilal Banarsidass, 1991.
Nagel, Thomas. *The View from Nowhere*. New York: Oxford University Press, 1986.
Needham, Joseph. "Human Law and Laws of Nature." In *The Grand Titration: Science and Society in East and West*, 299–331. Toronto: University of Toronto Press, 1969.
Neuner, Josef, and Jacques Dupuis, eds. *The Christian Faith in the Doctrinal Documents of the Catholic Church*. New York: Alba House, 1982.
Newton, Isaac. "First Letter to Bentley, 16 Dec. 1692." In *Opera quae exstant omnia*, vol. 4, edited by Samuel Horsley. London: Nichols, 1782.
———. *Philosophiae naturalis principia mathematica*. Translated by Andrew Motte. Revised and edited by Florian Cajori. Berkeley, CA: University of California Press, 1934.
Niebuhr, H. Richard. *Christ and Culture*. 1951. New York: Harper & Row, 1956.
Nolan, Daniel. "Recombination Unbound." *Philosophical Studies* 84 (1996) 239–62.

North, Pierre. "Le principe anthropique ou la place de l'homme dans l'univers." *Fac-réflexion* 36 (1996) 4–19.
O'Donovan, Oliver. *Resurrection and Moral Order: An Outline for Evangelical Ethics*. Leicester, UK: InterVarsity, 1986.
Oakley, Francis. "Christian Theology and the Newtonian Science: The Rise of the Concept of the Laws of Nature." *Church History* 30 (1961) 433–57.
———. *Omnipotence, Covenant, and Order: An Excursion in the History of Ideas from Abelard to Leibniz*. Ithaca, NY: Cornell University Press, 1984.
Oberman, Heiko A. "Reformation and Revolution: Copernicus' Discovery in an Era of Change." In *The Cultural Context of Medieval Learning*, edited by John E. Murdoch and Edith D. Sylla, 397–435. Dordrecht: Reidel, 1975.
Omnès, Roland. *The Interpretation of Quantum Mechanics*. Princeton Series in Physics. Princeton: Princeton University Press, 1994.
Osler, Margaret. "From Immanent Natures to Nature as Artifice: The Reinterpretation of Final Causes in Seventeenth-Century Natural Philosophy." *Monist* 79 (1996) 388–407.
Palmerino, Carla Rita. "The Mathematical Characters of Galileo's Book of Nature." In *The Book of Nature in Early Modern and Modern History*, edited by Klaas van Berkel and Arjo Vanderjagt, 27–44. Leuven: Peeters, 2006.
Pannenberg, Wolfhart. "Contingency and Natural Law." In *Toward a Theology of Nature: Essays on Science and Faith*, edited by Ted Peters, 72–122. Louisville, KY: Westminster John Knox, 1993.
———. "The Doctrine of Creation and Modern Science." In *Toward a Theology of Nature: Essays on Science and Faith*, edited by Ted Peters, 29–49. Louisville, KY: Westminster John Knox, 1993.
———. "God and Nature." In *Toward a Theology of Nature: Essays on Science and Faith*, edited by Ted Peters, 50–71. Louisville, KY: Westminster John Knox, 1993.
———. "Die Kontingenz der geschöpflichen Wirklichkeit." *Theologische Literaturzeitung* 119 (1994) 1049–58.
———. "Die Subjektivität Gottes und die Trinitätslehre." In *Grundfragen Systematischer Theologie: gesammelte Aufsätze*, vol. 2, 96–111. Göttingen: Vandenhoeck & Ruprecht, 1980.
———. *Systematic Theology*. 2 vols. Translated by Geoffrey W. Bromiley. Grand Rapids: Eerdmans, 1994.
———. "Theological Questions to Scientists." In *Toward a Theology of Nature: Essays on Science and Faith*, edited by Ted Peters, 15–28. Louisville, KY: Westminster John Knox, 1993.
Pascal, Blaise. *Pensées*. Edited by Léon Brunschvicg, with chronology, introduction, and notes by Dominique Descotes. Paris: Flammarion, 1976.
Petcher, Donald N. "The Interplay between Science and Belief: A Case Study in Modern Physics." In *Facets of Faith and Science*, vol. 2, edited by Jitse M. Van Der Meer, 257–720. Lanham, MD: University Press of America, 1996.
Peters, Ted. "Cosmos as Creation." In *Cosmos as Creation: Theology and Science in Consonance*, edited by Ted Peters, 45–114. Nashville: Abingdon, 1989.
Pickstock, Catherine. *After Writing: On the Liturgical Consummation of Philosophy*. Oxford: Blackwell, 1988.
Plato. *Parmenides*. Translated by R. E. Allen. New Haven, CT: Yale University Press, 1997.
———. *Timaeus*. Translated by Donald J. Zeyl. Indianapolis: Hackett, 2000.

Polanyi, Michael. *Knowing and Being*. Edited by Marjorie Grene. London: Routledge, 1969.
———. *Personal Knowledge: Towards a Post-Critical Philosophy*. Chicago: University of Chicago Press, 1958.
———. "Science and Reality." *British Journal for the Philosophy of Science* 18 (1967) 177–96.
Polkinghorne, John C. "The Metaphysics of Divine Action." In *Chaos and Complexity: Scientific Perspectives on Divine Action*, edited by Robert J. Russell, et al., 147–56. Vatican City: Vatican Observatory, 1995.
———. *Science and Theology: An Introduction*. London: SPCK, 1998.
Popper, Karl R. *The Open Universe: An Argument for Indeterminism*. Postscript to the Logic of Scientific Discovery 2. New Jersey: Rowman & Littlefield, 1982.
———. *A World of Propensities*. Bristol, UK: Thoemmes, 1990.
Putallaz, François-Xavier. "Historiographie du nominalisme médiéval." In *Saint Thomas au XXe siècle: Colloque du centenaire de la "Revue thomiste"* (Toulouse, 25–28 March, 1993), edited by Serge-Thomas Bonino, 233–46. Paris: Saint-Paul, 1994.
Putnam, Hilary. "There Is At Least One A Priori Truth." *Erkenntnis* 13 (1978) 153–70.
Quine, Willard Van Orman. "Two Dogmas of Empiricism." In *From a Logical Point of View*, 2nd ed., 20–46. Cambridge: Harvard University Press, 1980.
Rad, Gerhard von. *Wisdom in Israel*. Translated by James D. Martin. Harrisburg, PA: Trinity, 1993.
Railton, Peter. "Explanation and Metaphysical Controversy." In *Scientific Explanation*, edited by Philip Kitcher and Wesley C. Salmon, 220–52. Minnesota Studies in the Philosophy of Science 13. Minneapolis: University of Minnesota Press, 1989.
Redhead, Michael. *From Physics to Metaphysics*. Tarner Lectures, Cambridge 1993. Cambridge: Cambridge University Press, 1995.
Rees, Martin. *Our Cosmic Habitat*. London: Weidenfeld & Nicolson, 2002.
Renault, Laurence. *Dieu et les créatures selon Thomas d'Aquin*. Paris: PUF, 1995.
Rosier-Catach, Irène. *La parole efficace: signe, rituel, sacré*. Preface by Alain de Libera. Paris: Seuil, 2004.
Ross, James. "The Crash of Modal Metaphysics." *Review of Metaphysics* 43 (1989) 251–79.
Rudavsky, Tamar, ed. *Divine Omniscience and Omnipotence in Medieval Philosophy: Islamic, Jewish and Christian Perspectives*. Dordrecht: Reidel, 1985.
Russell, Bertrand. *The Philosophy of Leibniz*. 1900. Reprint. Nottingham, UK: Spokesman, 2008.
Russell, Bertrand, and Frederick C. Copleston. "A Debate on the Existence of God." In *The Existence of God: A Reader*, edited by John Hick, 167–91. London: Collier MacMillan, 1964.
Russell, Robert J. "Contingency in Physics and Cosmology: A Critique of the Theology of Wolfhart Pannenberg." *Zygon* 23 (1988) 23–43.
Russell, Robert J., et al., eds. *Chaos and Complexity: Scientific Perspectives on Divine Action*. Vatican City: Vatican Observatory, 1995.
Scott, Robert Balgamie Young. *Proverbs, Ecclesiastes: A New Translation with Introduction and Commentary*. The Anchor Bible 18. Garden City, NY: Doubleday, 1974.
Settle, Tom. "Stones that the Builder Rejected: An Essay Recommending the Critical Approach in Both Science and Religion." In *Facets of Faith and Science*, edited by Jitse M. Van der Meer, vol. 1, 307ff. Lanham, MD: University Press of America, 1996.
Sherringham, Marc. *Introduction à la philosophie esthétique*. Paris: Payot, 1992.
Silk, Joseph. "Holistic Cosmology." *Science* 277 (1997) 644.

Smolin, Lee. "Cosmological Natural Selection as the Explanation for the Complexity of the Universe." *Physica A* 340 (2004) 705–13.

———. *The Life of the Cosmos*. London: Orion, 1998.

Sober, Elliot. "Simplicity (in Scientific Theories)." In *Routledge Encyclopedia of Philosophy*, vol. 8, edited by Edward Craig, 780–83. London: Routledge, 1998.

Spinoza, Baruch. *The Ethics*. Translated by R. H. M. Elwes. Middlesex, UK: Echo Library, 2006.

———. *Theological-Political Treatise*. Cambridge Texts in the History of Philosophy. Translated by Michael Silverthorne and Jonathan Israel. Cambridge: Cambridge University Press, 2007.

Stauffer, Richard. *Dieu, la création et la Providence dans la prédication de Calvin*. Basler und Berner Studien zur historischen und systematischen Theologie 33. Berne: Lang, 1978.

Stump, Eleonore. "Non-Cartesian Substance Dualism and Materialism without Reductionism." *Faith and Philosophy* 12 (1995) 505–31.

Swartz, Norman. *The Concept of Physical Law*. Cambridge: Cambridge University Press, 1985.

———. "Laws of Nature." In *The Internet Encyclopedia of Philosophy*, 2001. No Pages. Online: http://www.iep.utm.edu/lawofnat/.

———. "A Neo-Humean Perspective: Laws as Regularities." In *Laws of Nature: Essays on the Philosophical, Scientific and Historical Dimensions*, edited by Friedel Weinert, 67–91. Berlin: de Gruyter, 1995.

Swinburne, Richard. *The Existence of God*. 2nd ed. Oxford: Clarendon, 2004.

Thomas Aquinas. *On Being and Essence*. In *Selected Writings: The Principles of Nature, On Being and Essence, On the Virtues in General, On Free Choice*, translated by Robert P. Goodwin, 33–70. Indianapolis, IN: Bobbs-Merrill, 1965.

———. *Summa contra gentiles*. 5 vols. Translated by Anton C. Pegis et al. Notre Dame: University of Notre Dame Press, 1975.

———. *Summa theologiae*. 60 vols. Translated by Thomas Gilby et al. New York: McGraw-Hill, 1964–73.

Thorson, Walter R. "Legitimacy and Scope of 'Naturalism' in Science (Part I): Theological Basis for a 'Naturalistic Science.'" *Perspectives on Science and Christian Faith* 54 (2002) 1–11.

Torrance, Thomas F. "Ultimate and Penultimate Beliefs in Science." In *Facets of Faith and Science*, edited by Jitse M. Van der Meer, vol. 1, 151–76. Lanham, MD: University Press of America, 1996.

Tresmontant, Claude. *Études de métaphysique biblique*. Paris: Gabalda, 1955.

———. *The Origins of Christian Philosophy*. Twentieth Century Encyclopedia of Catholicism 11. Translated by Mark Pontifex. New York: Hawthorn, 1963.

Trueman, Carl R., and R. Scott Clark, eds. *Protestant Scholasticism: Essays in Reassessment*. Carlisle, UK: Paternoster, 1999.

Turner, Denys. *How to Be an Atheist*. Inaugural lecture, University of Cambridge, 12 October, 2001. Cambridge: Cambridge University Press, 2002.

Van Der Meer, Jitse M. "The Role of Metaphysical and Religious Beliefs in Science." In *Studies in Science and Theology: Yearbook of the European Society for the Study of Science and Theology*, vol. 5, edited by N. H. Gregersen et al., 247–56. Aarhus, Denmark: University of Aarhus, 1999.

Van Fraassen, Bas C. "Against Transcendental Empiricism." In *The Question of Hermeneutics: Essays in Honor of Joseph J. Kockelmans*, edited by Timothy J. Stapleton, 309–35. Dordrecht: Kluwer, 1994.

———. "The Charybdis of Realism: Epistemological Implications of Bell's Inequality." In *Philosophical Consequences of Quantum Theory: Reflections on Bell's Theorem*, edited by James T. Cushing and Ernan McMullin, 97–113. Notre Dame: University of Notre Dame Press, 1989.

———. "Constructive Empiricism Now." *Philosophical Studies* 106 (2001) 151–70.

———. *The Empirical Stance*. New Haven, CT: Yale University Press, 2002.

———. *Laws and Symmetry*. Oxford: Clarendon, 1989.

———. "Science, Materialism, and False Consciousness." In *Warrant in Contemporary Epistemology: Essays in Honor of Plantinga's Theory of Knowledge*, edited by Jonathan L. Kvangig, 149–81. Lanham, MD: Rowman & Littlefield, 1996.

———. "The Theory of Tragedy and of Science: Does Nature Have Narrative Structure?" In *Aristotle and Contemporary Science*, edited by Demetra Sfendoni-Mentzou, vol. I, 31–59. New York: Lang, 2000.

———. "The World of Empiricism." In *Physics and Our View of the World*, edited by Jan Hilgevoord, 114–34. Cambridge: Cambridge University Press, 1994.

Van Inwagen, Peter. "Dualism and Materialism: Athens and Jerusalem." *Faith and Philosophy* 12 (1995) 475–88.

———. "Quam Dilecta." In *God and the Philosophers: The Reconciliation of Faith and Reason*, edited by Thomas V. Morris, 31–60. Oxford: Oxford University Press, 1994.

Van Til, Cornelius. *A Christian Theory of Knowledge*. Nutley, NJ: Presbyterian & Reformed, 1969.

———. *Common Grace and the Gospel*. Philadelphia: Presbyterian & Reformed, 1974.

———. *In Defense of Biblical Christianity*. Vol. 2, *A Survey of Christian Epistemology*. Ripon, CA: Den Dulk Christian Foundation, 1969.

———. "Kant or Christ." 1942. In *Christianity and Idealism*, 133–39. Philadelphia: Presbyterian & Reformed, 1955.

Van Till, Howard J., et al. *Portraits of Creation: Biblical and Scientific Perspectives on the World's Formation*. Grand Rapids: Eerdmans, 1990.

Vanhoozer, Kevin J., ed. *The Trinity in a Pluralistic Age: Theological Essays on Culture and Religion*. Grand Rapids: Eerdmans, 1997.

Warfield, Benjamin B. *Evolution, Science, and Scripture: Selected Writings*. Edited with introduction by Mark A. Noll and David N. Livingstone. Grand Rapids: Baker, 2000.

Weinberg, Stephen. "Can Science Explain Everything? Anything?" *New York Review of Books* 48.9 (2001) 47–50.

Wells, Paul, ed. *Quel est le but principal de l'homme? les textes de Westminster*. Aix-en-Provence: Kerygma, 1988.

Westfall, Richard S. "The Changing World of the Newtonian Industry." *Journal for the History of Ideas* 37 (1976) 175–85.

Westphal, Merold. "Hermeneutics as Epistemology." In *The Blackwell Guide to Epistemology*, edited by John Greco and Ernest Sosa, 415–35. Malden, UK: Blackwell, 1999.

Wheeler, John A. "Beyond the End of Time." 1971. In *Black Holes, Gravitational Waves and Cosmology: An Introduction*, 286–307. New York: Gordon & Breach, 1974.

———. "How Come the Quantum?" *Annals of the New York Academy of Sciences* 480 (1986) 304–16.

———. "On Recognizing 'Law without Law.'" *American Journal of Physics* 51 (1983) 398–404.

Wheeler, John A., and Kenneth Ford. *Geons, Black Holes and Quantum Foam: A Life in Physics*. New York: Norton, 2000.

White, Andrew D. *A History of the Warfare of Science with Theology in Christendom*. 2 vols. 1896. Reprint. New York: Dover, 1960.

Wittgenstein, Ludwig. *Philosophische Untersuchungen: eine kritisch-genetische Edition*. Edited by Joachim Schulte. Frankfurt: Suhrkamp, 2001.

Wolfson, Harry Austryn, *The Philosophy of the Church Fathers*. Vol. 1, *Faith, Trinity, Incarnation*. Cambridge: Harvard University Press, 1956.

Wolters, Albert M. "Creation as Separation: A Proposed Link between Bible and Theory." In *Facets of Faith and Science*, vol. 4, edited by Jitse M. Van Der Meer, 347–52. Lanham, MD: University Press of America, 1996.

———. *Creation Regained: Biblical Basics for a Reformational Worldview*. Carlisle, UK: Paternoster, 1996.

———. "Dutch Neo-Calvinism: Worldview, Philosophy and Rationality." In *Rationality in the Calvinian Tradition*, edited by Hendrik Hart, Johan Van der Hoeven, and Nicholas Wolterstorff, 113–131. London: University Press of America, 1983.

Woodward, James. "Realism about Laws." *Erkenntnis* 36 (1992) 181–218.

Wybrow, Cameron, ed. *Creation, Nature and Political Order in the Philosophy of Michael Foster (1903–1959): The Classic Mind Articles and Others, with Modern Critical Essays*. Lampeter, UK: Mellen, 1992.

Young, William. "Herman Dooyeweerd." In *Creative Minds in Contemporary Theology: A Guidebook to the Principal Teachings of Karl Barth, G .C. Berkouwer, Dietrich Bonhoeffer, Emil Brunner, Rudolf Bultmann, Oscar Cullmann, James Denney, C. H. Dodd, Herman Dooyeweerd, P. T. Forsyth, Charles Gore, Reinhold Niebuhr, Pierre Teilhard de Chardin, and Paul Tillich*, edited by Philip E. Hughes, 270–301. 2nd ed. Grand Rapids: Eerdmans, 1969.

Author Index

Adams, Marylin McCord, 15–16, 39
Adams, Robert M., 23–24
Agazzi, Evandro, 83–84
Ailly, Pierre d', 40, 71
Alain (Chartier, Émile-Auguste), 162
Alexander, Samuel, 81
Anselm of Canterbury, 112
Aratos, 33
Aristotle, xxiv, 10, 14, 26–29, 41, 52–53, 66, 91, 125, 159–60
Armstrong, David M., 73–75, 133, 153, 155
Athanasius, 5
Augustine of Hippo, xxi, 4, 9–10, 14, 19, 36–38, 46, 62, 68, 70–71, 87, 120, 122, 139
Averroès, 41

Bachelard, Gaston, 81
Bacon, Francis, 66
Balthasar, Hans Urs von, 94
Barr, James, xxiii
Barth, Karl, xi, 31
Bartmann, Bernard, 113, 139
Basil of Caesarea, 7, 38
Bavinck, Herman, xxi, 4, 6
Beauchamp, Paul, 79
Bell, John S., 91, 93
Berkeley, George, 56
Berkhof, Louis, 32

Berkouwer, Gerrit C., 95
Beuttler, Ulrich, 52
Bilynskyj, Stephen S., 61, 77
Bitbol, Michel, xvi, 59, 63, 90, 92, 115, 143, 161–62, 165
Blocher, Henri, v, xvi, 2, 5, 16–17, 34, 44, 96, 117, 169
Bohr, Niels, 109, 114
Boltzmann, Ludwig, 145
Bonaventure, 71
Born, Max, 146
Boyle, Robert, 25, 49–50, 54–55
Broad, Charlie D., 81
Brooke, John H., xvi, xx, 156
Brun, Jean, 119
Brunschvicg, Léon, 121
Buridan, Jean, 39–41
Burkhardt, Helmut, 33

Calvin, John, vii, xi, xxi, 9–11, 17, 23, 41–49, 55, 77, 87–88, 120
Cao, Tian Yu, 141
Carroll, John, 77, 133
Carter, Brandon, 152
Cartwright, Nancy, 54, 64, 75–76, 83–86, 100–101, 134, 155–56
Cassirer, Ernst, 53, 108, 128
Chalmers, Alan F., 54–55, 77
Chesterton, G.K., 1
Clark, R. Scott, 41

Clarke, Samuel, 68
Clavier, Paul, 151, 155, 162
Clayton, Philip, 82
Clouser, Roy A., 3, 17, 80
Cochrane, Charles Norris, 5
Collingwood, Robin G., 52, 58, 80, 83, 85
Collins, C. John, xxiii, 56, 61
Copleston, Frederick C., 159
Cotes, Roger, 13
Courtenay, William J., 49, 70–71
Craig, William L., 152
Curiel, Erik, 142

Dales, Richard C., 41
Damian, Peter, 56
Darwin, Charles, ix, 68, 146
Davidson, Donald, 116
Davis, Edward B., xix, 13
Dionysius (pseudo-), xxi, 47–48
Denzinger, Heinrich, 126
Derrida, Jacques, 96–97
Descartes, René, ix, 8–9, 11, 17, 40, 50–51, 56–57, 99–100, 116, 145
Deutsch, David, 145–46
Dooyeweerd, Herman, xxi, 27, 29, 55, 79–80, 84
Dowe, Phil, 93
Duhem, Pierre, 40, 68
Duns Scotus, John, 15, 38

Earman, John, 152
Eichrodt, Walter, 2–3, 62
Einstein, Albert, 69, 91–92, 105, 117, 138–40, 143
Emery, Gilles, 34–35
Engels, Friedrich, 68

Feyerabend, Paul, 105, 110, 163
Fishacre, Richard, 70–71
Force, James E., 68
Ford, Kenneth, 144
Forrest, Peter, 153
Foster, John, 134–37, 156
Foster, Michael, xviii, xix, 8, 37, 52, 66
Funkenstein, Amos, 12, 65

Gadamer, Hans–Georg, 110
Galileo, ix, xviii, 58, 63–65, 83
Gay, John H., xxi
Geertsema, Henk G., 104
Gilson, Etienne, xxiii, 8, 16, 128
Gisel, Pierre, 8, 14, 26, 62, 96
Grant, Edward, 10, 40
Gregory of Nyssa, 38
Grene, Marjorie, 145
Guerlac, Henry, 51
Guillaume d'Auvergne, 70
Gunton, Colin, 5, 38
Guth, Alan, 147

Haarsma, Deborah B., 151
Haarsma, Loren D., 151
Hacking, Ian, 151–52
Hamilton, Victor P., 62
Hampe, Michael, 52
Harper, Charles L., 96
Harré, Rom, 133–34
Harrison, Peter, 40, 103–4
Hawking, Stephen, 147
Heidegger, Martin, 109–10
Heisenberg, Werner, 77, 90–91, 100, 109, 114
Helm, Paul, 17
Helmholtz, Hermann von, 108
Heschel, Abraham J., 5, 34
Hesse, Mary, 133
Hillion, Daniel, xvi, 157
Hintikka, Jaakko, 26
Hooykaas, Reijer, xxi
Hopkins, Gerard M., 64
Horgan, Terence, 81
Humboldt, Wilhelm von, 108
Hume, David, 73, 118–19, 124, 132–35, 142–43, 151, 155, 159–63
Hüttemann, Andreas, 50–51, 54
Hyman, Arthur, 13

Irenaeus of Lyons, xx

Jaki, Stanley L., 68
Jastrow, Joseph, 158
John Paul II, 126
Jüngel, Eberhard, 34

Justin (pseudo-) 3

Kaiser, Christopher B., 98
Kant, Emmanuel, xi, xix, 59, 64, 95–96, 108–10, 118–19, 124, 127–28, 160–68
Kierkegaard, Søren, xi, 125
Kilwardby, Robert, 70
Kistler, Max, 156
Klaaren, Eugene M. xxi, 39, 41, 49
Knuuttila, Simo, 14–15
Koyré, Alexandre, 52
Kretzmann, Norman, 10
Kripke, Saul, 131
Kuhn, Thomas S. xvii, 105–6, 110
Kuyper, Abraham, xxi, 79, 112

Langton, Douglas C., 15
Laubier, Patrick de, 68
Laughlin, Robert B., 142
Lecerf, Auguste, 4, 96, 120, 127
Lecourt, Dominique, 56
Leibniz, Gottfried Wilhelm, 13, 18–24, 27, 112
Lemaître, Georges, 69
Leslie, John, 138, 151
Lewis, Clive Staples, 116, 149
Lewis, David K., 75, 133, 153
Lipton, Peter, xvi, 54, 134
Livingstone, David N., 68
Locke, John, 51
Lombard, Peter, 34
Lovejoy, Arthur O., 14, 26–27
Lucretius, 150–51
Luther, Martin, 41–42

MacKay, Donald, 87
Madden, Edward H., 134
Maier, Anneliese, 41
Malebranche, Nicolas, 56
Marion, Jean-Luc, 100
Maula, Erkka, 26
Maxwell, James Clerk, 155
McGuire, James E., 51
McMullin, Ernan, 65
McTaggart, John, 16
Melanchthon, Philipp, 41–42

Mersenne, Marin, 8, 56–57
Merton, Robert K. xviii
Michon, Cyrille, ix–xi, xvi, 10
Milton, John, 38, 52
Mittelstaedt, Peter, xvi, 90–91, 93, 143, 146, 165
Monod, Jacques, 89
Morel, Georges, 123
Morgan, C. Lloyd, 81
Morgan, John, xviii
Murphy, Nancey, 116

Nagarjuna, 155
Nagel, Thomas, 109
Needham, Joseph, 52
Newcastle, William Cavendish, 56
Newton, Isaac, ix, 13, 40, 51, 67–68
Nicolas of Autrecourt, 39, 56
Nicholas of Cusa (Cusanus) xxi
Niebuhr, H. Richard, xxi
Nietzsche, Friedrich, 68
Nolan, David, 153
North, Pierre, 150

O'Donovan, Oliver, 98, 104, 113, 121, 130
Oakley, Francis, 27, 39–40, 42, 56
Oberman, Heiko A., 39–40
Omnès, Roland, 143
Oresme, Nicole, 40
Osiander, Andreas, 46
Osler, Margaret J., 52

Pannenberg, Wolfhart, 2, 12, 36, 67–68, 74, 128
Pascal, Blaise, xi, 121
Petcher, Donald N., 84
Peters, Ted, 67
Philo of Alexandria, 36, 41
Philoponus, John, 38, 63
Pickstock, Catherine, 39
Pines, David, 142
Planck, Max, 142
Plato, xxiv, 26, 36, 63, 101
Plotinus, 14, 27
Podolsky, Boris, 91
Polanyi, Michael, 105–7, 110, 145

Author Index

Polkinghorne, John, 93
Pollard, William, 93
Popper, Karl R., 89, 91, 116
Putallaz, François-Xavier, 38
Putnam, Hilary, 17

Quine, Willard Van Orman, 17, 145

Rad, Gerhard von, 9
Railton, Peter, 132
Redhead, Michael, 149
Rees, Martin, 148, 150
Renault, Laurence, 29, 35
Rosen, Nathan, 91
Rosier-Catach, Irène, 70–71
Ross, James, 17
Russell, Bertrand, 19, 21, 159
Russell, Colin A. xviii
Russell, Robert J., 12

Schelling, Friedrich Wilhelm Joseph von, 27, 68
Servet, Michel, 43
Settle, Tom, xxiii
Shellard, Paul, 150
Sherringham, Marc, 3, 6, 12, 108
Silk, Joseph, 148
Smolin, Lee, 146–48, 153–54
Sober, Elliot, 133
Solovine, Maurice, 140
Sorabji, Richard, 63
Spinoza, Baruch, 7, 12–14, 18, 20, 22, 27, 92
Stauffer, Richard, 43–44, 47
Stump, Eleonore, 116
Swartz, Norman, 155, 157
Swinburne, Richard, 129–34

Tempier, Étienne, 13, 40

Thomas Aquinas, xxi, 10, 27–32, 34–35, 40–41, 65–66, 71, 101, 116, 124–25, 129–30, 159
Thorson, Walter R., 74
Torrance, Thomas F., 13
Tresmontant, Claude, 3, 13, 97, 101
Trueman, Carl R., 41
Turner, Denys, 159

Van der Meer, Jitse M. xvi, xxi, 4
Van Fraassen, Bas C. xix, 52, 73, 75, 93, 96, 119, 121, 134, 150, 154
Van Inwagen, Peter, 116, 157–58
Van Til, Cornelius, xxi–xxii, 12, 16–18, 35–36, 74, 84–85, 89, 96–99, 102, 122, 127, 131–32, 159
Van Till, Howard J., 74
Vaughan, Jonathan, iii, xv
Voltaire, 18

Warfield, Benjamin B., 68
Wedderkopf, Magnus von, 19
Weinberg, Stephen, 142
Westfall, Richard S., 51
Westphal, Merold, 110
Wheeler, John Archibald, 143–46, 148, 156
White, Andrew D. xviii
William of Ockham, 15–16, 39–40, 71
Wittgenstein, Ludwig, 158
Wolfson, Harry A., 36
Wolleb, Johannes, 4
Wolters, Albert M. xxi, 6, 79
Woodward, James, 54
Wybrow, Cameron, xix

Young, William, 80

Zwingli, Ulrich, 42

Scripture Index

Genesis

1:1	xiii, 1, 7, 126
1:2	31, 62
1:3	59, 95
1:4	79
1:6	79
1:9	79
1:11f	2
1:12	2, 59, 79
1:14	79
1:18	79
1:21	59, 79
1:22	2
1:24	79
1:25	59
1:26f	32, 115–16
1:28	2
1:31	2, 44, 59
2:1–3	3
2:7	78
3	103
3:22	32
4:17–22	111
5:1	32
5:3–32	111
6:18	69
8:21f	69, 72
9:6	32
9:8–17	69
9:9–13	69
10	111
12:3	69
15:18	69
17:2ff	69

Exodus

6:3	32
20:11	3
24	69
31:17	3

Numbers

33:52	32

Deuteronomy

1:39	32
6:7	112

1 Samuel

2:8	60

2 Samuel

7:12–17	69
14:17	32
19:36	32

Scripture Index

1 Kings
3:9	32

2 Kings
17:25	2

1 Chronicles
16:30	60

Job
1:6	33
4:18	44
15:15	44
25:5	44
26:5–14	56
26:10	61
26:11	15
28:25–27	60
28:28	112
33:4	32
38:4—39:30	56
38:4–6	60
38:8–11	61
38:10	86
38:25	60
42:7	44

Psalms
2:7	33
19:1	169
19:1ff	45
24:2	60
33:6	95
39:6	32
73:20	32
78:3f	112
82:6	33
89:3	69
89:28–37	69
93:1	60
96:10	60
97:5	15
104:9	61
104:30	31
111:10	112
115:3	15
119:89–91	56, 60
119:91	61
135:6	15
139:5–6	98
139:6	82
139:17–18	82, 98
148	61

Proverbs
1:7	112, 126
8:22–31	60
8:27–29	61
8:29	86
8:30	9
16:33	87

Ecclesiastes
3:11	98
7:13	15

Isaiah
7:15f	32
14:27	15
40:12–14	82
40:13	98
40:13f	15
42:8	4
43:13	15
44:24	15
46:10	2, 15

Jeremiah
5:22	61
5:22–24	56
10:12	15
27:5	15
31:31–34	69
31:35–36	61, 86
31:37	82
32:17	15
33:14–26	70
33:20–21	70
33:22	82
33:25	61
33:25–26	70

Ezekiel

16:17	32
37:26	69

Hosea

1:2	2

Amos

8:9	15

Joel

3:3-4	15

Matthew

1:1-17	111
3:9	14
10:28	78
19:26	14
20.1ff	70
22:1ff	70
26:28	69
26:53	14

Luke

1:37	14
3:23-38	111
3:38	33

John

1:1	38
1:1-3	60, 95
1:3	31
1:14	38
8:32	120
10:34	33

Acts

3:25	69
17:28	33

Romans

1:18-21	128
1:19f	45
1:20	9
1:22-27	113

1 Corinthians

11:2	112
11:3	113
11:7	32
14:33	61
15:38	7

2 Corinthians

3:17	122
4:16	78

Galatians

4:4	106

Ephesians

1:11	7
3:15	131
4:18	102
5:31f	113

Colossians

1:16	31, 106
2:5	78
3:10	32

1 Timothy

4:4	44
6:15-16	16

Titus

1:15	102

Hebrews

1:3	31, 95, 106
1:11f	16
8-9	69
11:3	45

James

1:17	8, 16
3:9	32

1 Peter

3:4	78

2 Peter
1:4	3, 33
3:10–13	15

1 John
1:1	38

Jude
3	112

Revelation
4:11	7
19:13	38

Subject Index

analogia entis (analogy of being) 25–31, 41–49, 80
angels, 29, 43–49
Aristotelianism, 13–16, 27–28, 41, 52–53, 56–57, 75–76, 125, 156
art, 108–109
atheism, ix–x, xvi, 75, 130, 140, 159

Big Bang, 69
Buddhism, xvi, 155

capacities. *See* dispositions.
causality, xxiii, 22, 41, 53, 69–72, 87–88
    causal network, 72
    sine qua non, 71–72
chaos, 39, 51, 61, 86, 104, 144–45
chance, xiv, 22, 59, 61, 86–90, 93, 144, 151–52
Christ, 6, 59, 95, 106, 111, 125
contingency
    of the natural order, 66–69, 92, 115, 149
    of creation, 8–24
    of the laws of logic, 8, 10–12, 15–19, 56, 144–50
covenant, 69–72
creation
    dependence on the Creator, 2–4, 31, 49, 120, 126–27, 130, 156

ex nihilo, 3–4, 16, 20, 25–28, 37, 43, 62–66
existence distinct from God, 2–3, 74, 78
freedom, 7–11
imperfection, 43–44
incomprehensibility, 82, 85, 102
link with the Trinity, 31–38
of matter, 28–29, 62–63
stability, 56, 60, 71–72

demiurge, 3, 26, 62, 66
determinism, 12–14, 87–89, 122
dispositions, 54–57, 75–77, 137, 155–57
duality of body and soul, 78, 116, 122

election, 9, 21, 87, 120
emergence, 82, 89, 145–46
empiricism, 95–96, 135–37, 154–60, 170
evil, 6, 9–11, 32, 53, 104
evolution
    biological, ix, 67–69, 81, 88
    cosmological, 146–48
explanation, 38, 51–53, 63–64, 72–77, 123–65

Fall, the, 103
forms, substantial, 25–49, 66
fortune, 86–87

genealogies, 111
God
    faithfulness, 61, 69-72
    freedom, 3, 7-12, 18-24, 67
    incomprehensibility, 78, 98-102, 167
    legislator, 12-13, 39, 51-52, 134-37, 156
    "of the gaps" x, 93
    omnipotence, 14-16, 49-51
    omniscience, 82, 99-100, 102
    proofs of existence, 123-37, 159
    pure action, 28-30
    righteousness, 10, 43-46
    sovereignty, xxi, 4,-5, 9, 55-56, 61-62, 86-88
    triune, 8, 31-38, 80-81
    will, 3, 7-11, 16, 18-24, 37-39, 49-51, 55-56, 67, 73, 76, 86-89
    wisdom, 9-11, 45, 50, 60-63, 88
    word, 2, 41-42, 59-60, 95-97, 168

hierarchy
    of knowledge, 107-8
    of beings, 26, 38-39, 47-52, 80, 124-25
human beings
    freedom, 9, 88, 115-22
    historical rootedness, 111-12, 122
    image of God, 32-33, 45-48, 78, 82, 115-16, 165
    responsibility, 9, 121-22
    sexual differentiation, 112
    status of creature, 9, 98-102, 112, 120, 170
    understanding, 96, 119, 134-35, 160-66

ideals, Platonic, 8, 19, 36-39, 50
idol, idolatry, 4
incarnation, 6, 37, 106
instrumentalism, 75

Jansenism, 56, 103
Judaism, xvi, 34, 36, 60

Kantianism, 119, 127, 143, 160-68

knowledge
    affected by sin, 102-5
    dependence on God, 126-28
    freedom, 115-22
    limits, 83-85, 98-102, 159-67, 171
    naturalized, 117-18
    personal nature, 105-9, 139
    situated nature, 109-12

laws of nature
    ceteris paribus, 53-57
    contingency, 66-69
    established by God, 13, 56, 61-62, 82-85
    evolution, 146-48
    modern science, 49-53
    necessity, 72-77
    subject to change, 68
    stability, 71
    universality, 61, 77-78
logos, 36-39, 59-60, 95-97, 104-6, 109

mathematics, 8, 17, 23, 51, 56, 58-59, 62-65, 73, 77, 85, 92, 143-45, 152, 163
matter, 3-4, 25-29, 36, 50, 62-66, 67, 77-78, 85-86, 90-91, 101-2, 122, 160, 163
miracles, 12-13, 53, 61, 93, 158-59,
monads, doctrine of, 19-24, 112
monotheism, 2-16, 77, 80
multiverse, 147-53

naturalism, 74-75, 84, 129-35, 141-43, 149, 154, 157, 162-65
necessity
    logical, metaphysical, 12-13, 143-44
    physical, nomological, 12-13, 42, 72-77, 135, 157
Neo-Calvinism, xxi, 79-80
Neo-Kantianism, xiv, 108, 119, 160-63

order, natural. *See* laws of nature.

pantheism, 7, 10, 20, 26, 42, 47, 113, 137-41, 170

Platonism, 19, 36–38, 75–76, 101
plurality, 82–85
polytheism, 62, 138
positivism, logical, 105
possibility, 12–24
potentia, potentialities, 14–17, 26–30, 47–49, 90–91
predestination. *See* election.
principle
    anthropic, 150–53
    of plenitude, 14–16, 26, 148, 152, 154
    of reason, 20–24

quantum mechanics, xiii–xvii, 59, 77, 86, 90–93, 109, 114–15, 141–47

rationalism, 18–24, 89, 98–100, 160
realism, 113–18, 153–54, 169–70
redemption, 6, 46, 53, 111
reductionism, 77–85, 88–89, 100, 107–9, 116, 142
Reformation, 41–49, 103
relativism, 113–14, 163
revelation, xi, 6, 95–97, 99, 168

salvation, 42, 111, 120
skepticism, 155–60, 167

science
    Greek, 25–49, 63, 65, 83, 90–91
    limits, 78, 83–85, 148–50
    modern, xvii–xxiv, 39, 49–57, 67, 78, 83, 100
    scientific method, 26, 58–59, 49–50, 64–69, 72–73, 82–85, 100, 105–9, 115–17, 160–65
scientism, 141–150, 170
sin, 102–4
soul, 30, 43, 116
Stoicism, 40, 42, 51, 60, 88. *See also* determinism.

theology, natural, x–xi, 123–37, 160, 164
theory
    Darwinian, 67–69
    of everything, 82, 142–43
    unified physical, 141–42
Trinity, 33–38, 106, 113, 139

universals, 75–77, 133, 155
universes, multiple, 147–53

word, God's, 2, 41–42, 59–60, 95–97, 168
worlds, possible, 15–24, 153

Biosketch

After completing postgraduate studies in physics and mathematics—including research in theoretical solid state physics—at the University of Cologne (Germany) and in theology at the Seminary for Evangelical Theology in Vaux-sur-Seine (France), Lydia Jaeger obtained her Ph.D. in philosophy at the Sorbonne on the possible links between the concept of law of nature and religious presuppositions, under the supervision of Michel Bitbol (CNRS, France). She holds a permanent lectureship and is academic dean at the *Institut Biblique de Nogent-sur-Marne*, an interdenominational Evangelical Bible college near Paris, which trains pastors and other church workers at an undergraduate level, and lay people in extension programs.

Since 2000, Lydia Jaeger has had several short study leaves in the Department of History and Philosophy of Science at the University of Cambridge (Great Britain), where she is also an associate member of St. Edmund's College and of the Faraday Institute for Science and Religion. From 2005 to 2009, she held a four-year research professorship in philosophy of science and contemporary thought, jointly based at the Seminary for Evangelical Theology in Vaux-sur-Seine and the *Institut Biblique de Nogent-sur-Marne*. Her current research interests are natural order, the epistemological and ethical implications of the doctrine of creation, the theology of science and our understanding of human persons in the light of evolutionary biology, neuroscience, and philosophy. She is a member of the American Scientific Affiliation (ASA), Christians in Science (CiS), the Fellowship of European Evangelical Theologians (FEET), the International Society for Science and Religion (ISSR), and the Tyndale Fellowship; she is a founding member of the Société de Philosophie des Sciences, the Réseau des Scientifiques Evangéliques, and the Réseau Evangéliques et Sciences Humaines. She is the author of five books and several articles on the relation between Christianity and the natural sciences.

Correspondence:
Institut Biblique de Nogent
39, Grande Rue
94130 Nogent-sur-Marne
France

Website: http://ljaeger.ibnogent.org.

www.ingramcontent.com/pod-product-compliance
Lightning Source LLC
Chambersburg PA
CBHW031357230426
43670CB00006B/568